EDWARD BOND

Plays: 6

The War Plays
A Trilogy

Part One:
Red Black and Ignorant

Part Two:
The Tin Can People

Part Three:
Great Peace

Choruses from
After the Assassinations

Methuen Drama

METHUEN DRAMA CONTEMPORARY DRAMATISTS
This collection first published in Great Britain in 1998
by Methuen Drama

The War Plays first published in 1985 by Methuen London
Revised edition 1991
Copyright © 1983. 1991 by Edward Bond
Commentary on *The War Plays* copyright © 1991 by Edward Bond
Poems for *The War Plays* first published in *Poems 1978-1985*
by Methuen London
Copyright © 1987 by Edward Bond
Choruses from After the Assassinations first published in a volume
with *Derek* in 1983 by Methuen London
Copyright © 1983, 1998 by Edward Bond
Copyright in this collection © 1998 by Edward Bond
The author has asserted his moral rights

ISBN 0 413 70400 9

A CIP catalogue record for this book is available at the British Library

Transferred to digital printing 2002

Contents

Edward Bond: A Chronology

PLAY	*First performance*
The Pope's Wedding	9.12.1962
Saved	3.11.1965
A Chaste Maid in Cheapside (*adaptation*)	13.1.1966
The Three Sisters (*translation*)	18.4.1967
Early Morning	31.3.1968
Narrow Road to the Deep North	24.6.1968
Black Mass (*part of* Sharpeville Sequence)	22.3.1970
Passion	11.4.1971
Lear	29.9.1971
The Sea	22.5.1973
Bingo: Scenes of money and death	14.11.1973
Spring Awakening (*translation*)	28.5.1974
The Fool: Scenes of bread and love	18.11.1975
Stone	8.6.1976
We Come to the River	12.7.1976
The White Devil (*adaptation*)	12.7.1976
Grandma Faust (*part one* of A-A-America!)	25.10.1976
The Swing (*part two of* A-A-America!)	22.11.1976
The Bundle: New Narrow Road to the Deep North	13.1.1978
The Woman	10.8.1978
The Worlds	8.3.1979
Restoration	21.7.1981
Summer	27.1.1982
Derek	18.10.1982
After the Assassinations	1.3.1983
The Cat (*performed as* The English Cat)	2.6.1983
Human Cannon	2.2.1986
The War Plays	
Part I: Red Black and Ignorant	29.5.1985
Part II: The Tin Can People	29.5.1985
Part III: Great Peace	17.7.1985
Jackets	24.1.1989
September	16.9.1989
In the Company of Men	1.2.1992
Lulu (*translation*)	2.3.1992
Olly's Prison (*TV*)	1.5.1993
Tuesday (*TV*)	1.6.1993
At the Inland Sea	16.10.1995
Coffee	27.11.1996
Eleven Vests	14.10.1997

The War Plays
A Trilogy

for Maria Carmela Coco Davani

Part One: Red Black and Ignorant

ONE

Introduction

The MONSTER *comes on.*

MONSTER.

1

Alone of creatures we know that we pass between birth
   and death
And wish to teach each new mind to be as profound as a
   crystal ocean through which we may see the ocean bed
   and from shore to shore

2

We speak of our children before they are born
Carry them before we can hold them
Fold their clothes and lay their bed before they can wake
Sew and harvest and market their food before they can
   eat
For them we build streets before they can walk
And guard them from sickness before they can draw
   breath
For three seasons they grow in the womb while the world
   may age ten thousand years
When they are born the hands of mechanics housekeepers
   masons pilots designers administrators drivers garden-
   ers are held together to receive them
No exiled hero could return to a land more welcoming
No president be received into office with such
   preparation
No victor be greeted with so much joy
We should not wonder that in the past children thought
   the world was watched over by gods

3

But now we kill them

The MOTHER *comes on.*

MOTHER.

1

In the past there were survivors to tell that suddenly the
world became a place of toys
A huge red ball inflated in the sky
Houses shook as dolls' houses shake when they're carried
by children
Small things became big and big things vanished
Many reported that the cloud glowed like a bonfire
And that the wounded babbled in the strange tongues
spoken by children when they pretend to be foreigners

2

I did not see or hear these things
I sat alone in my room
That morning the child had moved in my womb as if it
wanted to run away from the world
Through the womb's wall it had felt the world's fear
Now my head was bent as I listened
I was so intent I did not hear the explosions and passed
into death without knowing
My body's spasm crushed the child
My flesh burst open and threw him into the furnace of
my burning house

The MONSTER *sits on the bench beside his* MOTHER.

MONSTER. When the rockets destroyed the world every-
thing whistled
Every hard surface and hard edge whistled
Mouths of medicine bottles and whiskey bottles

Cornices of law courts and office blocks
Cracks in rocks
Whistled in derision
As the tyres stopped screeching the winds whistled in the
broken windows
Doors and wheelchairs – some empty, others carrying
sick and maimed – whistled as they flew high over the
great plains
The mountains whistled
The last breaths whistled from dead mouths
And as the flesh burned from faces the skulls whistled
Surfaces too soft to whistle burned and the fires whistled
The heart leapt like a bird in its burning cage and the
ribs whistled
The earth whistled in derision
In final derision at the lord of creation
In derision derision
That drowned the sounds of explosions and the last
screams of the world's masters
The whole earth whistled in derision at the lord of
creation

MOTHER. This is the child my womb threw into the fire

The MOTHER *goes out.*

MONSTER. Now we will show scenes from the life I did not
live
If what happens seems such that human beings would
not allow it to happen you have not read the histories
of your times

The MONSTER *goes out.*

TWO

Learning

MONSTER. Learning

A BOY *comes on.*

BOY. I'll wait in this corner of the playground and stop her
   as she leaves school

A GIRL *comes on.*

   Come out with me tonight
GIRL. Been stood up?
BOY. No
GIRL. Why you asking so late?
BOY. You kept dodging me
GIRL. Where to?
BOY. Disco
GIRL. Disco's boring weekdays
BOY. The club has good groups on Wednesdays

The MONSTER *comes in.*

MONSTER (*flatly*).
   In lessons a blowtorch ran over my body
   My nerves are burned out so I felt no pain
   The flame poked me like a finger attracting my attention
      and then pointed to the ground
GIRL. Who else've you asked?
BOY. It'll be just the two of us

The BOY *casually spits.*

   O I spat on you
MONSTER. O
BOY. Its on your jacket
GIRL. Urgh

BOY. Sorry
   I wasnt looking where I spat
GIRL. Urgh its running down his sleeve
MONSTER. It doesnt matter
GIRL. Aint it horrible!
   All gob
   Mucky bastard
BOY. Have you got a tissue?
MONSTER. No
BOY. I'll tear a page from my exercise book
GIRL. You'll get reported
BOY. Have you got a tissue?
GIRL. Im not a chemist shop
BOY. I'll tear out the page at the opposite side of the book
   and then the teacher wont know the book's been
   vandalised
MONSTER. I don't want to get you into trouble
BOY. I meant to spit on the ground
GIRL. He'll blame you for walking into his spit

The BOY *tears a sheet of paper from his exercise book and
gives it to the* MONSTER.

MONSTER. Thank you

The MONSTER *wipes the spit from his jacket sleeve with the
sheet of paper. The* BOY *tears out the opposite sheet from his
exercise book, folds it carefully and puts it into his pocket.*

GIRL. The paper's too stiff
   It's not absorbent
   You're rubbing the phlegm into the fabric
   Urgh
   Mucky bastards
MONSTER. Its coming off
BOY. Dribble more spit on it to loosen the bits
GIRL. Leave it till you get home

BOY. Double the paper and scoop it up with the thick edge
Six o'clock all right?

GIRL. Im not going anywhere afterwards

BOY. There's always a good group at the club

GIRL. Dont drop the paper on the ground for people to look at
Urgh

MONSTER. Im going to the washroom

The MONSTER *sits on the bench and the* BOY *and* GIRL *go out.*

MONSTER. I spent my life putting together the bits of a jigsaw
It was complete and I looked at the picture
But then a friend kicked the table
The pieces of jigsaw flew into the air like startled pigeons and settled down again into the picture
But the picture is different
A bullet has passed from side to side of my brain

A TEACHER *comes on.*

TEACHER. Why are you sitting in the washroom?

MONSTER. Sorry sir

TEACHER. Headmaster forbids loitering in the washrooms

MONSTER. Yes sir

TEACHER. Dont pretend you've discovered how to think and came here to practise in quiet

MONSTER. I was spat at

TEACHER. Where?

MONSTER. In the playground

TEACHER. Who spat at you?

MONSTER. It was an accident

TEACHER. Then why are you sitting alone in the washroom?
I've watched you for twenty minutes

MONSTER. A bullet passed from side to side of my brain
and left a vapour trail across the sky

TEACHER. What is this nonsense?
You say the spit fell on you accidentally
You are innocent in the matter

MONSTER. Yes sir

TEACHER. Then it is self-indulgent to brood as if you were
guilty
You're not a martyr
I've noticed you often give yourself airs
If it happens again you'll go on report
Who spat at you?

MONSTER. Robinson sir

TEACHER. At what part of you did he spit?

MONSTER. My sleeve

TEACHER. Nauseous
You are to go to Robinson and tell him
'It is against school rules to spit in the school buildings
or the school playground
Spitting is unhygienic and loutish
Furthermore it may lead to unforseeable circumstances
By this spit you might have forfeited my friendship'
Then you will spit on Robinson's sleeve
After that you will both shake hands

MONSTER. But I dont –

TEACHER. Robinson is approaching
No doubt seeking some other unsullied spot to make
offensive with his ubiquitous saliva
I shall watch from the common room window

The TEACHER *goes out.*

MONSTER. My friend had forgotten he had spat on me
He was devising ways of making the girl take the long
way home through the park after the club

The BOY *comes in.*

MONSTER. It is against school rules to spit in our school
   buildings or in our playground
   It is unhealthy and shows disregard of others' feelings
   Its my duty to help you break a habit you should have
   outgrown with infancy

The MONSTER *spits on the* BOY's *sleeve and then holds out
his hand.*
The BOY *automatically shakes it.*
A moment's paralysis.
They fight, rolling over and over on the ground.

MONSTER. I had not yet learned to hate
   That knowledge is gained in higher schools
   So far I knew only the basis of hate: fear
   We struck at each other as two men caught in the drum
      of a cement mixer would strike each other when they
      were using their arms and legs only to stop the drum
      spinning
   The effort of the struggle made us sweat
   As we grappled we smelt each other's sweat
   It smelt of dust

The MONSTER *and the* BOY *go out.*

THREE

Love

MONSTER. Love

A WOMAN *comes on.*
She is beautiful.

WOMAN. He is beautiful

His legs are as subtle as trees bending in spring wind on
    hills over the city
His chest is as broad as fields
In his arms is the fullness of autumn
And his eyes are as sharp as frost to see the approach of
    the enemy

The MONSTER *comes on.*
Bandages have unwound from his arms and legs and trail
behind him.
He contorts and jerks like kindling in a fire.
The WOMAN *does not change her mood.*

You are beautiful
Your hands move as steadily as the hands of a cleaning
    woman scrubbing the table for her daughter's new
    house
I wish our children to inherit your beauty so that when
    they grow and I am old I shall see you again with a
    young woman's joy
Your smile shines with the lights of a city
I place my hand on your stomach where each hair is like
    a diagram of a dance
MONSTER. My blood stinks: pools on factory floors: acid
My bandages burn with acid
Words uproot my teeth: the stumps of old trees
They rattle in my mouth: dice!
I spit them out and count: the end of the world!
WOMAN. And my love is not selfish
    You make all things beautiful as all things in the sun
        show its light
    People shopping walk as if they were gathering the fruit
        of paradise
    Even fool's babble takes on the meaning of children's
        songs

I take your body into mine as a tree devouring its own
  fruit

MONSTER. Bandages: rags: rotted in blood
  I tried to strangle myself: they tore: the noise of laughing

The MONSTER *stands.*

WOMAN. In bed I notice your warmth
  The warmth in your legs is different from the warmth in
    your neck
  The warmth in the back of your neck is different from
    the warmth in the front

As the MONSTER *goes out he cries like a child.*

When I see you I smile as the goddesses smiled when the
    beautiful were given to them in the festival
  I watch you join the brown blue and yellow-and-green
    wires to the electric plug
And you make flowers grow inwards on my face

The WOMAN *goes out.*

FOUR

Eating

MONSTER. Eating

The MONSTER *comes on and sits on one end of the bench.*

MONSTER (*calls*). I cant find my book
WIFE (*off*). You left it on the bus
MONSTER (*calls*). I didnt take it on the bus
  I cant read on buses
WIFE (*off*). Then its still here

MONSTER (*calls*). Try to remember where you put it when
     you cleaned up
   It has a blue cover

The WIFE *comes on with a loaf and a breadknife. She sits
on the end of the bench opposite the* MONSTER *and cuts the
loaf.*

WIFE. I've made it a rule never to touch your books

Fractional pause.

If it was a library book the name of the library would
     have been inside (*Fractional pause.*) and when you left
     it on the bus it would have been returned

Fractional pause.

Then when you reported the loss to the librarian you'd
     have learned that it had been found
   The cover was green

She gives the MONSTER *a slice of bread.*

The plate's hot
MONSTER. Thank you
   If I wasnt intelligent enough to know the colour of the
     cover I'd hardly be trying to read what was inside it
WIFE. You give me many opportunities to watch you
     reading your books
   That's how I acquired the habit of noticing the colour of
     the covers
   When it changes you've bought a new book
MONSTER. A book cant vanish
WIFE. Buy another one
   Arent you going to eat?
MONSTER. Im not hungry
WIFE. Why didnt you tell me that before I cooked?
MONSTER. I was hungry

Now Im not

WIFE. I suppose now I've cooked your meal you expect me
    to scrape it off the plate for you into the pedal bin
    You can afford your luxuries because I struggle to pay
    for the necessities
    Buy books if you must read
    But its not fair to waste good food I struggled to buy

Quietly needling.

You deserve to lose your appetite when you argue

MONSTER. I merely asked where you'd hidden my book

WIFE (*eating*). All this because you've mislaid a book with
    a green cover
    If you're not going to eat your bread I'll eat it

She takes his slice of bread and eats it.

I thought children sulked over food

MONSTER. The sound of grunting doesn't give me an
    appetite

WIFE. You'll eat when you're hungry

The MONSTER grunts.

Was it a book of manners?

*The MONSTER stands, picks up all the bread, tears it apart,
throws the pieces on the floor and stamps on them.*

MONSTER. Eat it off the floor!

He pushes his WIFE onto the floor.

Eat it up!
Go on!

He tries to force pieces of bread into her mouth.

Grunt grunt!
Eat your meal off the floor and lick it clean!

Gobble up your swill!

Pause. He tries again to force her to eat.

WIFE. Are you satisfied now the food's wasted?

MONSTER. If you want to behave like a pig live like a pig!
Perhaps you'll be more interesting to talk to!

He tries to force pieces of bread into her mouth.

Eat it! Eat it!

WIFE. You behave like a monster

MONSTER (*turns away and groans*). The charred squirrel
leaps from the burning tree through the broken
window: its trapped in the burning room

Its blazing fur spreads the fire its running away from: its
pitiful cries

Out in the street an old general runs between skeletons
stealing their medals

WIFE. Im not cleaning up after you

The WIFE stands and goes out as the MONSTER talks.

MONSTER (*calmer*). At every turn we break the oath we
make when we're born to human reason

Even in hell to walk with decorum

With each little rage we tear pages from the dictionary

From the first drop of rain we catch the icy sickness that
will kill us

Soon we set fire to the bread-lorries before the rows of
starving children on the camp square

And when the storm comes take down the sick people's
hovels stone by stone

*The WIFE comes on with a brush and pan and sweeps the
bread from the floor.*

WIFE. Do it once more and I shant cook
If you cant control your anger you'll have to shout at me

But we cant afford this waste

The MONSTER *goes out.*

As nature doesnt define what shall make us angry
We define ourselves by the things we allow to make us
    angry
If we choose these wrongly or are wrongly taught we are
    blind with rage even when we're most calm

The WIFE *goes out.*

FIVE

Selling

MONSTER. Selling

The BUYER, *the* MONSTER *and his* WIFE *come on.*

BUYER. I am the buyer
    The Register of Births records the birth of your son
    He is now at an age to learn to speak
    I have come to buy him
WIFE. Let us keep him to ourselves for a little longer
    He's too small to sell
BUYER. You want him to grow to be strong with a good
        character
    We'll give him regular health checks and training in
        discipline
    He will learn to think and behave in such a way that the
        community will welcome him
    Later we may give him work
    If not he'll need us even more
    Surely you wont deny him our help and protection?
WIFE. I didnt expect you so soon

BUYER. Training must begin early to have full effect
  You will be paid enough to feed and clothe him
  There will even be toys
  The child wont know its sold
  But if you wait till its older before you sell it it would
    think you treated it as your property
  There'd be dissension in the family
  I hope you're not among those misguided parents who let
    their unfortunate children run wild
  When the time finally comes for such children to be sold
    they suffer as much as a living animal sealed in a can
    on a supermarket shelf
  Some can never be sold
  They're scattered like dry beans on the supermarket floor
    and no buyer can gather them up to be weighed and
    priced
MONSTER. How much?
BUYER. According to the livestock book he comes from a
    good strain
  He's your only produce
  Provided the screening tests show no –
WIFE. He's perfect in wind and limb
BUYER. Subsistence for twenty years
MONSTER. But you want him for life!
BUYER. In twenty years he'll have his own child to sell
WIFE. What if he doesnt?
BUYER. Then he must sell someone else's child
  In his situation it would be up to him to find someone
MONSTER. Twenty-five
MAN. I consulted your records before I quoted my price
  They show you were sold for twenty years and your wife
    for eighteen
MONSTER. Times have changed
  There've been political struggles
  Now people have rights

We live in a free country

There's no freedom if you can't fix your own price

BUYER. There are always more of you coming on to the market so the prices are set by the buyers

If the price is too high we dont take

There are many types of incineratory devices for disposing of unsellable goods which if left lying about would create a health hazard

Take the twenty years

The economic situation is bad and prices will fall

MONSTER. Fetch our son

WIFE. Dont take less than twenty-three

The MONSTER'*s* WIFE *goes out.*

BUYER. With the money I offer you'd live in greater comfort than your parents did

The end of twenty years is a long way off

Who knows if anyone will be here by then?

You're jeopardising your son's future for three years that may never appear on any calendar

If he's all you say he is in twenty years he'll be a buyer himself!

Then when he reads my report of this interview in the files he'd disown his family

Even worse: suppose the list of applicants for a major chairmanship had been reduced to your son and one other

The computer would take as a deciding factor his parents' non-co-operation with the state

The good citizen is satisfied more by serving than being served

MONSTER. That's what you'll train him to think

BUYER. Certainly

And then he wont object will he?

His opinions will be formed even before he knows the
   subjects on which he holds them
Could life be more trouble-free?

The MONSTER'S WIFE *brings on a child made of newspaper
papier mâché and wrapped in newspaper sheets.*

WIFE. He was one of the first house-trained in his batch at
   clinic
Never cries for food or dribbles it when he gets it
His cot blanket's so tidy you'd think it was a three-piece
   suit
A whole day passes and there's not one wrinkle on it
Sometimes its uncanny

The BUYER *ignores the child and eagerly examines the sheets
in which its wrapped.*

BUYER (*reading*). The paper says at Birmingham Crown
   Court a man was given twenty-three life sentences for
   robbing old ladies of their shopping bags
He was caught when the battery powering his wheelchair
   ran out as he tried to escape from the scene of his last
   offence
WIFE. His smile is worth three years
The prime minister would tell the chauffeur to stop so
   that my son could be photographed standing on the
   curb and smiling into the official limousine

The BUYER *takes the baby from the wife and reads from the
print on its face.*

BUYER. The paper says a university professor has made it
   possible to fire military beams through the earth to
   reach their targets with a saving of several seconds
   formerly lost in following the earth's curvature
As he received the Government Science Medal he said
   that his next invention would –

MONSTER. We'll take twenty

BUYER. I name this child mine

WIFE. Its for the best

MONSTER. If the screening tests are good perhaps you
could increase it to –

BUYER. I must hurry
My days are full of sales

Snatches a newspaper sheet from the child.

I'll just take page three
The nude has a dagger in her breast
Last Thursday they showed the moment when the hair
of the blond with the lovely smile which had been
drenched in petrol was being set alight by the winner
of the week's lucky number

The BUYER *goes.*

MONSTER (*turns aside and gently hugs his arms and chest as if
they still smarted from the fire*). They are so greedy they
stuff food into their anus
People starve and the guts of the granaries burst
In the fish farms piles of rotting fish rise from the middle
of the black lakes under piles of screaming gulls
But I who have never tasted milk tell of the time when
the eater and the food are consumed by one fire

The MONSTER *and his* WIFE *go out.*

SIX

Work

MONSTER. Work

A WOMAN *is trapped under the bench. The* SON *comes on.*

SON. A woman walked in the centre of the decaying city
   A wall of a derelict warehouse fell into the street and a
      concrete beam from the wall pinioned her to the
      pavement
WOMAN. Help me
SON. Every day there are cries for help in this part of the
      city
   No one answers them
   Often the person who cries is a decoy
   Even when they arent people say they have only them-
      selves to blame for coming to this savage place
   They couldnt have been going about lawful business
      because here nothing is lawful
   The city centre stands outside the human community
      and so no help can be given
   It lies open to the skies like a broken coffin
   And from the walls seep dust and the damp smells of
      exploitation that began with the makers of bricks and
      the builders of walls
WOMAN. Help
SON. From the distance I've seen the wall collapse and bury
      the woman in this blanket of stone
   I know her: she is a friend

The SON *goes to the* WOMAN.

WOMAN. Thank god a friend came!
   I was afraid my calls would bring thugs to rob me and
      then kill me so that I couldnt give evidence against
      them
   Help me
   I cant carry the weight of this concrete beam much longer

The SON *pretends to try to lift the beam.*

SON. How heavy it is!

WOMAN. I'm carrying the weight so two people must be
    able to lift it
    If we lift it three inches I could crawl out
SON. The beam is too heavy for us to lift
WOMAN. Quickly my strength is going!
    Lift with me when I give the word
    Now!

The WOMAN *and the* SON *try to lift the beam.*
He stops lifting.

SON. Its heavy
WOMAN. Please help me
SON. Let the rubble take the beam's weight and I'll pull
    you from underneath
WOMAN. No
    Why're you on this street?
    You're going to the factory
    Yesterday I told you there was a job vacant
    You're going to ask for it
SON. Take your hands from the beam
    It wont fall on you
WOMAN. You want my leg to be crushed so that you get
    the job
    You are my enemy!
SON. No
    Let me run to fetch help
    With two or three to help we could lift the beam
WOMAN. You'd tell anyone you met not to come into this
    street because more walls were going to fall
    Take the job
    Im powerless
    You can swagger off to the factory and feel no more
    shame than a dog pissing in the street
    No one who feels shame will succeed in this city
    But send anyone you meet to help me!

Even if their parents' blood was wet on their hands they
   couldn't be as cruel as you
SON. I look anxiously along the empty street afraid someone
   will come
   I see my father at the corner
   He comes towards me

The MONSTER *comes on.*

WOMAN. Help!
MONSTER. Someone's calling help
   Why d'you stand with your hands at your sides?

The SON *steps between the* MONSTER *and the beam.*

SON. Father a woman's trapped in the rubble
   The beam is supported by fallen debris
   If we move the beam the debris will be dislodged and the
      beam will crush her
   Run for the security
   They'll bring heavy rescue equipment
   I'll stay to make sure she isnt robbed

The MONSTER *reaches for the bench.*

MONSTER. The beam isn't heavy
   Two of us can lift it
   She's lucky I came along!

The MONSTER *tries to lift the beam.*

SON. There's a job in the factory at the end of the street
   This woman and I want it
   Her qualifications are better than mine
   If she's incapacitated for a little while I'll get the job
WOMAN. Your son was my friend!
MONSTER. You'd let a friend's leg be broken so that you
      could get work?
   Monstrous!

The MONSTER *strains to lift the beam.*

SON. Father
This may be my last chance to get work
Without work Im an outcast
The community wont give me the power to control my
 life
What have you done for me?
A junk school – job training for nothing
I've been buried in rubble for years
Father the woman is nothing to you
I am your son: I have a right to your help
MONSTER (*groans*). If her leg breaks she could be crippled
 for life
Even if she recovered she'd feel great pain
WOMAN. Help me
I will be grateful
I wont go for the job
SON (*snarling at the* WOMAN). If the fisherman throws the
 fish back into the water the fish doesn't give him back
 his bait
MONSTER (*leaves the beam on the* WOMAN *and wanders away
 in pain*). If you walked away tomorrow you might hear
 of a better job
Then you'd regret your cruelty!
WOMAN. The beam moved!
SON. Why should she have the job?
Its chance her brain is better than mine just as it was
 chance the beam fell on her
Five minutes and it could have fallen on me

The SON *raises his fists to hit the* MONSTER.

WOMAN. Its breaking my leg!

The MONSTER *pushes his* SON *to the ground.*

MONSTER. The world isnt just!
    Justice is made by people!
    If I do what is right I have the strength of a hundred
        men!

The MONSTER *goes to the bench.*
He lifts it over his head and poses in triumph.
His SON *and the* WOMAN *look up at him.*
A heroic snapshot: as the WOMAN *talks it fades . . .*

WOMAN. I look at the face of the one who helped me
    Without thinking we smile at each other
    He turns to look at his son: and as he smiles his brow
        creases into a frown
    It isnt easy to be just in an unjust world

The SON *stands.*

SON. You would call my father good and me evil
    No – the pittance paid to the workless ensures that all seek
        work
    The government rules by creating two classes of citizens
    I am second class: I have no work
    I cant afford to behave as if I were first class
WOMAN. When the wall fell I was hurrying to the factory
        to ask for the vacant job
    As I hurried along and saw the smoke rising from the
        factory chimneys I sniffed the air to catch the smell
        and my mouth watered as the sight of others eating
        makes the mouth water
    That's why I didnt hear the wall's warning rumble and
        was trapped
MONSTER.

1

In bad times it should be human to do good
But in bad times good cannot be done

Where there is too little to go round to give to one is to
take from another
Ten naked children huddled under one sheet
The parents pull at the sheet to stretch it to cover the
children
The sheet is torn to tatters and blown away in the wind
Those who would change the world by kindness should
learn
Where kindness is most needed it cannot be given

2

When the rich man gives a pound to the poor man
That night enter the rich man's house and steal all that
he has more than the poor man
The rich man gives a meal to the poor man's son
Take the rich man's son and do not return him to his
father till the poor man's son is fed *every* day
How else will there be justice?
When you come running with the rich man's charity the
poor man will be dead
You will put food into the mouth of a corpse
We are not taught to understand the world
The dead man seems to be humming with satisfaction
but the sound is made by the fly buzzing in his gaping
mouth

The MONSTER, *his* SON *and the* WOMAN *go.*

SEVEN

The Army

As the SON *sings, the* MONSTER *and his* WIFE (*and the other characters if they are played by other players*) *help the* SON *to put on a bullet-proof army jacket and combat helmet and give him a rifle.*
When they have dressed him they go.

SON.

The Army Song

1

I am the army
My legs are made of tanks
My arms are made of guns
My trunk is made of nukes
My head is made of bombs
I am the army

2

I am the army
My breath is toxic gas
My eyes are radar beams
My pulse is tickertape
When I speak a siren screams
I am the army

3

When a soldier heaves a grenade what does he see: a
    body explode like a bottle on a wall
When a soldier slits a belly what does he see: guts spill
    like clothes from a suitcase
When a soldier fires a bullet what does he see: blood
    spurt like water from a hosepipe

That is the soldier's reward for his skills: the pleasure of
seeing the way he kills

4

I see nothing

5

I am the army
My feet are on the earth
My hand is on the moon
My head is out in space
Dont whine to me in fear
Dont plead for the human race
Dont show me children huddled in dread
I am the army
I shit on the earth from the stratosphere
And wipe my arse on the lists of the dead
Bow down and worship me

The SON *goes.*

EIGHT

No one can willingly give up the name of human

MONSTER. No one can willingly give up the name of human

The MONSTER *comes on.*

MONSTER. When my son reached the age at which I
fathered him
There were so many rockets the world looked like a
hedgehog
It could have been destroyed as easily as if it had been a

little apple and a giant stood up in space and devoured
   it in one bite
People walked on tiptoe in the street as if they feared the
   vibration of their steps would set off the rockets
They stopped moving the furniture in their houses: the
   movement might show up on radar screens and bring
   destruction on them and their neighbours
Security was so great all were suspected
Even as they lay in their silos the rockets destroyed the
   societies they were said to protect

The SON *comes on with a gun.*

MONSTER. Anyone see you enter the house?
SON. Why?
MONSTER. It would be marked as the home of a soldier
   Why d'you carry guns in the street?
SON. To protect ourselves from you mother-stranglers

The MONSTER's WIFE *comes in.*

WIFE. My son

She embraces him.

   Are you on leave?
SON (*takes off his helmet*). There's an action
WIFE. Dont talk about it now
   Have you eaten?
SON. Not since yesterday
WIFE. I thought the army ate
SON. The civvie-corpses ambush our trucks and steal our
   fodder
WIFE. Come into the kitchen
   I'll get you a meal
MONSTER. He does things he cant tell his parents
WIFE. He's in the army because he couldn't work as a civilian
      You stopped him

SON. Its an offence under martial law to slander soldiers
  You're the sort who turn out with the corpse-mobs of
    mother-stranglers when they shoot us up and then
    bellyache because we're armed
WIFE. Both of you stop it
SON. There's nothing wrong with him a good postmortem
    wouldnt put right
WIFE. The army wont let him out and if he didnt obey
    orders he'd be shot
  Can you change that?
SON. I like the army
  When you're a soldier all your problems are solved by
    training
  Kill or be killed
  No apologies or explanations
  You always gab about right and wrong
  Do what's right? – its as much use as an overcoat to a corpse
  In a storm the gaps between the raindrops dont stop you
    getting wet
  Can you *stop the storm*?
  Im not ashamed to tell you why Im here
  Every squaddie's been sent back to his own street to
    shoot one civvie-corpse
  He chooses which
  Make the decisions hard
  Test the potential
  Know yourself
  When you've got gunsights for eyes and triggers for
    fingers you can call yourself a soldier
MONSTER. You'd do that?

As the SON *talks the* MONSTER *turns away in pain.*

SON. Following the reason yeh
  You think this is a famine?
  Next year you'll be so hungry you'll be like corpses who

eat the nails out of their coffin and then look round for
something else

He takes off his jacket and gives it to his MOTHER.

After this action you'll be so corpse-scared if we stood
you against the wall you'd offer to load our rifles in
case we did something really nasty

The streets'll be as quiet as a churchyard where the
mourners are deaf and dumb and the corpses've taken
a vow of silence

After that we can put down the food riots with a few
bursts of armalite and a few hangings from the helicop-
ter platforms

Otherwise we'd've had to go over you with the human
lawnmower

In the end the army's doing this for the public good

WIFE. There's only two families left on this street:

Us and the old couple still in the house on the corner

MONSTER. He's known them since he was a child

SON. We dont have to come up with a choice

The order says we could leave it to the officer

WIFE. No no no

He'd choose me or your father

He'd do it to punish you for being a coward

Dont argue with him

It torments him for nothing

He didnt make this mess: we're the ones who –

MONSTER. He sits there in human clothes and speaks our
language

Doesnt the food humans eat poison you?

WIFE. Stop it

Its easy to talk!

You're like a judge who gives a verdict in an armchair

MONSTER. Run and hide in the ruins

There are whole communities living outside the law

WIFE (*explaining plainly and simply so that he will under-stand*). No no I told you

    If he doesnt choose the officer wont even ask who else is left in the street

    He'll shoot *both of us* to punish him

    Two will have been shot instead of one

MONSTER (*flatly*). We live like prisoners in a death-cell facing death every day

    Once there were gaps between bars: they've filled them in

    If a pardon came they'd use it to make a list of the condemned

    Perhaps its better to die

WIFE. What if they shot me?

MONSTER. I hope it would be me but I cant help what happens now

WIFE. Then you're the monster not our son!

    What can we do in the end?

    Fight for our own

    Your son or your husband

    I'll fight for them!

    Tooth and nail!

    So would the woman on the corner!

She embraces her son.

    Poor boy

    I dont blame you

    Never never would I do that

    If you were free you'd help these people

    You were a kind boy

    You always whistled when you turned into the street

    I listen out for it

    Now your face is like stone at the top of a mountain

    Did you tell the officer you'd go to the corner house?

SON. No

WIFE. Silly silly

If you'd told him it would've all been settled now
It would be too late to let him choose: he'd punish you
   for changing your mind

Sudden suspicion.

Why did you come here?
Why didn't you go straight to the corner house?
SON. I don't know
WIFE. Its silly
   When you're given these things to do you must make it
      easy for yourself
   Otherwise they cant be done
   Quickly!
   Go and do it

She puts the SON *into his jacket*

I'll help you with your jacket
There, I'll fasten the buttons
My boy I'll help you as I did when you were a child
I'll always be here to help you whenever you need me
I'll go with you to the corner house
SON. No . . .
WIFE. Look: a loose button
   That must be sewn on when you come back
   There isnt time now

She gives him his helmet.

We cant let the officers see you without a button
They're so intolerant
Yes you look smart
Take your gun to the corner house

She gives him his gun.

They'll be home: the curfew's begun
Come back quickly

The SON *takes his gun and goes.*
The WIFE *sits on the bench.*
After the WIFE *has been speaking for a while the* MONSTER
goes to the bench and sits facing away from her.

He wont shoot the woman
The old man's ill
He's the one
Wouldnt last two days in a famine
I tell you when I saw him I wanted to run away
Crossed to the other side of the street
A dog put its head down and barked at him
Staring eyes and thin: my life! . . .
He had that white face you see on the freaks in the ruins
I thought he was carrying two big stones but they were
    his hands
The empty carrier bag she'd tied round his neck on a
    string had more in it than him
Perhaps our son will be lucky: if he could find him dead
    everything would be simple
Lift him out onto the floor and gently put a bullet in him
If I cook will he eat?
MONSTER. It's just another job for him
    He didn't go straight to the corner house because it didnt
    even occur to him to get it over quickly
WIFE. What planet d'you come from?
    No one's life was ever saved because they couldnt find
    someone to kill him!
If it says you're killed you're killed
Its better if he does it
He wont gloat or be crueller than he has to be
What d'you want from him?
Would it make killing more human if he was ashamed of
    doing it?
I know what they did to him before he could do it

Pity him

She lifts the MONSTER's *hand and with formal intimacy kisses the back of the wrist.*

Pity him . . .
How often are we allowed to live in our own century?
I've walked in it once or twice
Put my hands into it once or twice as if I was blindfold
    and groped inside a strange box
We lay the table and eat off the floor
We dont own our lives
They're owned by savages: that's why we're cruel
I'll prepare the meal and first we'll wait on him and then
    sit down and eat with him to show respect
Things may happen that will make today seem so trivial
    we'll forget it
As long as we can sit at our table its an ordinary day
The roof's over our heads: the walls arent burning
If we havent learned to sit at our table while the
    murderers walk the streets we dont know how our
    neighbours have had to live for years
If they put a pistol to my head I'll go on washing the
    dishes as if they hadnt entered my house
How else shall we live?

The SON *arrives at the* ALISON's *house (another part of the stage).*

SON.

1

When we were children we called this the corner house
    that stands where three roads meet

2

Mrs Alison
Its your neighbours' son
The soldier
Open the door
Is it all right to come in?
No I wont sit down
If you like

The SON *brings a chair and sits.*

3

You have to leave the house every week to collect your
    security?
You'll be all right if you hurry
Dont stop even for people you know
Has Mr Alison been to hospital?
No, his tie: its mostly only officials who wear ties
Your generation tries to keep up standards

4

Ten years since I played in the street
Now it'd be safer to play in a minefield
Thank god for the government child pens
I suppose the changes bewilder you
The old days wont come again
You're tired of the new ones
(You can shoot now they're calm)

5

The room seemed bigger when I was a child
I could touch the ceiling
My mother (why dont you kill him?) is cooking
Its late
(He'd lie on the floor like a raincoat in a jumble sale

For anyone to buy
You put it on and look in the mirror:
The stranger's still wearing it)
My mother said hurry
Bolt the door after me so that even I couldnt get in

The SON *leaves the* ALISON's *house. He stands lost. The*
MONSTER's WIFE *fetches a breadknife and the remains of a*
loaf, sits on the bench and cuts the loaf into slices. The SON
goes to the bench.

WIFE. You didnt let the meal get cold
That's right
Do your hands need a wash?
The supermarkets have soldiers to guard the tins
I'd like to see a full saucepan again

The MONSTER's WIFE *offers bread to the* MONSTER *and*
the SON.
The MONSTER *holds his bread in his hand.*
The MONSTER's WIFE *eats mechanically.*

I should go and watch with her
You sent her out of the room but she came back when
   you fired
I'd ask her here if I thought she'd come
She wouldnt speak to me
That'll pass
She'll have to put up with it like the rest
We live with what there is like bees getting honey from
   flowers on a litter heap
SON. Dad I couldnt kill him
He was old
His bones were as weak as a broken fence
A few sprawling sticks on an allotment that wouldnt keep
   out the three-legged dogs

The SON *shoots the* MONSTER.
The MONSTER *dies immediately: he drops his bread.*

WIFE. He's dead!
  You're mad!
  He's come to kill us all!

The MONSTER'S WIFE *runs out.*
The SON *picks up the pieces of bread and sits on the bench.*

MONSTER. Praise this soldier
  Why did he kill his father and not the stranger?
  Under his scars the flesh was whole
  Praise him as you would the first wheel
  The first pitcher that held water
  The first wall that stood on the earth as still as a startled
     animal
  The first cutting that gave fruit to a barren tree
  For all of us there is a time when we must know ourself
  No natural laws or legal codes will guide us
  Notions of good and evil will say nothing
  The problems these things solve are not serious
  We stand more naked than when we were born
  Our life can be crushed as easily as an ant by an army
  But at this time we could not be crushed even by the
     weight of the continent on which the army marched
  We know ourself and say: I cannot give up the name of
     human
  All that is needed is to define rightly what it is to be human
  If we define it wrongly we die
  If we define it and teach it rightly we shall live

  The first playwrights said know yourself
  My son learned it was better to kill what he loved
  Than that one creature who is sick or lame or old or poor
     or a stranger should sit and stare at an empty world
     and find no reason why it should suffer

The MONSTER *goes.*

SON. The massacre has begun in the streets
　　There is a string of clouds in the sky
　　Sit here for a while
　　Then go to the ruins where the people are

The SON *goes.*

NINE

Funeral

WIFE.
　　　　　　} Funeral
SON.

The MONSTER, *the* MONSTER'S WIFE *and* SON *come on*
(and the other characters if they are played by other players).
The MONSTER *carries two fistfuls of ash.*

WIFE. You who live in barbarous times
　　Under rulers with redness on their hands blackness in
　　　　their hearts and ignorance in their minds
　　Everything before your time was the childhood of
　　　　humankind
　　With the new weapons that age passed
　　But you went on building your house with bricks that
　　　　were already on fire
SON. If we'd lived we wouldnt have been content with your
　　　　savage stupidities
　　We would have learned
　　Everyday: small things
　　And big things: when the mind is unfurled like a banner
　　　　in the sky
MONSTER. You killed us for freedom

Democracy isnt the right to vote but freedom to know
and the knowledge based on knowing
Your democracy is the way truth is suppressed and
freedom hustled away to prison

What is the freedom you gave me?
Two fists of ash

He throws the ash on the ground.

Where is the freedom in that?

THE ARMY SONG

(1984)

Words by
EDWARD BOND

Music by
DAVID SHAW-PARKER

This score gives the parts for voice and piano; in addition, it is
strongly recommended that the use of harsh-sounding percussion
instruments be explored. All the piano chords should be played
as open fifths (no thirds) unless otherwise stated.

Music processed by Peter Washtell

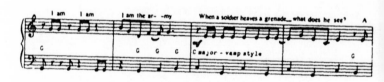

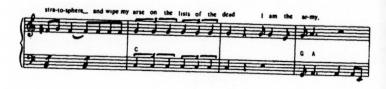

THE ARMY SONG
(1985)

Words by
EDWARD BOND

Music by
DAVID SHAW-PARKER

* All the guitar chords should be played as open fifths (no thirds).

© David Shaw-Parker.

Music processed by Peter Vasaltell

Part Two: The Tin Can People

Characters:

FIRST MAN
SECOND MAN
THIRD MAN
FIRST WOMAN
SECOND WOMAN
THIRD WOMAN
FOURTH WOMAN

The choruses should be spoken by individual characters.

Section One: Paradise in Hell

Section Two: The Tin Can Riots

Section Three: The Young Sages

SECTION ONE: PARADISE IN HELL

First Chorus

Years later a dust as white as old people's hair settled on
everything
The world looked like a drawing in lead on white paper
Hours after the explosions I walked over a bridge
The thirst caused by the fires was so severe that even the
drowning called for water
People fled in all directions from one hell into another
I thought the explosions had thrown strange sea creatures
onto the bridge whose ancestors had long ago retreated
under the ocean
(You see how confused I was)
These fish-shaped fin-footed creatures stood on one spot
and swayed
Green seaweed hung from their walrus heads
If in hell there are zoos they would have been shown in
them
Then I saw that they were people whose skin hung down
in knotted strips
I told them to die
They couldnt be helped and as everything was at an end
it was pointless to suffer
Many fell from the bridge onto the backs of others in the
river – it was already full of these strange creatures
The skin of one person clothed the bones of another
It was one animal with a hundred thousand legs and arms
and one body covered with mouths that shouted its
pain
One part of this animal crawled towards the docks and
another towards the commercial centre
As if it wished to pull itself apart

One

The FIRST MAN *comes on.*
He groans mechanically.

FIRST MAN. Organ grinder's music
   No monkey on shoulder
   Inside
   Pops out of skin – jumps up arm – dives into chest
   Howls in roof of mouth
   Look: its fingernails are me in a mirror
   Im a monkey house
   Nearer I am to death higher monkey jumps
   Laughs in one ear – jumps over face – flash of pink arse
      – laughs in other ear
   Give it a new name every day: today Benjamin
   He is my starvation
   Each hair of my starvation is real
   One day he'll open a door in my side and walk off without
      a name
   I steal grass from skeleton's teeth
   All I eat is bitter
   My body poisons my food
   My shit has more goodness in it than food
   No hares or birds or rats
   Bones of animals and people lie together on the road like
      broken picture frames
   The flies flew off: great swarms: I thought the sky was
      full of funerals: the drumming

The FIRST MAN *sees a tin on the ground.*

Tin
Food
Stood up
Side clean: no dirt splashed by rain . . .

A baby's skull sticking out of the ground

The FIRST WOMAN *comes on.*

FIRST WOMAN. Dont be afraid
A few of us survived
We live behind the slope
I saw you from the stones on the top
Can you see me?

No response.

I fetched some food and then ran to meet you
FIRST MAN. Your tin?
FIRST WOMAN. I'll open it
FIRST MAN. Stay there

The FIRST WOMAN *throws a tin-opener along the ground.*
The FIRST MAN *turns and walks away – still keeping an eye*
on her – and then turns towards her.

Trap
Not dying for one tin
FIRST WOMAN (*goes to tin and opens it*). Its not poisonous.
    (*Stands tin on the ground and walks away from it.*)
FIRST MAN. . . . More tins?
FIRST WOMAN. Yes – eat all of it
FIRST MAN. Poison at the bottom
FIRST WOMAN. I'll show you the other people
One of us has died
Now you're here . . . !

The FIRST MAN *picks up the tin.*

You're not used to being with anyone
We'll walk on opposite sides of the road

The FIRST WOMAN *and the* FIRST MAN *go.*

Two

The SECOND MAN *and the* SECOND *and* THIRD WOMAN *come on.*
The SECOND MAN *and the* THIRD WOMAN *carry a covered body on a stretcher.*

SECOND WOMAN. Wait
SECOND MAN. We cant stop again
    He must be buried
SECOND WOMAN. Its too soon: why should we make the
      world look emptier before we have to?
    He still looks alive . . .

No response.

    Im not going any further
    I'll go for a walk on my own on the hill
    Begin to get used to being without him
    I'll hear your spades when Im up there
    If anyone wants to say anything they should say it here
      on the road

The SECOND MAN *and the* THIRD WOMAN *put down the stretcher.*

SECOND MAN. Talk to us about him
    People used to talk about their dead
    It was one of the things that made them human
SECOND WOMAN. What's the use?
    Tomorrow we could all be dead from radiation
    Not even one of us left to bury the rest
SECOND MAN. We dont know what'll happen
    We can only hope that some people go on living
    That's why we must do all the things that human beings
      did

Otherwise they'll be forgotten and the survivors will become savages

Go and walk: we cant persuade you of anything now

We'll talk later

SECOND WOMAN. When he saw the blood in his urine he knew he'd die: he didnt deceive himself but he didnt tell me

Then I kept finding his hair on the pillows in the morning

So we spoke about it

There's been so much dying

We all gave up counting bodies in the first ten minutes

Then no one died for years – not even from radiation

Perhaps the bombs would even make us live longer – who could tell?

They didnt: we've been dead since they fell

So many died their deaths even counted for those who went on living

Our pulses are watches ticking on dead people's wrists

SECOND MAN. Shall we bury him now?

Today we're sad: there are so few of us one death is like a fatal epidemic

Yet we're lucky

In the first years after the bombs we came together

Perhaps there are other survivors but there've been no planes or search parties

The burning corn set fire to its seed – the trees burned their own fruit

Nothing grows: the dust of so many dead has stifled the earth

The animals are dead: their bones lie in the fields like broken traps

If a few live they keep out of our way

Yet we're in paradise

There's no need to work: we only do that when we dig tombs in the rocks to show respect for our dead

We have tins: millions: enough to live on for a thousand years

There's no exploitation – and so there are no enemies

If others came why should they attack us?

The pillar of the house doesnt pull down the other pillars

We wouldnt want anything from them except that they should be alive

They could share our tins

If they took our land we'd give them more

Houses? – each of us could have his own town

When a house needs repairing we move into another house

Its as if all the dead left us all they had in their wills – and as there were so many of them we've inherited the earth

We know what hell is – the fires – the shock wave: like being shoved by a team of giants – the long winter: clouds suddenly froze solid and ice blocks fell and crushed many who'd survived – and the long night when we were like ants crawling over a page of braille

Before the bombs we were strangers: now we're closer than children to their parents

All of us shared one common wound

We knew the deepest humiliation possible to us: to be with the dying and not able to help or comfort them

Now we live together in decency

Not because we're better than those who died but because when they destroyed each other they destroyed their problem: the conflicts that came from their struggles to sustain their lives: they left us their tins

Paradise was built in the ruins of hell: which is its only possible foundation

So we were lucky

SECOND WOMAN. We were children when we met: months after the explosions: his hair still stood on end

Our first words – obviously – is there anyone else?

We shook our heads

I thought I was meeting the other half of the world

The boats in the harbour were sunk or listing

We made a raft and put up a sheet for a sail

Drifted through the charred city

All the windows and doorways were empty

We shouted: no answer or movement

A crate was suspended from a crane: a few bones sat at the controls

The bridges were like trelliswork piled with creepers of skeletons – their heads and arms hung down like orchids

Nothing seemed itself anymore

We didnt use the word love: we needed each other to live: we were lovers whose great desire was for other people

We came to a place where the river was clogged with debris: bodies and doorways and bricks: swept there by the wave set up by the shock: as if a giant had flushed his toilet: this was the sewer

We left the river and walked till we came here

THIRD WOMAN. Why talk about it?

I used to think if I did I'd be able to live normally again

How can you talk about the destruction of the world and be normal?

My parents talk to me in my sleep: they dont know they're dead: I feel guilty as if Im keeping the secret from them

(*To the* SECOND WOMAN.) You haven't suffered more than the rest of us

I tried to help the wounded – there was no medical knowledge or drugs

The sick came together in a few places – crawled and limped along the streets – followed each other's cries

When the blind touched the walls they fell on them

I shouldnt have started to speak

In the mornings there were rooms full of the dead

I watched one old man on a heap of bricks – a whole day
   – blind

I saw him through the windows each time I passed

An ant crawling on a rubbish heap

He couldnt find his way off

I couldnt go to him – the floors were covered in wounded

I'd've been stopped at every step

To tell the truth – why dont you stop me? – it was a
   game to watch him: it took my mind off the work

I suppose in the end he fell in a hole

The next day I squeezed out through the door past the
   wounded coming in

In the street I saw maggots crawling from the dead onto
   the living: they were too weak to pick them off: they
   waved in their wounds like sea-anemones

Please interrupt me: I cant stop speaking

Of course babies suckled their dead mothers and mothers
   tried to give milk to their dead babies

But these things have been since the earliest times – put
   in books – I saw something I shouldnt have seen –
   because no human being should ever be in the world
   where it happened because they could never be at
   home there – when I came to a part of town I didnt
   know – where there was a great white square I hadnt
   seen before – no doubt it had been made by a bomb –
   and I walked over it – the heat had turned the ground
   to glass

And dotted across it were dark shapes – long black brown
   bundles – melted – gluey – I didnt know what they
   were – brown – streaked with red and yellow – and I
   thought they were giant's turds – the simplest explanation was that a giant had walked over the square and

shat – and as there were bones in the turds I saw they
    were bodies
So I said die die die
I walked over the square saying die as if I were saying
    good morning because that's what I'd heard other
    people say – in fact it had become the greeting in that
    city
I told everything I saw to die

The FIRST MAN *comes on carrying the open tin.*

THIRD WOMAN. A man!
SECOND WOMAN. Look! New!
SECOND MAN. Are there anymore? Are there anymore?

The FIRST WOMAN *comes on.*

SECOND WOMAN. Are you alone?
SECOND MAN. Where've you come from?
SECOND WOMAN. How did he get here?
THIRD WOMAN. Can he talk?
SECOND WOMAN. Can he see us?
SECOND MAN. Did he walk here?
SECOND WOMAN (*to the* FIRST WOMAN). Did you find
    him?
THIRD WOMAN. Where are you from?
SECOND WOMAN (*to the* FIRST WOMAN). Where was he? Is
    he alone?
SECOND MAN. Is there anyone else?
THIRD WOMAN. Anyone? Anyone?
FIRST MAN (*muttering*). People . . . people . . .
SECOND MAN. Are there any –
SECOND WOMAN. Shut up let him speak!
FIRST MAN (*sweeps with his arm*). White ash
  All over
  Footprints
  Years

    No one else

FIRST WOMAN. He was on the outside road by himself

SECOND WOMAN. Did you see any signs of people –
    settlements –

SECOND MAN. Or hear machines?

THIRD WOMAN. Is there anyone?

FIRST MAN. Spoke each day
    Ha! teach a ghost his arithmetic
    Kept words
    Passport for people
    Lists
    Spanner
    Towel
    Here lies one whose name was writ in water
    Humpty Dumpty
    A wheel came off my pushcart

FIRST WOMAN. He's been on his own for years – that's
    why he talks like that

FIRST MAN. Seventeen
    I know you're people because you're corpse-shaped

He goes to the stretcher and looks at the covered body.

SECOND MAN. He's dead

FIRST MAN (*ponders*). When there are people they cover the
    dead
    Why?
    Yes – they cant feel the cold
    (*He points.*) You are women – and men

The FIRST MAN *lies down and goes to sleep.*

SECOND WOMAN. He's gone to sleep

THIRD WOMAN. There are people! People!

SECOND WOMAN. Sh dont wake him!

SECOND MAN. We know there's one more person – we cant
    claim anymore than that

THIRD WOMAN. If there's one there could be thousands!
  Hundreds!
SECOND WOMAN. Perhaps they still know how to make
    things!
  They could drive here in a car!
  Send an aeroplane!
SECOND MAN. We must dig out the sign!
  If they sent an aeroplane and it didnt go straight overhead
    they'd miss it!
  Its full of dust!
  We're fools!
THIRD WOMAN. There are people! People!
FIRST WOMAN. People! People!
SECOND WOMAN. They're looking for us! They'll never
    give up till they find us – surely?
SECOND MAN. And light the beacon at night!
  It was stupid to stop it!
  We dont deserve to be found!
SECOND WOMAN. Why's he asleep?
SECOND MAN. He's like Lucifer – he thinks he's falling
    into hell: then he lands in a circle of friends offering
    him gifts!
  He's out of danger so suddenly all his energy goes!
  Like an alarm system switched off!
  Let him sleep!
  When he wakes he'll feel he's had a ten year rest
SECOND WOMAN. Yes he looks better already
FIRST WOMAN. See how he stood the tin upright before he
    slept
THIRD WOMAN. Shows he's careful
SECOND WOMAN. Sensible – a good planner
THIRD WOMAN. And he's got an excellent disposition: why
    else would he go to such pains not to be discourteous
    about our gift?
SECOND WOMAN. He's got engineer's hands

SECOND MAN. What did he say about himself?

FIRST WOMAN. Nothing
  I didnt ask
  I told him who we were
  (*To the other women.*) I spoke to him gently – as if he was
    a lost child

SECOND WOMAN. Look at his face – how peaceful
  Like an explorer sleeping on a new country for a bed

THIRD WOMAN. When the mouth's longer than the eye-
    brows it means a generous outlook on the world

SECOND MAN. Or he eats a lot
  You should've questioned him before he had time to
    invent a false story
  We mustnt get excited
  We have to be careful

FIRST WOMAN. You should've seen him eat from the tin
    with his fingers
  He made it look like a display of etiquette

THIRD WOMAN. Did he run when he saw you?
  I bet he runs like the wind!
  A person! Alive!
  We'll get him to run for us!

To the SECOND MAN.

  Challenge him to a race!

SECOND WOMAN. I'll take bets!

THIRD WOMAN. I know who I'll bet on!

FIRST WOMAN. Wait till you see him do his eating out of
    the tin!
  Its a work of art!

SECOND MAN. Did he run?

SECOND WOMAN. I bet he can dance!

THIRD WOMAN. And sing with that mouth!

The WOMEN *laugh and embrace each other.*

SECOND MAN. Look he's breathing
  Why did I think of sheep on a hill?
  There's no green grass now
SECOND WOMAN. He's one of us!
FIRST WOMAN *and* THIRD WOMAN. He's one of us!

  SECOND MAN *goes to the* WOMEN *and embraces them.*

SECOND MAN. One of us!
FIRST WOMAN. A new man!
THIRD WOMAN. In the middle of the funeral!

  The WOMEN *and the* SECOND MAN *go to the stretcher.*
  They are still smiling.

SECOND WOMAN. When we'd been together for a week he
    smiled
  Suddenly
  I'd forgotten a face could do that
  I was astonished

  She touches the edge of the cover.

  I wish he'd lived long enough to see the new man
SECOND MAN. He said there were others
SECOND WOMAN. Yes . . . people who could respect each
    other . . . not butchers who'd use the gravestones for
    a workbench
FIRST MAN (*wakes*). No! No! Not soldier!
  Too young!
  Look old: walk – bad food!
  Jacket from wardrobe!
  Didnt drop bombs!
  No gun!
  Speak your language!
THIRD WOMAN. Its all right
SECOND WOMAN. We're friends
FIRST MAN. Dreamt

On trial
Floorboards curled up – pointed – me
SECOND WOMAN. We're glad you're here
Look: a reserve depot was built in this valley
There are five warehouses full of tins
Millions! All ours! We'll never starve
SECOND MAN. They dropped a neutron bomb here
Killed the guards – left the tins
FIRST MAN. Not burned?
SECOND MAN. No – only some tins in a corner of one
warehouse
They were sucked into a liftshaft as if it was a giant
throat and melted at the bottom
We don't know why – they werent even by a door where
the blast could have moved them
No explanation
We'll show you
FIRST MAN. How many?
FIRST WOMAN. People?
SECOND WOMAN. Fourteen
Two are asleep
We never wake people when they sleep

She goes back to the stretcher.

I'll carry him
THIRD WOMAN. Walk at the side
SECOND WOMAN. No

The SECOND MAN *and the* SECOND WOMAN *carry out the body on the stretcher.*

FIRST MAN. You live in houses?
I've lived in houses
Took out the bones and lit a fire: all those tongues saying
one word
Why does the road bend when its going nowhere?

In the desert I found a skull eating a stone
Been clenched in its teeth to stop the pain
I shouted – a cliff – wind blew the echo back through the
    skull's mouth
It spoke
A bit higher – a woman's voice
Slept beside her in the sand
One of the rare dews: in the morning her cheeks were
    wet
If she'd've still had flesh I'd've got them to knit me into
    a jumper to cover her
Stayed several days so that she could speak
Then moved on
Must move
Keep going

THIRD WOMAN. You must tell us all that's happened to
    you: you can start this evening
We're glad you came

FIRST MAN. Im a sensible man
If I was mad you'd've found me dancing on the road as if
    it led to an asylum
In the desert – learned to tell one stone from another
Knew a stone after ten years – only seen it once before
Ants wore a path on it here (*He touches his forehead.*) –
    graggy moss for eyebrow
Now you people . . . as if stones could speak
Let me stay with you and my journey will've been a
    green track over the desert
Fetch your water – open your tins
All I want is – look at your faces – and speak
Look they're in a little queue behind the coffin following
    it along the bottom of the hill
From here they look like a black necklace
Can I walk with them?
I thought of how I'd first meet people

Not what they'd be like: wouldnt do that
Whoever they were I'd be polite
Sometimes I saw them in my head
Not like you: you're better than pictures
Cant trust anything in a dream
When you dream you're a deadman poking about with a
    torch

The THIRD WOMAN *falls down.*

FIRST MAN. She's dead
    Why did she do that?

The FIRST WOMAN *goes to the* THIRD WOMAN.

FIRST WOMAN. Its a coma – she's not breathing
FIRST MAN. Hit her chest!

He thumps the THIRD WOMAN's *chest.*

Breathe! Breathe!
You hit the chest!
That saves her!
FIRST WOMAN. She's not breathing!
    I think she's dead!
FIRST MAN. Yes but she's only just dead!
    Breathe

He thumps the THIRD WOMAN's *chest.*

Breathe! Breathe! Try!

He blows into the THIRD WOMAN's *mouth.*

FIRST WOMAN. There's no pulse!

The SECOND MAN *runs in.*

SECOND MAN. Get off her!

The SECOND MAN *pulls the* FIRST MAN *from the* THIRD
WOMAN.

FIRST MAN. She's only just dead – let me blow into her
  mouth – make her –
SECOND MAN. Animal! –

The FIRST MAN *picks up the* SECOND MAN *and holding
him horizontally takes him to the side and places him on the
ground and then goes back to the* THIRD WOMAN *and with
great gentleness warms her and massages her heart.*

FIRST MAN. Don't die!
  Breathe! Breathe!
  Its such a little thing
SECOND MAN (*gets to his feet*). Animal! Did he attack her?

He struggles to pull the FIRST MAN *from the* THIRD
WOMAN.

  Leave her alone –
FIRST WOMAN. He didnt attack her!
  She fell!
FIRST MAN. He thinks I stole the food but they gave it to
  me
FIRST WOMAN. She's dead!

The SECOND WOMAN *comes on.*

SECOND MAN. Dead?
SECOND WOMAN. Quick – if she's dying we can –
FIRST WOMAN. She's dead!
SECOND WOMAN. She cant be!

Frantically the SECOND WOMAN *sits the* THIRD WOMAN
up. The SECOND MAN *and the* FIRST WOMAN *help her to
try to get the* THIRD WOMAN *to her feet – she flops over.
They stand her up again and try to make her walk. The*
FIRST MAN *sits on the ground and watches.*

FIRST WOMAN. She's dead
SECOND WOMAN. Not possible! Dead?

FIRST WOMAN. She's stopped breathing

SECOND WOMAN. How could she stop? She didnt have –
there were no signs of – !

SECOND MAN. Its not radiation

FIRST WOMAN. She'd've warned us if she had that!

SECOND WOMAN. She must have warned us!
It'd be cruel not to warn us!
Surely she'd've told us!

They let the body of the THIRD WOMAN *fall.*

SECOND MAN. We'd've known – you cant hide radiation
She didnt say anything just now?

FIRST WOMAN. When she fell?

SECOND MAN. Yes

FIRST WOMAN. No she just fell

SECOND MAN. Its a new disease

SECOND WOMAN. It could be dangerous – this place – we
could be contaminated standing here
Or catch it from her

They back away.

SECOND MAN. If you can catch it we'll already've caught it

FIRST WOMAN. Im not ill – I dont feel ill

SECOND WOMAN. Nor did she

SECOND MAN. Didnt she say anything?
Think!

SECOND WOMAN (*points to the* FIRST MAN). Its him

FIRST MAN (*unsure*). Me? – what? – you said no trial –

SECOND MAN. You met people on your way here –

FIRST MAN. People?

SECOND MAN. Dont argue – you must have – at the
beginning
Did they die? Did they fall down like this?

SECOND WOMAN. He's on the run!
He's been turned out!

He's dangerous!

FIRST MAN. No

SECOND MAN. Did other people fall down when you spoke
   to them?

   Did you see anyone else make them fall down?

FIRST MAN. I was on a tall block

   It swayed like a string held upside down

   Wind

   Then it twisted

   People fell off – like water – sprinkled – the wind was
   wringing the tower out

FIRST WOMAN. He thinks you're asking about the bomb

SECOND MAN. Go back to –

FIRST WOMAN. But what if –

SECOND MAN. – the houses

   This is dangerous!

The FIRST *and* SECOND WOMEN *go out.*

You understand this woman is dead?

FIRST MAN. You wouldnt let me blow in –

SECOND MAN. See that small road?

   Take that – in two hours you come to a garage

   Wait there

   We'll bring you food and blankets – anything else you
   need

   You may be carrying a disease

FIRST MAN. No

SECOND MAN. All right all right – then give us time to
   think

   You dont want to harm your friends?

FIRST MAN. No no!

SECOND MAN. Good – then trust us

   We'll find a solution

   This isnt your fault

   I promise to do all I can to help you

FIRST MAN (*ingratiatingly*). What if she isnt dead?
  Dont go – I'll light a fire
  If there's a little life in –
SECOND MAN. You know how to get to the garage?
  Its a normal precaution to put you in quarantine
  But dont try any tricks

The SECOND MAN *goes out.*

FIRST MAN. Dead: seen it so often when I was with the
  bones . . .

He turns to face the THIRD WOMAN.

Three causes of death in her face
Legs – like a child's playing dead
Breast – empty paper bag – rummaged clean by a starving
  man
She's got a broken jar for a mouth
Hair moves – wind isnt interested in death – moves like
  a dog searching for its dead master
She counted on those fingers
Ruined houses throwing bricks at each other
Carry her till she's cold

The FIRST MAN *picks up the* THIRD WOMAN *and carries
her out.*

SECTION TWO: THE TIN CAN RIOTS

Second Chorus

The world was made into a crucible for an experiment
The effects couldnt have been foreseen
We called them the voice of the bomb

It spoke everywhere: we dont know how its orders were
put into effect

The tornadoes whirled like gambling wheels: where they
stopped someone might live

I saw one man who had stood by an iron railing when the
bombs fell

From the waist up the bars had been wrapped round him
and knotted so that he walked with his trunk and head
in a cage: his head nodded like a bird

It was chance

The laws of nature hadnt changed but doors locked at
the creation so that there could be life had been opened

Years after the explosions we entered a command pit

The steel doors and cement fields had kept out radiation
as efficiently as earth keeps air from a tomb

But the bomb's voice had spoken

The inside of the door was fouler than the outside

Stalactites hung from the roofs – not accumulations
through centuries but made in hours – minutes – after
the explosions

Skeletons sat before stone buttons and stone computers

Stone politicians and stone officers bent over stone maps
of cities they had made dust

Our ancestors who sheltered in caves painted the walls
with scenes of life

These had covered them with charts of death

They were like pharaohs who killed their servants and
took them into their tomb with food and weapons

And their accountants to reach an agreement with the
managers of the dead

But even the food had turned to stone

Even the rats stealing the food: their theft was captured
forever in stone

So reckless and foolish were these people that when they
lived it could have been said they haunted the dead

One

The FIRST *and* SECOND WOMAN *wait.*
The SECOND MAN *comes on.*
They all stand apart from each other.

SECOND MAN. We'll have to kill him
SECOND WOMAN. How?
  We cant get close enough to do it with a knife or hammer
    – he'd run for it
  There arent enough of us to stone him
  When they stoned people it took a whole town
FIRST WOMAN. We mustnt panic – try to think!
SECOND WOMAN. I feel so helpless
  It was easy for the bombs to kill millions!
  How d'you kill just one?
FIRST WOMAN. We dont know there is a disease – and if
    there is we dont know he brought it
  She could've had it for months
  Perhaps it has symptoms you dont see or feel
  Even if someone else dies – we wouldnt know it came
    from him – it could've come from her
SECOND WOMAN. O god you were with him an hour when
    you brought him to us and we all stood round him
    when he slept
  We'll all have it by now!
FIRST WOMAN. Think! – we mustnt waste time killing him
    when this might be our last chance to save ourselves!
  Any one of us could be carrying the disease . . .
  If we suspect anyone – even ourselves – we must say
  Did anything happen in the last few months – did we see
    anything – suspicious?
SECOND WOMAN. Nothing nothing
FIRST WOMAN. Look – even if there is a disease it doesnt
    mean we'll die

If he has a disease it hasnt killed him!

Perhaps only some people are vulnerable

FIRST MAN. Think about all that later

What we know for certain is that when he came one of us
died

The probability's so great it'd be insane not to act on it!

FIRST WOMAN. But he's the first new person to come here
for thirteen years

If we're going to be sick we'll need him even more!

He's young – and he must be strong or he couldnt have
walked so long

To kill him . . .

SECOND MAN. There are so few of us my dear

Its our duty to protect ourselves

Make a weapon

FIRST WOMAN. There are trollies in the warehouses

Why dont we load them with tins and build a depot for
him out in the desert?

He couldnt harm us out there

He'd be on his own but he'd have the tins – it'd be a
better life than he'd had so far

SECOND MAN. Even that's too risky

FIRST WOMAN. Then tell him to go

SECOND WOMAN. He wouldnt

FIRST WOMAN. Try

When he understands that if he stayed he might kill us
he'll see we could never be his friends

So if he stayed what would he get?

Go or stay he'd be on his own

SECOND WOMAN. Dont tell him that – any fool could work
it out: he'd stay and get the tins

FIRST WOMAN. We said he looked like a good man

SECOND WOMAN. Where could he go? – back where he
came?

After a week he'd turn round again and come here just to
see us – we're like sight to the blind to him

FIRST WOMAN. If he went further on he might meet other
people

SECOND WOMAN. And contaminate them

SECOND MAN. We're like people doing a jigsaw with one
piece missing and one piece in our hand – and we're
arguing if it'll fit!

We have to kill him – not only for our sake but for the
sake of anyone else there might be

Anything can be used as a weapon

Knock him down with a chair

Put out poisoned tins

SECOND WOMAN. We'd have to puncture them: he'd see
the marks

He's bound to be suspicious

SECOND MAN. The crow bars we used for digging the tomb

One of us creeps up on him with a crowbar while the rest
distract his attention

You'd all better carry crowbars as a precaution

No its too risky

He might see the person creeping up on him – then he'd
have to throw the crowbar and if he missed he'd arm
himself with it

There are two points: one we mustnt get close enough to
him to risk more contamination and two we need a
missile that's good enough to hit the target first time
and work

I'll make a spear

The SECOND MAN *goes out.*

FIRST WOMAN. We could be the last people on earth

If we killed him it would be like committing the crime
the bombs were dropped to punish

SECOND WOMAN. Well god knows we were punished so
    we're entitled to commit the crime
Suppose he blackmailed us?
Moved into our houses so we had to move out
He could go to the stores and contaminate our tins
He'll realise that once we tolerate him here he can do
    what he likes – get away with murder
I dont want to kill anyone but what sense does it make to
    worry about one death anymore?
If anyone came looking for him they'd never even find
    his body in this charnel house
We live in dead people's clothes – eat their food – we
    took the store keys from dead soldiers' pockets
One more wont make the skeletons cry

The SECOND MAN *comes back with a metal rod and a
hammer and immediately kneels and begins to make a spear.*

SECOND MAN. He didnt go to the garage
He's up on the hill where he can see what we're doing

Hammering.

John and Irene are watching him
I told everyone to assemble here: we must all be respon-
    sible for the action we take today
They used this rod for pulling down tins from the top
    shelves
Heavy enough to go through bone
Im flattening the flange to improve its penetrating power
Needs a sharper point

Still hammering.

Come in!: I'm making a spear
We'll hunt him together – not too near – circle the hill –
    then send a raiding party over the top – drive him down
You pretend to have guns

The grease guns from the stores will look like automatics
    from a distance if you keep your cool and remember to
    hold them like soldiers
I'll kill him
I run best
I need to get close in to hit his head: one blow'll do it
The chest is a bigger target

*He stops hammering and weighs the spear in his hand to find
the point of balance.*

I'll go for the chest

Hammering.

Come in!: this is going to be our spear
The soldier should kill quickly and cleanly so as to limit
    the enemy's sufferings to the necessary minimum
But the soldier's main concern must be self-preservation:
    cant risk three deaths in a week!
When I've killed him I'll break the spear and live on my
    own for six months
Not out of guilt: he has to be killed for the community's
    sake
Six months will be a sign of the respect we owe all the dead
And it'll show anyone who heard we'd killed him that we
    did it reluctantly
After six months you'll come and welcome me back
In the meantime you'd better live apart in twos
Then any disease will be isolated
If anyone develops symptoms they must shout them
    across to the others so that they can watch for them in
    themselves
What happens after he's dead depends on chance
Perhaps this disease broke out in other places – years ago

He stops hammering.

It could be why there are no search planes
Even why we cant have children – the two might be
    connected
Without children we'd have died out anyway – perhaps
    the disease will only bring the end quicker
Let's be grateful we had so long together

He restarts hammering.

Whatever happens this is the most important day in our
    history since the bomb
Strange to kill someone we waited for so long
We have to save the community
If we kill him we'll be as safe as anyone can be
I give you my word he'll be dead in an hour
Burn the body and get rid of the ashes
No I can do that!

He stops hammering and drops the spear.

No no no its useless! Stupid! Im talking nonsense!
What time have I got to practise?
I could throw the spear and miss
He'd know we wanted to kill him
He'd go on the rampage and kill god knows how many
    before we killed him – or run berserk and contaminate
    the lot of us!
I'll have to grapple with him: hold him with one hand
    and knife him with the other
Go up to him smiling and say we've proved he wasnt the
    cause of death
Hold out my hands as if Im welcoming him and then
    push him on the ground
After I've burned the body I'll take the ashes away with
    me
He could have carried the disease for seventeen years –
    and it could be the same with me

I cant come back
Dont try to change my mind
We have to make certain he dies: I'll sacrifice myself for
the community
It'll be some repayment for the time I've spent in our
paradise

As the SECOND WOMAN *speaks, the* SECOND MAN *picks
up the spear and holds it in the war-memorial pose of a
soldier preparing to go into battle.*

SECOND WOMAN. When you're gone we wont forget you
We'll come to the boundary and shout out our news
We'll find a cliff where we can drop tins without damag-
ing them – you must heap up more dust at the bottom
– and we'll bring you fresh blankets and clothes
We know the loneliness of living by yourself in ruins
You've chosen to behave in the way the best human
beings behave
SECOND MAN. Thank you
Now no one must come with me: I'll go alone
FIRST WOMAN. Wait a moment
If you can touch him when you kill him any of us can do
it
It doesnt have to be the best runner
We'll draw lots – or choose the one we can most afford to
lose
SECOND MAN. No something could still go wrong: he could
make a dash for it or there could be a scrap – he's
strong
I dont have to play the hero to you: you were all heroes
when the bombs fell
Lets obey the logic of the situation
That decides everything
What? – did one of you speak to me?

Make sure the others know the path you took when you
   brought him to the funeral
Then put it out of –

The SECOND MAN *falls to the ground. The others stare at
him in silence.*

FIRST WOMAN. He cant be dead
SECOND WOMAN. O god
   Dont go near him
FIRST WOMAN (*shouts at the* SECOND MAN). No! No! No!

Shouts and claps.

   Did his eye move?
SECOND WOMAN. He's dead – you can see it
FIRST WOMAN. No! No!
SECOND WOMAN. Keep away from him you fool!
FIRST WOMAN. Terrible!
   Is it all going to end now?
SECOND WOMAN. Yes we'll all die!
   No one'll escape!
   No he was only the carrier!
   The sickness's died with him!
   Thank god the danger's over!
   We're saved!
   But how could it die with him?
   I dont know!
   What can we do?
   Run a sweepstake on whose turn is next?
   No no I didnt say that!
   Fool – tempting providence!
   What can I do?
   They killed millions with their bombs – and now they're
      dead they're killing the rest of us with their diseases!

The FOURTH WOMAN *comes on.*

FOURTH WOMAN. Quickly! We're in danger!
  John's died!
FIRST WOMAN. Are you sure?
FOURTH WOMAN. Yes!
FIRST WOMAN. Did you see him?
SECOND WOMAN. You didnt touch him?
FOURTH WOMAN. No I could tell he was dead!
FIRST WOMAN. How did it happen?
SECOND WOMAN. When?
FOURTH WOMAN. Just now
FIRST WOMAN. Tell us exactly how
FOURTH WOMAN. He fell down – no warning – he didnt
    look ill – just looked down – then fell
  I ran straight here

She sees the SECOND MAN.

  He's dead
FIRST WOMAN. Yes
FOURTH WOMAN. When?
SECOND WOMAN. A minute ago
FOURTH WOMAN. Its an epidemic: we'll all die
SECOND WOMAN. You didnt go near the new man?
FOURTH WOMAN. No why should we?
FIRST WOMAN. To speak to him
FOURTH WOMAN. Didnt go nearer than a mile
FIRST WOMAN. We'll get knives and cut a record on a stone
  Spend all the time we've got on that
  If other people come here they'll know that till this
    happened we lived in peace for seventeen years
  It'll be a message of hope: they could even be in a worse
    state than we are
  And we must warn them the place may be contaminated
  Even the tins: we called them the fruits of paradise
  Close the house and burn it

The FIRST WOMAN *goes out.*

SECOND WOMAN. By the time they've stood there long
enough to read it they'll be dead
I should stop speaking: all the words sound like insults
When will it end?
I saw maggots crawl off the dead
We cant crawl off: human maggots on a dead earth
The dead sit up and eat us: tuck in their shrouds for bibs
FOURTH WOMAN. I ran here so fast!
Never so fast before!
Jumped down that hill – over the wall!
Where did the strength come from?
The illness affects people differently!
It's possible!
It makes some of us feel more alive!
Fevers can do that!
The lucky ones dont have to die!
Tell me where I got the strength to run so fast!
It must have come from somewhere!
SECOND WOMAN. You were always so slow!
They called you the snail on crutches!
FOURTH WOMAN. Perhaps if we keep moving?
John was standing still when he died
SECOND WOMAN. *He* was standing still!
FOURTH WOMAN. They were all standing still
We must keep moving! Its as simple as that!
SECOND WOMAN. Walk!
FOURTH WOMAN. Take turns to watch the others while
they sleep!
Keep waking them up – stand them on their feet!
Make them jump!
SECOND WOMAN. Move your arms!
FOURTH WOMAN. Wave! Kick your legs!
We dont have to die!

SECOND WOMAN. But careful – dont waste energy!

FOURTH WOMAN. No – just walk!

SECOND WOMAN. Walk
Its the bomb – it never stops its destruction
The houses are weak: open a window and the roof shakes
Look at a tree and it falls down
We're like birds whose feathers turned to lead overnight

FOURTH WOMAN. John was watching a man condemned to death
She was at a funeral

SECOND WOMAN. And he was making a weapon to kill someone

FOURTH WOMAN. They were all doing things to do with death!
You see – we dont have to die!
Have nothing to do with death!
We've had too much to do with it!
That's why we're dying!
If someone dies we wont even look at them!

They run faster and faster

SECOND WOMAN. And eat!

FOURTH WOMAN. Yes eat!

SECOND WOMAN. Eat and eat and eat!

FOURTH WOMAN. Eat all the tins! Carry tins round with us!

SECOND WOMAN. Open them and stack them in rows
Always have food in your mouth and more ready to eat!

FOURTH WOMAN. This is why they dropped the bombs
I knew there was a reason!
They wanted to see who could survive!

SECOND WOMAN. It was a test!
They'll send planes to fetch us
Take us somewhere else
Its obvious: they want us for something important

FOURTH WOMAN (*stops running*). What will it be?

SECOND WOMAN. They were talking about planets before
the bombs

Planets were always on the radio

Move you silly cow! – your eyes are popping out as if you
were caught in the blast!

FOURTH WOMAN (*running*). A planet – not bombed!

SECOND WOMAN. That's why they left the tins

They couldnt let us die – it'd've ruined their experiment

FOURTH WOMAN. That's why they left the tin-openers!

They'll be surprised when they see us

SECOND WOMAN. No they knew we'd survive – they had to
prove it to some of the others – you always get the doubters!

FOURTH WOMAN. All the bombs and fires and dust –

SECOND WOMAN. Were the test

Perhaps its not another planet: its the earth – they've
cleared out the destructive elements – now we'll colon-
ise it

We'll have the good life – our own swimming pools – we
must be ready

Behave like people who've been chosen to represent
others – move and speak calmly – quietly –

(*Stops.*) Look at him in his shirt

He wasnt chosen in spite of all the boasting

That shirt's better than the ones we've got

It could've been my shirt

As good as stole it from me

He was downstairs and he made me search upstairs

When I came down he was buttoning up the shirt

Get it off him

That's my shirt

Together the SECOND *and* FOURTH WOMEN *strip the*
SECOND MAN.

FOURTH WOMAN. Mind the buttons!

Look at him clinging to it!

Hasnt got the strength to break a cracked egg

SECOND WOMAN. Of course it was paradise for him: he got
what he wanted!

Not us!

Now he cant even choose a shirt to be buried in!

I knew why he wanted to go to the new man on his own:
to send him here to infect us

FOURTH WOMAN. Would he? God we had an escape!

SECOND WOMAN. It wasnt past him

It's because there are people of his sort that bombs get
dropped!

FOURTH WOMAN. Kick him kick him

SECOND WOMAN. Harder

You have to kick hard to make him feel now

Hard – for all the people who died!

FOURTH WOMAN. Kick him!

SECOND WOMAN. When we were all dead he'd've killed the
new man and kept everything to himself

FOURTH WOMAN. Then what would he have done?

SECOND WOMAN. Sold the tins

FOURTH WOMAN. The swine the swine!

Kick him for selling our tins!

SECOND WOMAN. Put on his shirt and strutted round with
a trolly till he came to some starving people –

FOURTH WOMAN. Our tins!

Stole our tins and hid them!

The shelves are empty!

He only left the front rows!

We never looked!

The cunning pig!

They kick the SECOND MAN *around the stage. Then they
stop and stare at him.*

FOURTH WOMAN. To think it was him all the time: and
then he came here to watch us suffer

She looks at the SECOND WOMAN – *afraid.*

Dont be upset – we found him out – we're safe now

No response.

Try your shirt

She holds the shirt against the SECOND WOMAN.

It looks pretty on –
SECOND WOMAN. Take it off!
  It stinks of him!
  Roll it in some shit till it smells better!
  Lets take him downstairs
  Open the door and stand him in the doorway so he can
     see the street
  Then burn his house

The SECOND *and* FOURTH WOMEN *drag out the* SECOND
MAN.

Third Chorus

  Before the bombs dropped people lived in the cold
     shadows at the feet of stone idols
  How could they know what is true when the oracles and
     newspapers and radios lied?
  The lake doesnt sparkle when you fill it with wrecked
     cars
  You wouldnt ask people to swim oceans or put out
     volcanos with bare hands
  Yet you asked them to practise virtue when they worked
     for thieves
  Be philosophers when they lived in noisy blocks where
     no one could think

Learn the arts of peace when each must fight his neighbour for work
Or be generous when they must beg for the state handout
And be restrained when the leaders arm themselves for
terror

And yet they turned each link of their chains into the
bright eye of a child
They grew and the chains sank into their flesh till they
bound their bones – yet they walked upright
They shone like a flame in the full blast of the storm
On bare branches in the harsh sleet of winter they put
out fruit full of the ripeness of summer
As the axe cut the tree-trunk the wood grew again
They were too kind too generous too given to reason

Dont judge – but wonder the parents didnt sit on their
doorsteps cursing their children and the children
murder their parents as they slept at night
That they didnt burn down their neighbour's house and
loot the city centre

Deadmen were trained to perform one action: press with
the button-finger
Their leaders discarded the world as if they threw a
cigarette pack into the ashcan
Wonder that not till the bombs were dropped did these
people run mad

Two

The FIRST MAN *comes on.*

FIRST MAN. If there were gods they'd come here to learn!
I went to the street – asked for food
Them: opening tins – wasting food – covered in it – they

looked turned inside out – as if you could see what
they were made of

Threw stones at me – stones smeared with food: is this
how they feed their beggars?

They shouted – dirt poured out of their mouths: are they
the people who shit from the face?

They'd've eaten me but too full to run

They set fire to stores – reeked – an army's kitchens

Huge fires – tiny voices – as if they were playing old
tapes of executions in the flames

Tins melted – stank – acid

Tins pounded in fire – up and down – like teeth

Man fell off roof: little black squiggle under microscope

Fell into fire – tins ate him

Rest went on eating – couldnt tell him from food – ate
both together

All day the sun pale behind black smoke – clouds of flies
in ruins – like wigs blowing off mourners – tumbling
over churchyards

Night – find room – dark

Breathing – dark bundle in corner

Lie down

Didnt hit me – didnt run away

Touched legs

Smelt food

It's a woman

Fires died down now

Red hot girders: straight lines in sky – or mixed up –
squiggled – string on ground

The SECOND WOMAN *comes in carrying the spear and
wearing the* SECOND MAN'*s shirt. She is dirty and dishevelled and her clothes and skin and hair are smeared and
saturated with food.*

SECOND WOMAN. You were talking

Thought you had a gang of your friends

The fires brought them here – saw the reflections on the
clouds

FIRST MAN. I dont know if I have a disease

Couldnt know – never met anyone before to know if I
harmed them

We survived the bomb: now help each other

Let me –

SECOND WOMAN. Help?

Since you came seven of us have died!

One hanged herself: her face was the same colour as the
rope – it looked as if she'd unwound it from inside her

One of us even died before you came: as if he knew you
were coming

You leave bones behind you – not footprints

FIRST MAN. Watched a plough turning a field: I was a boy

Pebbles fell out of ground like tears

I dont leave bones behind me: they are already on the
road in front of me

Let me go

SECOND WOMAN. You'd contaminate others

FIRST MAN. There's no one else

SECOND WOMAN. Perhaps not

That's why no one came to find us

Some must have survived – even the radiation

Perhaps they caught your disease even before you had it

It kills everything off – the last disease

Why dont you kill yourself?

FIRST MAN. No

SECOND WOMAN. No you survive – you walk for seventeen
years and start to kill the moment you get here

We waited for you – got a place ready for you in this
paradise

Now we've made ruins out of the ruins – like savages
digging up the dead to mock them

FIRST MAN. Why is she crying?

  I thought after the bombs no one would cry till more
    bombs fell

SECOND WOMAN. When you came we discussed what we
    could do

  Thought it all out

  Some of those who died were cleverer than the rest:
    we've had the benefit of their decision

  They said kill you: now they cant change their mind

  If you'd come here holding a child by the hand . . .

  We dont have children – we dont know why

  Most knowledge was destroyed by the bombs

  Are men sterile or women or both?

  When you came we thought perhaps you'd be our first
    father

  It could have been

  You were young and strong – you'd been able to walk so
    far

  Instead you brought death – to this graveyard!

She picks food from her shirt and tastes it.

  My shirt smells of food: makes me hungry

  When I came up here I said I'd kill you: the wind blew
    and the sleeve on my arm carrying the spear nodded yes
  What does it matter?

  Even before they had the bombs they killed like children
    pretending they had them: statesman bang-bang mil-
    lions dead

  They started killing so early in the mornings one half of
    the window was in light and the other in dark

The FIRST MAN *takes out a knife.*

FIRST MAN. I dont want to kill or hurt you

SECOND WOMAN. Kill me?

  (*Calls.*) Help! Help!

I dont need help: I want them to see me kill you
(*Calls.*) Help! Help! He's killing me! Im bleeding!
   Quickly!
That'll fetch them
Enjoy your last minutes
I wont kill you till they get here
Mind the point: its sharp

The FIRST WOMAN *and* THIRD MAN *come on: both are dishevelled and filthy, and their clothes and skin and hair are smeared and saturated with food.*

FIRST WOMAN. Wait!
   No one else has died
   It's possible the fire's burned the disease out
   There're still six of us alive
THIRD MAN. The others are licking food off the bricks

The FOURTH WOMAN *comes on: she is even filthier and more dishevelled than the others. The* SECOND WOMAN *makes threatening feints at the* FIRST MAN *with the spear. He defends himself.*

FOURTH WOMAN. My mother called me in from the open
   window
   Then the house was gone
   After the bomb I saw a hat with a feather soaring over
   the street but it was a roof – high up – with a child
   clinging to it
   My arm's shaking: its the vibration from the bomb
THIRD MAN. We've finished it off: illiterates in the library:
   children playing with calendars: an army wiping its
   arse on history books
   Tower block – cylinders – blew every window out –
   frames in the street – giants' spectacles trodden on in a
   fight

Cut myself on a tin: ate with bleeding fingers: phew! my
  hands stink of cannibals
FOURTH WOMAN. If we pretend to be dead we'll survive
  The hen pretended to be dead – the fox laid her in the
    grass – shut his eyes to scratch himself – scritch scritch
    with the hind leg

As the THIRD MAN *talks the* FOURTH WOMAN *slowly
walks about pretending to be dead.*

We must practise how to be dead
THIRD MAN. The stores were laid out by a military man
  One for soup
  One for main courses
  One for tinned prunes to minister to army bowels
  We tucked in in any old order
  Like mad waiters galloping round a restaurant and
    snatching grub from the diners' plates
FOURTH WOMAN. If I sit with the dead till I reek of them
  I wont be found out
THIRD MAN. Even someone who thinks he's a tree knows
    what a tree is
  There are grounds for hope
  For every bomb that exploded ten failed to explode: it
    could've been worse
FIRST WOMAN (*to the* FIRST MAN).
  You did this to us!
  Your stupid stutterings – staring eyes – clutching at us!
  You had seventeen years – couldnt you have taken *one*
    turning that would have led you away from us!
FIRST MAN. No – if I could've only found a sweet paper
    you'd dropped here on the road – I'd've come for that
FIRST WOMAN. The last two deaths came more slowly
  There was a gap of four hours then nine and now no
    more for twenty

The disease may be dying out: perhaps we're immune now

As many of us must survive as possible: even this fool: we cant kill him

THIRD MAN. We'll survive the disease and die of starvation

To the SECOND WOMAN.

You poured cans of paint and paraffin onto the burning tins

Emptied trolly loads down the shoots

FIRST WOMAN. Why did you have to destroy?

I panicked – I ate – but I didnt destroy!

I went to hide in a hole and when I woke up you were still screaming like kids in a playground!

And now you have to kill!

The SECOND WOMAN *half lowers the spear.*

SECOND WOMAN. Did I push someone into the fire?

There was a black figure with outstretched arms

Perhaps I was throwing away my overcoat in the heat

I dont know what to do: I wiped the tears from a dead face and now there are more tears on it

If we kill him it will be easier

We'll have done all there was left to do

Then we can rest

THIRD MAN. I think he only has the disease when he's here

We've lived so long together – worked out how to behave

Another human being is worse than a bomb

Someone from another planet could stand between you and the sun and not know he was depriving you of anything – because the sun is so far away

It's not his fault

He's real – we're in a dream: we cant suddenly eat real food – or lose real blood

We cant let anything be real after the bombs
If its beautiful – makes you happy – kill it
The dead cant bear to be with the living: we only ask to
be buried
With or without his disease he has to be killed

The SECOND WOMAN *lunges with the spear at the* FIRST
MAN. *They fight.*

FIRST MAN. We – fight like animals on an abattoir floor!

The FIRST WOMAN *struggles with the* SECOND WOMAN
and takes the spear from her.

SECOND WOMAN. Every brick was crushed or scorched
Our beds could have been slashed with razors
The trees were stripped bare
There were so many bodies they buried the earth
If the people who did that had come to your house first
you'd have asked them in and cut their throats
The suffering must have taught us something
We'll do what was decided

The FIRST WOMAN *drops the spear and puts her arms round
the* FIRST MAN.

SECOND WOMAN. Dont touch him!
FIRST WOMAN. Its finished
I'll sleep with you –
SECOND WOMAN. No!
FIRST WOMAN. There could be children
SECOND WOMAN. Diseased! Diseased! If they grew up
they'd have to kill each other!
FIRST WOMAN. In a few years we'll be old
This is our only chance
SECOND WOMAN. Someone else might have come
tomorrow!
A plane might come!

FIRST WOMAN. It's too late – if we must let's die!
   What we had wasnt worth saving!
   It was like the time before the bomb!
FIRST MAN. Let me tell you!
   It was you in the room – in the riot? – in a coma?
   It was you
   I fucked you

The THIRD MAN *picks up the spear and spears the* FIRST
MAN. *He falls.*

THIRD MAN. It was a shame not to see if it worked
   He took such trouble over it before he died

The FIRST MAN *lies on his back – his arms and legs move
slowly like an upturned tortoise's.*

Look he's like a baby: nurse him

The FIRST WOMAN *picks up the spear.*

FIRST WOMAN. Pick him up
   Take him to the first aid
   Quickly – or I'll kill you

The THIRD MAN *and* SECOND WOMAN *carry out the*
FIRST MAN. *The* FIRST WOMAN *follows them.*
The FOURTH WOMAN *has gone – still practising being dead.*

SECTION THREE: THE YOUNG SAGES

Fourth Chorus

Why were the bombs dropped?
If that could be told simply they wouldnt be dropped
Suppose we said bombs were better food on one plate
     than on another?
Or money in an account while somewhere in the same
     city people are in debt for a few sticks of furniture?
Or one school in green fields and another on a waste lot?
That would be hard to understand

Injustice is harmful when its seen: when its unseen the
     disaster is terrible
To justify injustice words beliefs opinions faith passions
     – all are corrupted
Soon people need an interpreter to understand the words
     that come from their own mouth and would have to be
     someone else to know the passions in their own breast!
That is even harder to understand

And so the bombs lie among the crumbs on your kitchen
     table and the books on the school desk
Are propped on the walls of lawcourts and workshops
Football fans wave them over their heads wrapped in
     team-scarfs
And every night they are locked in the safe by a junior
     cashier
You must create justice: and what chance do you have of
     that, you who must eat bread baked in the bomb-
     factory?

We make ourselves as much as we make the houses in
     which we live

But we make ourselves without plans: and even our tools
    we have to invent as we work
These are the convulsions of history
Truly you live in a new age: as you enter your house to
    complete it you bring with you your new tool, the bomb
We can only tell you: you must create justice

One

The FIRST MAN *comes on. He sits.*

FIRST MAN (*calls*). Come and sit here. It's still warm

The FIRST WOMAN *and the* FOURTH WOMAN *come on.
They sit.*

FOURTH WOMAN. We dont learn from other people's
mistakes – not even from most of our own. But knowledge is collected and tools handed on. We cant go back
to the beginning but we can change the future.

The FIRST WOMAN *and the* FOURTH WOMAN *sit.*

FIRST MAN. A tree grows but it doesnt own its own field.
The owner can come along anytime and cut it down and
burn it. It's the same with us. When the things we need
to live are owned by someone else, we're owned – we can
be cut down and burned at any time. Now no tins – so
we can only own what we make and wear and use
ourselves. That's the only difference – but it means that
at last we own ourselves.

FIRST WOMAN. Im too scared to hope. It would make it
worse if we had to go back to the nightmare.

FOURTH WOMAN. In two generations – or a hundred –
they'll bring children to see where we lived. They'll say
'This is where the tin can riots occurred. After that they

had to make their own lives.' Then they'll show them our library –

FIRST MAN. Library?

FOURTH WOMAN. – where we kept the records we made of what we knew about machines and history and all the other things we remembered. Then they'll show them the first generator we made from spare parts and the first tractor. They'll say 'This is the first field. The soil was sterile till they worked it and irrigated it for a long while. Then the first shoots stuck up like green nails on the inside of a door. And while they worked they heard their children playing in the ruins. That's how they turned the chaos into a new world.'

FIRST MAN. And bombs'll be as old to them as stone axes are to us.

FIRST WOMAN. Yes if we survive. They'll look back at us and say we lived in prisons. They'll live in justice. Justice is a stone woman sitting in a stone room trying to make human gestures. If our children live she'll learn to make them – and then the stone will be as human as these hands which open tins. Lets go in before its dark.

As the three go the others come with a light to welcome them.

Part Three: Great Peace

Characters:

CORPORAL
PEMBERTON
SOLDIER 1
SOLDIER 2
SOLDIER 3
SOLDIER 4
SON
OFFICER
MRS SYMMONS
WOMAN
WOMAN 1
MOTHER
DAUGHTER
MAN
MIDDLE-AGED MAN
YOUNG MAN

ONE

Military Post

An ARMY CAPTAIN. *A* CORPORAL *marches on a* SQUAD OF
SOLDIERS.

CORPORAL. Squad 'alt – squad right turn – squad stand at
    ease (*Salute*.) Sir squad paraded ready for orders
CAPTAIN (*salute*). Thank you corporal
    Stand easy men

SQUAD *stands easy*.

Food supplies are already limited and the situation is
    deteriorating
Famine among the civilian population is unavoidable
(When you see what *that* is you wont complain about
    canteen food)
Under government emergency regulations food will be
    restricted to civilian elements needed to assist in the
    recovery programme
The number of young needed to replace older elements
    as they become inoperative is limited
The harsh truth is that most of them would die of
    malnutrition in the fullness of time
But not before their parents had spent valuable energy
    and supplies in nursing them – thus squandering
    resources needed for the recovery programme
To prevent this waste every soldier will return to his
    place of civilian domicile and eliminate one child: as
    young as possible and not above five years
Immediately thereafter he will report the body's where-
    abouts to the Civil Defence for disposal under the
    sanitary regulations

A year ago this order would have been inconceivable because it would not have been necessary

Now the nuclear exchange has destroyed our community's economic foundation

You'd think the population was made up of individuals with one hand and two mouths!

No age group is exempt from modern war, the ancient tilth and tithe

Disobedience to this order will be summarily dealt with under field regulations

In the meantime all leave cancelled – no hint of this must get outside beforehand

You're entrusted with this mission because you're trained to undertake whatever is necessary to meet the challenge of our times and secure the welfare of the community

You will act promptly and as humanely as the job to be done allows

You have my full confidence

Thank you corporal

CORPORAL. Squad stand at ease – squad shun – sir (*Salute.*)

CAPTAIN (*salute*). Thank you corporal – carry on

CORPORAL. Sir

The CAPTAIN *goes.*

CORPORAL. Squad stand at ease – stand easy

The SQUAD *stands easy.*

Right – civilian domicile means yer permanent place of abode outside the army's arms or in your case the 'ouse where yer last screwed a tart two nights runnin if any of yer was capable of such a feat

PEMBERTON. Make a packet out of this corp: I know what sod'll cough up in our street

CORPORAL. Wrap up Pemberton

Anyone got any intelligent questions?

SOLDIER 1. What if we ain got no local kids?

PEMBERTON. If its your street it'll be full of bastards

CORPORAL. Yer proceed t' the next street an so on till yer strike lucky

SOLDIER 2. Why d'we 'ave t' pick 'em corp?

SOLDIER 1. On the look out for leadership potential

PEMBERTON. 'Oo's interested in your potential?

You ain the broom you're the shit on the bristles

SOLDIER 3. Down ourn they'll pay yer t' get rid of the bastards

SON. They wont put up no welcome sign next time we come 'ome

CORPORAL. Next time there wont be no 'ome t' come 'ome to

You pick the kids so they can cut down on paper work

SOLDIER 2. They dont wanna accept responsibility: we pick an they say it was squaddies on the rampage

SOLDIER 3. They'll put a couple of us in the glass 'ouse t' prove it

SOLDIER 1. Nah they're stirrin up the civvie-shit

They get them against us so's we're trigger 'appy when they give us an order t' corpse 'em

CORPORAL. I said *intelligent* questions

You ain 'ere t' ask why you're 'ere

Squad stand at ease – squad shun – squad right turn – quick march

Hup

The CORPORAL *and the* SOLDIERS *march out.*

TWO

The Woman's House

The WOMAN's *neighbour* MRS SYMMONS *sits on a chair.*

MRS SYMMONS (*voice raised*). No power for the stock lift
   but they still 'ave illuminated displays in the shop
   windows
   Carried cartons up them stairs all day
   I told the guard searchin me when I left: if the bloke 'oo
   designed the stores 'ad t' carry cartons the stairs'd be
   in a different place
   'As she bin good?
WOMAN (*off*). 'Er usual grizzles till she dropped off didnt
   you love?
MRS SYMMONS. She doesnt cry when I 'ave 'er
WOMAN (*off*). P'raps she prefers 'er own cot
   That's why I asked for one of 'er pillows – thought that
   might settle 'er
MRS SYMMONS. I wonder if she's warm enough

   The WOMAN *comes in carrying* MRS SYMMONS's *child.*

WOMAN. I can't afford extra 'eatin
   Too warm makes 'em susceptible t' colds
MRS SYMMONS. Im sorry the grizzlin must get on your
   nerves
WOMAN. I'll 'ave t' ask for more money
MRS SYMMONS. I cant afford no more
   It wouldnt be worth me going out t' work
WOMAN. I put off askin as long as I could
   Everythin goes up in price
   I'd be better off goin out t' work meself
MRS SYMMONS (*takes her baby*). I wasnt complainin about
   the cold

Its just as cold in our place
We're lucky we've got you t' 'elp us
If she was anywhere else I'd worry all day
Some places they'd eat the food I left for its dinner
You mustnt mind if I grumble

WOMAN. You're free t' grumble as much as yer like – but
I'll 'ave t' ask for another ten quid

MRS SYMMONS. O no

WOMAN. What with the cost of food, runnin the 'ouse –
lightin an 'eat – an its gettin colder – I dont mind 'er
for a profit but I cant be out of pocket
You'll find somethin: dont matter 'ow well yer sweep the
floor there's always fluff under the sofa
You get discount tins from your store
Flog them up the other end
They cant afford your tins round 'ere: bet 'alf of 'em owe
yer
You've got t'be smart now you're responsible for the
little one

MRS SYMMONS. I cant go up the other end
No transport – I'd 'ave t' walk
Could you take tins instead of money?
There's a foreman in goods inwards – 'e's pally with the
lorry drivers – 'e must get 'is 'ands on no end of tins
'E 'asnt got a family so 'e doesnt give 'em t' them

WOMAN. I dont like t' ask

MRS SYMMONS. I might be able t' get clothes

WOMAN. Money would be best – though I might be willin'
t' take tins

MRS SYMMONS (to the baby). What a problem my precious
is to 'er mummy

WOMAN. We'll say ten pounds startin Friday fortnight
That gives you time t' make some arrangement with the
foreman
If its tins I cant take any muck

MRS SYMMONS. Im not sure about the foreman – I'll try –
'e keeps tellin me 'e used t' watch me run 'ome from
school
You'd worry about 'er if she was with someone else
WOMAN. Yer cant look after 'em for ever
Yer 'ave t' let 'em go someday – just 'ope they finish up
'appy
MRS SYMMONS. Thank you – 'bye
WOMAN. Bye

MRS SYMMONS *goes out with her child.*

THREE

The Woman's House

The WOMAN. *Her* SON *comes in. He wears uniform and carries a kitbag.*

WOMAN. Son! You're 'ere! Come in! Let me look at yer –
yes!
SON. Mum
WOMAN. Sit down – the 'ouse is so empty without yer
(*Kitbag.*) I'll take this through – dont want the place t'
look like a barracks while you're 'ome
Weighs a ton
Must be dead on your feet
I'll get somethin t' eat
SON. No
(*Looks round.*) Still copin . . .
WOMAN. Yeh dont let it get me down
Must've known you were comin': washed the curtains
You look well: the army feeds yer
Sit down
I 'eard they wanna put us in camps?

'Ave you 'eard anythin?

SON. Its easier t' protect civvies if they're concentrated in a
few places

Shouldnt listen t' rumours

There's some tins in the sack

WOMAN. Bless yer thats why its so 'eavy

(*Looks in the kitbag.*) Peas – pulped apple – that's full of
vitamins – I'll put these in my secret store!

You 'avent bin goin   without for us?

SON. No its not army: pick 'em up on some of the searches

WOMAN. I wont ask, just be grateful

Let me open one?

SON. No they're for you an the kid

WOMAN. Yer 'avent seen it

The WOMAN *goes out and returns in a moment with her
baby.*

WOMAN. Wont wake 'er: might wake itself when it 'ears
your voice

SON. You look tired

WOMAN. It's just the excitement of seein you

Things seem t' go from bad t' worse – makes everythin a
strain

SON. Yer cant run a country when 'alf yer own people are
against yer

WOMAN. Saw some young men an girls standin on a street
corner in their shirt sleeves

Police wouldn't let yer get near – they'd found some
weapons in a 'ouse

'Ad t' come round by Lychfield Road an I 'ad the pram

We 'ad squatters in number twelve – they make even the
rubble look clean

They took them away an nailed up the doors an windows

Daft, they could easy get in through the roof

The army want t' clear the rubble out the streets

If they 'ad t' come down 'ere in an emergency they'd 'ave
    t' use a tank
Anythin could –
SON. All right
WOMAN. Just an encouragement t' rats
SON. We 'ave t' get rid of the 'uman rubbish first

Doorbell.

WOMAN. Mrs Symmons – 'er 'usband's bin taken in

The WOMAN *puts the tins back into the kitbag and lowers
the flap. She goes to the door and lets in* MRS SYMMONS.
MRS SYMMONS *carries her baby.*

WOMAN. My son's 'ome
    (*Removes the kitbag.*) Made me a present of 'is dirty
      washin
    (*To her* SON). Yer didnt say 'ow long you'd got
SON. Few 'ours
WOMAN. That all?

The WOMAN *goes out with her own baby and the kitbag.*

MRS SYMMONS (*to* SON). 'Ello
WOMAN (*off*). 'Ow's my little grizzler t'day?
MRS SYMMONS. She 'asnt bin cryin
WOMAN (*off*). P'haps she's going t' treat us t' one of 'er
    quiet days
MRS SYMMONS (*to* SON). When the soldiers searched our
    'ouse they made a noise – broke things
    I didnt think she'd noticed but since then she's developed
    a habit of cryin

The WOMAN *comes in and takes the baby from* MRS
SYMMONS.

WOMAN. P'raps she misses 'er dad – dont you my love?
MRS SYMMONS. I might be able to manage the ten quid

WOMAN. That's right dear
I put myself out for you an you do the same for me
MRS SYMMONS. But you mustnt ask again
WOMAN. No dear we'll only do what's fair
You're a good girl an yer dont take advantage of anyone's
soft nature

The WOMAN *goes out with* MRS SYMMONS's *baby.*

MRS SYMMONS. Your mother worries about you
SON. She knows Im better off in the army than standin on
street corners
MRS SYMMONS. Yes
When the soldiers left our 'ouse one of them came back
an said 'we didnt find anythin'
There wasnt anythin t' find, my 'usband only 'ad the
leaflets – 'e'd been 'andin them out on the streets in
broad daylight
But it was 'is way of tellin me they 'adnt planted anythin
SON. What's left after some of the terrorist skylarks'd turn
a corpse's stomach
I 'ave t' clear it up
They wanna 'and em over t' the victims' family
MRS SYMMONS (*calls*). Bye
(*To* SON). 'Ave t' 'urry I'm late

MRS SYMMONS *goes out.*

WOMAN (*off*). That wasnt nice about victims' families

The WOMAN *comes on with two plates of pap and two
spoons.*

Get 'em fed an settled down – you can feed 'er's
SON. I cant
WOMAN. Trainin for when yer get married
She might as well get used t' bein 'andled by strangers

The WOMAN *goes out and returns with the two babies.*

SON. Do we 'ave t' do this now I –

WOMAN. What's the matter yer fed a baby before
I'll manage 'em
You're tired 'auling them 'eavy tins

SON. Im out of fags

WOMAN. Yer might find some in the dresser if you're lucky

SON. Not scroungin yours – we'll feed 'em an then you pop
down the shop

WOMAN. I can go now

SON. Feed 'em first

WOMAN. Yes then they'll be good as angels

The WOMAN *gives the* SON *a saucer and spoon. He feeds*
MRS SYMMONS'*s baby. The* WOMAN *feeds her own.*

SON. Skin like a frog – all gob

WOMAN. Let the poor little mite enjoy it while she's got
the chance
With '*er* father she's already got a mark on 'er file
There did it dribble its little chin?
Make 'er swallow slow or she sicks it up

SON. What did 'er father get up to?

WOMAN. 'Anded round leaflets
Tried t' 'old up deliveries of cement t' the new silos
What good's that?
If the army wants silos they'll get 'em

SON. There was more in it than leaflets

WOMAN. They'll probably 'ave 'er in for questionin an this
kid'll go in an institution
That's a good love
You need a flannel?

SON. No

WOMAN. Use the side of your finger
Bein 'ungry makes em clean eaters

That one'd chew the spoon
SON. She's got white spots in 'er gums
WOMAN. Milk teeth
   Funny way t' grow: see 'ow they make the skin sore
   Let me look: yes they're comin nicely

Takes MRS SYMMONS's *baby.*

Did she leave us a nice clean plate she did?
An now we'll settle down an be a good quiet girl to say
   thank you to the nice soldier 'oo fed us

She puts the babies beside each other.

Fags – you must be dyin for a smoke
Need anythin else from the shop?
SON. No
WOMAN. Shant be long if he dont keep me talkin

The WOMAN *goes out. The* SON *rolls up his sleeves.*

SON. Wash up this mess

The SON *takes out the saucers and spoons. He comes back
drying the wet saucers on a tea towel*

Does daddy talk t' keep you quiet?
'Shoot the corpsin soldiers'

Doorbell. The SON *puts away the saucers and tea towel and
opens the door.*
PEMBERTON *comes in.*

PEMBERTON. Ready?
   (*Sees the babies.*) Two? What for? 'Avin a clear out?
SON. Neighbour's kid – leaves it while she's out t' work
PEMBERTON. That's 'andy
   Get up there quick then?
   Few drinks iron out the wrinkles
   Stroll in the park

Get comfortable for the evenin

SON. Me mum's gone out for some fags

PEMBERTON. 'Onestly I'd rather watch a corpse shit

SON. Eh?

PEMBERTON. You come round our place t' pick me up
    I'd've give yer a copy of the post mortem not stand
    there like a corpse wonderin if its got BO

Two! – it ain as if yer 'ad t' go out lookin

SON. 'Ow did I know yer'd be round so soon?

PEMBERTON. This ain soon!

What's the matter? – give it time t' write its memoirs?

Pity the poor bleeder in your 'ands – shouldnt let you
    loose on a fossile chicken

SON. Corpse off!

Me mum was 'ere – I'm supposed t' ask 'er t' 'old it?

PEMBERTON. I'll wait outside

SON. Come 'ere with all your corpse-shit! It was goin all
    right – got the ol' lady out the 'ouse –

PEMBERTON. Look corpse that (it ain goin t' put up a
    fight) then get inside a clean civvie shirt an you'll be a
    new man

Cant go on the streets in army gear after this – the
    mums'll be out with their 'atchets

SON *goes out.*

(*Calls.*) Mine was three doors down. Crep in the back
    window. 'E's stood there. Told 'im why I'd come. 'Is
    class dont panic: read the papers with no pictures.
    Zonks 'is bed over the room. Thought 'e was tryin t'
    sledge me. No, lifts up the floorboard. Like an alliga-
    tor's gob. Keeps 'is under the bed. Twenty thousand
    US dollars. Says I get the rest when 'e sees the body.
    Got it all sussed: 'e sees the body 'e knows 'is kid's
    safe. I dont kill two. 'Is sort know 'ow t' 'andle money.
    'E as good as put me under contract.

SON (*off*). Should've corpsed the bugger's nipper out of
   spite
PEMBERTON (*calls*). 'E knows 'e ain dealin with a lunatic.
   I took the body round in a carrier bag. 'E drops the
   money on top – if Im buried in that way I'll come back
   t' life. Wants the body 'id so nobody knows 'e's bought
   'is nipper off. Said next time Im on leave 'e'll drop me
   some business. I reckon 'e's got me on the cheap.

   The WOMAN *comes in.*

WOMAN. 'Ello Perry
PEMBERTON. Bin fetchin the lad's fags?
   Old enough t' run 'is own errands
WOMAN (*calls*). Fags
   (*To* PEMBERTON.) 'E's run plenty of errands for me
   You two goin out?
PEMBERTON. Up the other end

   The SON *comes in wearing civvies.*

WOMAN. You changed!
   Look smart in your uniform – pull all the girls
SON. I'll spend a proper week indoors next time – do yer
   decoratin
WOMAN. Dont you let me interfere with your pleasure
   Go an enjoy yourself
   There's no need t' rush back: Im all right now I've seen
   yer
PEMBERTON. 'E still ain found 'is shoes
   I'll go on – if yer dont catch me up we'll be in the Yellow
   Brick when its gettin dark
WOMAN. Go with 'im – there's your fags
   'S not the end of the world if I spend the day on me own
   Once you start that decoratin I wont let you through the
   door till Im satisfied with the finish results
SON. I'll catch yer up

PEMBERTON. Cheerio then
WOMAN. Bye Perry

> PEMBERTON *goes out.*

Now you've let 'im down
SON. 'E ain cryin
  (*Fags*). What do I owe yer?
WOMAN. Dont be daft
SON. I've got t' kill a child
WOMAN. What? You've got t' kill a child?
SON. Its an order
WOMAN. An order?
  What d'you mean? – you've got t' kill a child
  I dont understand
SON. Its an order
WOMAN. An order? 'Ow can it be?
  Is that why you're 'ere?
SON. Yeh
WOMAN. Kill a kid? What kid?
SON. Any kid
WOMAN. Yer cant
SON. Its an order
WOMAN. They cant give an order like that
SON. The army can
  Kids eat too much – you two are all right, I drop you the
    tins – yer must've seen the others are starvin!
  Its gonna get worse
  They'd die anyway
WOMAN. Starving yes – I get tins – but – why order – ?
SON. For corpse sake its an order!
  I forgot t' ask the CO if 'e meant it!
WOMAN. You must say no – leave the army – run away
  Why *you*?
SON. It was all of us
WOMAN. You mean – Perry – (*Gestures to door.*) – ?

SON. Yeh – for cash

WOMAN. An came 'ere – in my 'ouse?

SON. 'E wiped 'is boots

WOMAN. Dont talk t' me like that!

Order order!

Tell them t' do their own orders!

My baby! (*Suddenly goes to her child and picks it up.*)

What'll you do?

SON. Carry out the order

'Ow else can they sort this mess out?

Too many kids, they die of starvation, the government's blamed, riots, high-jack food convoys, no doctors – it'd drag on for months. They 'ave t' do somethin t' stop the disaster.

WOMAN. Why our street?

What about the streets that cause trouble?

Loot – stone army trucks?

What about the terrorists 'oo maim kids with bombs?

Their children ought t' suffer first

No they send them t' special schools and we pay the bills!

Im sorry (*Goes to* MRS SYMMONS's *baby and looks at it.*)

Children cant pay for their parents' crimes

SON. That's nice civilised talk but it dont 'elp!

There 'as t' be a child from this street – its in the computer: one child for the Civil Defence t' burn

WOMAN (*puts down her own child and picks up* MRS SYMMONS's). But there arent any other children in this street

If I spoke to the officer – if the mothers spoke –

SON. What d' you think an army is?

Anyway its too late – its already started

WOMAN (*nurses* MRS SYMMONS's *baby*). Yes – but this baby – look 'ow we took care of it – fed it an clothed it even in these times!

We'll hide it!

SON. There 'as t' be a body
  You give them your kid?
WOMAN. Dont say such wicked things!
  I'll 'ide both of them – 'er mother can say 'er's was stolen
    while she was at work
  Give them one that's already dead
  If they're starvin there must be dead ones!
  The army wont care as long as you give them somethin!
SON. Where do I get one?
WOMAN. The 'ospital!
  I'll go – the doctors'll understand – no they might be in
    with the army – I'll talk t' the nurses – or they'll give
    you one that's going t' die – that wouldnt be so cruel
SON. So many kids'll die what difference does one more
    make?
WOMAN. But give them one that'll die today – or t'morrow!
  Try – go to the 'ospital – steal one that's sick –
SON. They're guardin the 'ospitals
WOMAN. 'Ow d'you know?
SON. They told us – 'ospitals 'd be the first thing they'd
    think of!
  They want t' cut down on the number alive not top up
    the number of dead!
WOMAN. At least ask! One of the guards might –
SON. There's no point – I know the sort of guards they'll
    be!
WOMAN. What d'you know? – it all comes t' nothin!
  Cant do this cant do that!
  What can yer do?
  Dustbins – search the dustbins
  When must you 'ave it?
SON. In the mornin eight-thirty
WOMAN. The papers say they find kids in dustbins
SON. The other mothers'll've ransacked the dustbins by
    now

Yer might as well ask me t' find another army with a
    different order!

WOMAN (*gets her coat*). I'll try

SON. That kid's mother'll be 'ere soon

WOMAN. No she works till six

SON. The other streets' kids'll be dead
    'Er customers – she'll get it from them

WOMAN. What? She'll come 'ere?
    Good! We'll both go away with the kids – we'll –

SON. One body or –

WOMAN. Then find one!
    Dont come t' your mother an' tell 'er such things!
    Go somewhere else!
    There must be a place for people like you
    Some shop or morgue where they sell dead children!
    'Avent they started that yet?
    My god is that why you sent me out for fags? – so that
        you could – ?
    Dont sit there in the clothes I washed!
    Get in your uniform so we know 'oo you are!
    You wont 'arm these children – not even touch 'em – in
        my 'ouse!

SON. You stupid bloody woman . . .
    If I dont give them a body Im shot
    Desert? – they'd shoot both kids an you an probably the
        'ole street
    What's the use of that, for one kid?

WOMAN. Good! – if they shoot you that'd be somethin!
    And me! They must shoot the mothers next – we bring
        the brats into the world
    Why d'you say such stupid things!
    They wont catch us – we'd stand a chance – we can run
        – these kids cant run without us!

SON. The worse an order is the more they make sure its
    obeyed

This is just a little corner of the war
If I dont do it someone else will
Give it t' me an go outside

WOMAN. I cant. Im sorry

SON. It wont know – it dont even know its wrong – no
more sense than the muck it eats – you women do its
sufferin for it – be grateful an go outside an cry
All this works itself out so we can all find our own way
through it
We should all be grateful

WOMAN. They didnt give this order

SON. Perry got it right
'E didnt take money for killin the child
That was an order – 'e couldnt get out of it
But he didnt be'ave like a button they pressed
'E was as smart as the lot 'oo give orders: 'e used it for
somethin for 'imself –
Screwed loot out of a crook: 'e took money t' stay 'uman

The WOMAN *walks away from the babies.*

WOMAN. I cant think

SON. Yer shouted at me, now its too 'ard t' think!
Then dont call me names
You cheat an stab each other in the back an cheer when
the army goes by
Its a great army in peace!: keeps everyone in their place
so they can go on swindlin an cheatin
When there's a war an it be'aves like an army: we didnt
know, we didnt think . . .
Well dont 'ave an army an expect your kids t'be safe . . .
Not every mother loses 'er kid
The ones 'oo dont'll still cheer when they see us, most of
em – an the rest'll shut up when their kids eat
Once this is over it wont trouble 'em anymore than a
corpse goes on sufferin what it died of

I've seen it before
When its done, go anywhere yer like, get the people
    t'gether an put us on trial an they'll say: well, its the
    army an we cant live without an army

The SON *goes to the two babies and picks up* MRS
SYMMONS's.

WOMAN. Make sure you've got the right one
SON. I 'ave
WOMAN. She leaves me 'er key for emergencies – on the
    dresser
SON. Forget it mum: Im sorry I shouted
WOMAN (*gives him the key*). Don't 'urt it
SON. Like a fly
    It wouldnt know even if it was grown up

The SON *goes out with* MRS SYMMONS's *child. The*
WOMAN *picks up her own.*

WOMAN. Dont open your eyes
    Not a sound
    The shawl!
    (*The* WOMAN *picks up* MRS SYMMONS's *child's shawl and
    then puts it down.*) No dont call 'im – dont 'old 'im up

Walks.

There's still time
    'E's not even at 'er 'ouse – I could call 'im an . . .

Doorbell.

WOMAN. 'Oo is it?
MRS SYMMONS (*off*). Mrs Symmons – I've come for my
    baby
WOMAN. So early? 'Ave you got the day off?
MRS SYMMONS. I want my baby! Give me my baby!
WOMAN. Whatever is it? You sound upset

MRS SYMMONS. Where is she?

WOMAN. What's the matter?

MRS SYMMONS. Open the door!

WOMAN. Dont speak t' me like that!

MRS SYMMONS (*off*). Give me my baby!

WOMAN. Your baby? Of course you'll 'ave your baby!
  What is the matter with you?
  Im not lettin you in in that state!
  You'll give the kid a shock – you know 'ow she grizzles

MRS SYMMONS (*off*). Open this door!

WOMAN. Are you alone?

MRS SYMMONS (*off*). Open it!

WOMAN. Just a minute while I fetch the key
  My son made me lock the door from the inside

MRS SYMMONS (*off*). Please open the door!

WOMAN. I cant find the key
  You wouldnt believe 'ow forgetful I am
  It should 'ave its own proper place by rights
  My son was quite cross with me for not lockin that door
  Said there are terrible people about
  With two kids in the 'ouse yer 'ave t' take care

MRS SYMMONS (*off*). 'Ave you found it?

WOMAN. Yes

The WOMAN *opens the door and* MRS SYMMONS *comes in.*

MRS SYMMONS (*searching*). Where is she? Give me my
  baby!
  She's not 'ere!
  I'll kill you if 'e 'urts 'er!
  My baby!

MRS SYMMONS *goes towards the door.*

WOMAN. Dont go out

MRS SYMMONS. Where's your son?

WOMAN. 'E took 'er for a walk – the fresh air –

Is there anythin wrong?

MRS SYMMONS. You're lyin! –

Dont you know?

WOMAN. Whatever is the matter dear?

Why're you so upset? Is there somethin I should know?

If you stand still so a body can –

MRS SYMMONS. 'Elp me!

WOMAN. Of course I'll 'elp you! But you must tell me 'ow!

MRS SYMMONS. People in the store – said children – bein
killed –

I started t'leave – manager tried t' stop me – laughed!

WOMAN. Is that all? I am relieved

I 'eard the same silly story when I went down t' the shop

You know 'ow people gossip

Our soldiers wouldnt kill children

They take care of us

MRS SYMMONS. Its true its true!

Women in the street! Cryin! I saw!

Where's your son?

'E came 'ere for my baby!

WOMAN. No no 'e wouldnt 'urt your baby

I'd – I'd've known – 'e couldnt 'ide that from me – an
I'd've stopped 'im

'E took 'er out for some fresh air

Come an sit with me

We'll wait t'gether

MRS SYMMONS. Where did 'e take 'er?

I cant run everywhere!

(*Through clenched teeth*.) Give me my baby

WOMAN. I dont know where your baby is

MRS SYMMONS *starts to go*.

Dont go out! Dont go 'ome!

MRS SYMMONS. Why?

WOMAN. I'll tell you where she is – not at 'ome!

I can see I should've told you straight off but I didnt
  want t' frighten you
'E knew what was 'appenin so 'e took 'er where she
  wouldnt come t' 'arm
'E wont 'urt 'er – 'e fed 'er with me
I dont know, I dont know
What can I tell you?
You poor woman we must trust 'im – an wait

The WOMAN *tries to touch* MRS SYMMONS. MRS SYM-
MONS *breaks away.*

MRS SYMMONS. 'E came t' kill 'er!
  You're keepin me 'ere on purpose!
WOMAN. There's nothin we can do for 'er – we must wait
MRS SYMMONS. I'll look in the street
WOMAN. If you make a disturbance they'll run you in
  Then what'll 'appen t' your kid?
  Stay 'ere – I'll 'elp you – take care of you

MRS SYMMONS *goes out.*

Poor woman let 'er run 'erself out
She'll need me t'morrow
Poor little kid – two mothers an no 'elp

FOUR

Mrs Symmons's House

MRS SYMMONS *sits alone. She wears her outdoors coat.*
The SON *comes in carrying her baby. His clothes are dirty and
his shirt is torn. A grazed bruise on his head has bled slightly.*
MRS SYMMONS *stands.*

MRS SYMMONS. Is she all right?

(*Takes her child*.) Yes

You didnt 'urt 'er

SON. I give 'er some water – she's 'ungry

MRS SYMMONS. I thought I would see 'er again

I 'oped I'd see 'er body – I wouldnt let myself think she'd be alive

My baby . . . not a scratch –

SON. Dont leave your door open

MRS SYMMONS. You've given 'er back . . . ?

I walked all day

There were women cryin in the street – bein taken t' their relatives

I asked if they'd seen my baby – looked an cried – I dont think they 'eard

I went back t' your 'ouse

I thought you was inside

Your mother wouldnt let me in

Then I thought no – search the streets

I couldnt walk anymore

I sat on a wall

Thought if she's dead its my place t' know

So that I share it with 'er

If I dont its like she smiled an I didnt smile back

Or she cried when I was in the room and I didnt 'ear

(*To the baby*.) It was as bad as if I wanted t' get rid of you . . .

So I came back

You've got a dirty shirt

Cut on your 'ead

SON. Some women chased me

I told them I was the father but they called some men from a garage

MRS SYMMONS. They cut your 'ead?

SON. No – I ran or they'd've taken 'er from me

I cut it on a fire escape

MRS SYMMONS. Why didnt you come straight 'ere?

SON. I took 'er out t' kill 'er but I couldnt find anywhere t'
      do it

   Then I ran t' stop the others takin 'er . . .

MRS SYMMONS. I 'avent got any money – no you dont want
      that

   You should wash your 'ead

   There's a bottle of disinfectant in the cabinet

   Its the baby's – you mustnt dilute it

SON. Its not bleedin'

MRS SYMMONS. What'll the army do t' you?

   You shouldnt've become a soldier

   Im sorry I cant 'elp you

   You'd better go

SON. Dont worry I wont change my mind!

   You've got 'er 'avent yer?

   Corpsin-jesus you ungrateful bitch!

MRS SYMMONS. Dont shout!

   You'll scare 'er!

   Why didnt you bring 'er straight t' me?

   I waited the 'ole day

   What were you doin in the street?

SON. I must go

MRS SYMMONS. They wont send some more soldiers?

SON. No its all over

   Stay indoors a few days

   When somethin like this's 'appened its best t' stay out of
      sight

   You'll 'ave a job managin on yer own

   Yer wont see your 'usband again

   Got relatives yer can go to?

MRS SYMMONS. No

   They took my travel permit

SON (turning). Right

MRS SYMMONS. I didnt want t' get rid of you

I wanted t' 'ave the child t' myself
SON. Your spare key from my mother's
MRS SYMMONS. I'll lock the door after you

MRS SYMMONS *takes the key from the* SON *and follows him out.*

FIVE

The Woman's House

The WOMAN. *Her* SON *comes in.*

WOMAN. Where've you bin?
  I sat 'ere all day!
  Are you all right?
  She came round three times! Bangin the door!
  She ain in the street – she didnt see you come up?
SON. No I left 'er in 'er place
WOMAN. So its . . . ?
  Where've you bin?
  You should've told your mother if you was stoppin out
  Look at your shirt – your 'ead
  Did she do . . . ?
SON. No
WOMAN. Dont tell me if its . . . ?
  We'll forget it
  They make us do it, they cant make us remember it
  Let it go sour in their own 'eads
  Take that shirt off an give it t' me t' wash
  It'll soon dry in front of the fire
  A proper mend wont show under your jacket
  What a shame, its your favourite shirt – I liked ironing
    that one
  When you didnt come I thought you was with your mates

'Ave t' stay in with the lads when you're in the army

Such a long day: made me think what *you* go through

All I did was shout: that dont 'elp

Well I learned my lesson

You did it for our sake

You're a good boy

Dont be cross with me – I dont see much of you, dont
    waste it bein angry

I know you better now: you're a new son t' me t'day

Thank you

SON. I didnt kill it

WOMAN. You didnt kill it

You found one

SON. 'Where was I?' Runnin round the streets like a rabbit
    on the race track

The 'ole day

All the doors was closed – yer'd think I was locked in the
    streets tryin t' get out

Me throat ached – goin so fast – me 'ead pushed back
    . . . !

We do some daft things to ourselves

WOMAN. Yer 'avent got a child t' give 'em

SON. I turned out the dustbins

Kept runnin past dogs sittin in 'eaps of rubbish I'd made

WOMAN. Where's 'er key?

SON. What?

WOMAN. I give you 'er key when you went out

You put it in your pocket

SON. Give it back

WOMAN. 'Ow did yer get your bruise?

SON. I was chased

'Id in an old 'all

Should've 'eard the fire escape rattle when I ran up

WOMAN. What'll we do?

SON. It'll 'ave t' be sorted out by the mornin

Leave it a bit

WOMAN. Would Perry do it for us?

That child the father bought off – that ain right

'E could give them that

'E's done it once, it wouldnt put much on 'is conscience

SON. No

WOMAN. I can pay

I've always bin strict about puttin a bit by: it adds up

I meant it for the family

'E'd do it for me

I know its wrong t' say these things but what else can I do?

I'll ask 'im, you mustnt – it'd be embarrassin

SON. No

'E'd 'ave a few drinks an blab – an it'd get back t' the officers – some of the squad'd jump at the chance!

Then chop! – I was told t' do it meself

Leave it – let me empty me 'ead till mornin – somethin'll turn up

WOMAN. It'll be too late!

We'll think of somethin we should've done while we was sittin 'ere!

. . . Well, there's 'ours yet

That shawl'll 'ave t' go back

She got that give 'er at 'er store

Thought she'd finished with it so I'd 'ave it

Tryin t' be practical t' make it easier

We 'ave t' give them a kid

We was ordered!

If we dont they'll come 'ere an take my kid!

That one's father's put a mark on it – it's bin pushed around till its sickenin t' go . . . ! – that's why it grizzles

It'll be dead in a year – there's no proper money comin

in that 'ome – they stopped 'er allowance when 'e went inside

If only you'd done it while I was out for the fags . . .

It could all be over now

It was possible then . . . an I shouted

I looked after you all these years an when the time comes I needed t' rely on you: I stopped yer

Now your mate's out spendin 'is wages

If only 'e'd bin my son!

'E wouldn't've listen t' me: told me t' get off!

'E wouldnt've dared cross my door till it was dead

Waited outside 'er 'ouse an caught 'er when she left for work – yes

Not bring 'is problems 'ome cryin at 'is mother's apron strings

Wouldnt even've told me, god bless 'im

No: come in, washed 'is 'ands, sat at the table an said grub

That's the sort of son 'oo 'elps a mother

And I 'ave t' 'ave one like you!

Why did yer listen t' me?

Yer 'avent got the sense yer was born with!

Dont yer know Im a stupid bitch – a silly cow?

Look at me now! Listen t' me!

'I wish 'e was my son'! – I bet 'e's bloody glad Im not 'is bleedin mother!

She wouldnt've stopped 'im – too much bloody sense!

But I be'ave as if I've got the right t' shout!

I wont make that mistake again

Next time I'll say what's best an stick t' it

. . . I dont want you t' be like your mate – but 'ow else can I manage?

You're trained for your job, 'oo trained me t' look after my kid?

Be yourself – I dont want t' change you – you're my kid
   too – I'll try t' 'elp both of yer

The WOMAN *picks up her baby.*

SON. Where you goin?
WOMAN. Give 'er 'er shawl
SON. Leave it till the mornin
WOMAN. I'll get it out the way

SIX

Mrs Symmon's House and the Street Outside

MRS SYMMONS *sits without her baby. She still wears her street
coat.*
The WOMAN *comes in with her baby.*

WOMAN. The pair of them
   Where were they all afternoon?
   I know why 'er child's alive
   No no 'e wouldnt . . . But she could make 'im!
   The child's there – explain that
   She couldnt pay 'im
   Ha! 'er sort dont 'ave money – they cant save!
   Bed bed bed that's what it was: bed!
   She didnt 'ave t' say dont kill it – no, lay there for 'im an
      'e's groanin I promise in 'er ear so's 'e can 'ave the bed
      creakin all day – that's 'ow she got it!
   No no my son wouldnt do that to us! Why not? As long
      as its bed they're 'appy!
   Where else was 'e all day?
   (*Puts the baby down.*) Hide there by the wall – no one'll
      'arm you my precious
   Dont make a sound – I'll be back soon

The WOMAN *goes to* MRS SYMMONS's *door and rings the bell once.*

Mrs Symmons dont be afraid
Im returning your baby's shawl
The poor little mite's so sickly Im worried it might get
    cold
I told you my son wouldnt 'urt it
'E does what 'is mother tells 'im
I've sent 'im back t' 'is barracks so 'e's out of mischief

Doorbell, once.

Its been a terrible day – I was so worried – just say one
    word so I know you an the kid are all right – then I
    can rest
MRS SYMMONS. We're all right
WOMAN. What a relief!
    You give me such a fright when you didnt answer
    For a moment I thought my son'd told me a lie!
    Why didnt you open the door when I rang?

Doorbell, once.

MRS SYMMONS. Please go away
WOMAN. Whatever's the matter?
    Open the door – Im not leavin you when you're in this
    state
MRS SYMMONS. Im all right
WOMAN. Then open the door an take the shawl
MRS SYMMONS. Leave it on the doorstep
    I dont need you to mind the baby anymore
    I can manage in future
    Thank you
WOMAN. Im glad t' 'ear that dear – you be independent
    A baby needs its own mother
    An you know if you ever need somewhere t' leave it for a

few 'ours – they might let you visit the prison per'aps
 – yer know where I am

MRS SYMMONS. Im going t' bed now

WOMAN. That's where we should all be

Im sorry I kept you up, but now I 'ave can I ask you a
little favour?: show me the kid through the window?

I'll 'ave a sleepless night if I dont see 'er

After this awful day 'er sweet little face'll put my mind at
rest

MRS SYMMONS. She's asleep

WOMAN. The precious, she can sleep through all this

Imagine, not even grizzlin . . . !

Doorbell, twice.

My son said you're t' bring 'er t' my 'ouse

You're not safe with no 'usband

The civilians've started killin kids: they're afraid of the
famine

'E says we're safe in my place 'cause its a soldier's 'ouse

MRS SYMMONS. I wont open the door

WOMAN. Dont upset me like this dear

Im so worried about that kid

I nursed 'er as if she was one of my own

Let me wrap 'er in 'er little shawl – yer cant begrudge
me that pleasure after all the 'elp I've give you

Doorbell, continuously. Starts to rattle the door.

Listen t' all this noise!

We'll 'ave the 'ole street up!

We mustnt let the neighbours know you've got a child in
there!

Now my son's gone Im on my own

Open the door so we can comfort each other

MRS SYMMONS. Go 'ome – I'll open it t'morrow

WOMAN. Yes you be cross with me dear – Im being
    silly . . .

The WOMAN *goes back to her baby.*

This is my only chance an Im wastin it!
(*Tears the shawl.*) 'Er kid should be dead! Its father!
They start the wars! They're why we 'ave bombs! Kill
    kids!
'E's safe under 'is concrete in prison an 'is kid's tucked
    up in its cot!
I'll tear it like this!

Tears the shawl.

Yes, tear it (*Tears the shawl.*) and stop (*Abruptly stops in
    mid-tear and holds the two sides apart.*) like this
Stupid cow! – tears a shawl! – weak weak weak
Yer might as well do nothin!
Yer go 'ome – you're already 'alf-way there – nothin
    decided
An later on she'll come for 'er shawl – an I'll 'and it back
    with the tear nicely stitched and tell 'er t' wrap 'er kid
    up an keep it warm – an she'll say 'thank you, you're a
    good woman' – an you'll be dead

The WOMAN *picks up her baby.*

You smile at me because yer dont know 'oo I am
These 'ands are killin yer but yer dont bleed
I stroke yer cheek: there's no scratch
I talk an say less than a child before its learned t' speak
What'll bring me t' me senses?
Im not fit t' 'old you in me 'ands
Im not cruel – cold – 'ard – cunning enough t' be a mother!

The WOMAN *puts down her child and goes back to* MRS
SYMMONS's *door.*

Mrs Symmons quick open the door

I went t' my 'ouse – I was so glad I'd 'eard your voice –
an soldiers were goin in my door!

Their truck was outside!

They want t' arrest me because my son didnt carry out
'is orders!

They'll kill my baby!

MRS SYMMONS. They wont

WOMAN. They will that's why they've come!

Remember I 'elped you!

Take the child in, dont matter about me: I'll go to the
soldiers an tell 'em its dead

Please

A mother's pleadin on your doorstep: is this where you
want them t' kill my child?

I think they've already killed my son!

Must I lose two children 'cause I saved yours?

MRS SYMMONS. I dont care what any of you do!

I wont open the door if you've got soldiers outside!

Im afraid!

WOMAN. When they find my flat empty they'll come
searchin

If they catch me 'ere they'll bring your door down!

Then it'll be your kid's turn

Open the door!

Just turn the key an let it open

MRS SYMMONS. Put your kid on the doorstep an cross over
the street

When I see you over there I'll open the door an take your
child in

Then go back t' the soldiers an say you threw your kid in
the river after a soldier'd killed it

They wont know anythin different!

Then our kids are safe

WOMAN. What if they see me across the street?

MRS SYMMONS. That's my last word
  Its all I can do t' 'elp
WOMAN. All right – yes dear that's best – I'll cross the –
  The child's on your doorstep: goodbye my precious . . .

The WOMAN *crosses to the far side of the street.* MRS
SYMMONS *looks to see that she's there.*

WOMAN. Quick before the soldiers come
  Let me see you take 'er in

MRS SYMMONS *opens her door and the* WOMAN *comes
forward.*

Thank you thank you
MRS SYMMONS. Stay there or I'll –
WOMAN (*still coming forward*). Dont be frightened my dear
    just a last look at my –
MRS SYMMONS. I'll shut the door!

The WOMAN *reaches* MRS SYMMONS *and tears at her coat,
searching for the child.*

WOMAN. Where is it! The bastard! In your belly!
  I'll get it!

The WOMAN *pushes past* MRS SYMMONS *and goes into the
house.* MRS SYMMONS *goes away down the road.*

WOMAN (*searching*):
  Bastard bastard bastard
  I'll kill it!
  Where's the little shit!
  Dont hide from me!
  I'll kill it!
  Its not 'ere – not 'ere – not 'ere!
  Nowhere?
  (*Going back to the door.*) Where's your bastard, please
    give me your bastard?

She sees that MRS SYMMONS *has gone.*

She's gone – it wasnt 'ere – she'd took it away – ha!
Both gone

The WOMAN *goes back to her child and picks it up.*

It was gone my darlin
All the time not there
We must go – its cold
Too many streets t' search, nowhere t' begin . . .
'Id in all them 'ouses
I played in this street once
'Opped after stones in the squares
They 'ad trees growin straight out of the pavements
What did grown-ups want trees for?
I still go down the street with you as if it was normal
They cut the trees down – they'll take the street away

SEVEN

The Woman's House

The SON *holding a wet shirt. The* WOMAN *comes in with her child.*

WOMAN. You washed your shirt
    There was no need
    I'd've done it
SON. She wouldnt let you in?
WOMAN (*half smile*): O your mother got in: there was no
        baby
    Sat there an 'ad me well fooled
    Clever woman
    She might've taken it round to 'er foreman friend's:

they're like that (*She crosses middle finger over index finger of her right hand.*)
Or 'id it on a bomb site
'Ow're you gettin us out of this?
Its your job – I cocked it up
Pass me that shirt its drippin on the ground

The WOMAN *puts down her baby and takes her* SON's *shirt.*

Per'aps she'll get 'erself picked up on the street with 'er child – then all this fuss'll be for nothin

The WOMAN *goes out.*

(*Off.*) Its a pity yer couldnt go up the other end an' see your mates drunk – that'd've shown you 'ow t' cope with all this

The WOMAN *comes back with a floorcloth, throws it to the* SON *to catch and goes out.*

(*Off.*) Mop that wet up before it stains

The SON *goes to the baby.*

(*Off.*) There's a town on our doorstep full of bodies
We could've dug in the ruins – one of 'em might've bin a kid
The dogs are at it now: we're above it

The sound of running water, off. The SON *covers the baby's face with the floorcloth.*

(*Off.*) Your suds're all round the sink
The army's supposed t' teach yer t' clean up
SON. Dont take long – please
Go quickly for 'er sake – dont let 'er come back
(*Looks at the baby.*) Still alive!

He covers the face with the floorcloth and moulds it to the face with both hands.

WOMAN (*off*). Is this the army's version of clean?
  It'll take more than an overnight soakin t' shift this
  I cant 'ave it ready for t'morrow
  Lucky you've got your other shirts

The sound of running water stops, off.

SON. Please dont take another breath . . .

He removes the floorcloth from the baby's face.

  That's just a movement – its not alive – dead – its the
    chest settlin down
WOMAN (*off*). When they see your cut they'll think you've
    bin in a brawl
  They wont 'ave a scratch on 'em after all they've done

The WOMAN *comes in. The* SON *stands with the floorcloth
in his hand.*

  What's wrong with the floor?

The SON *automatically flops the floorcloth onto the puddle.
The* WOMAN *goes uncomplainingly to the puddle and mops
it. The* SON *gets his jacket.*

  You ain goin out! I cant decide this on me own! You've
    got t' stay an 'elp me!
SON. I need a drink
WOMAN. I forbid yer t' go through that door
SON. No more – I must go out – you dont let me think – let
    me go

  SON *goes off.*

WOMAN. You wont think!
  You'll get drunk an forget!
  Spew it up in the gutter an the military police'll drag you
    back t' the barracks!
  I wont see yer! I'll be left t' deal with this on me own!

The SON *comes back with his kitbag.*

SON. I wont get drunk
    If I dont go the lads'll talk and that'll be –
WOMAN. What's the bag for?
SON. They've got a truck – drop it in that – save me luggin
    it in the mornin
WOMAN. You're runnin out on me yer little sod!
    Please dont go
SON. I'll be 'ere in the mornin!
WOMAN. O no yer wont yer little shit!
    You go through that door it'll be shut for ever!
    Im warnin yer!

SON *goes.*

(*Calls.*) I mean it!
Dont you come in this 'ouse again!

The WOMAN *goes to the puddle and finishes mopping it.*

You fool . . .
'Ow shall I get through the night
Not sit 'ere – but I wont go through the streets or pick at
    the rubble
My kid needs more than luck
But what . . . ?

The WOMAN *puts away the floorcloth, goes to her baby, sits
and picks it up.*

Let 'er keep 'er child
No grudge against them
Feed you first

Exposes her breast.

If Im calm I'll find a way
Wake up sleeper the smell of milk'll open your eyes

You're only small but yer make me be very good an very
   bad
Take your tit
Now I've got blood on me finger – smeared up the side
Did I cut meself on the floorboards?
Its out of your nose – one of your nose-bleeds
Wake up darlin
The blood's not comin – only when I lift your 'ead

Dabs at the child.

It's on my 'and – me wrist – dont mess mummy's –
Its –

She holds the baby up as if she was hanging a picture.

Its running from its nose
No no darlin dont do that
It wont stop runnin – it's goin down my arm –
Its bleedin – like a thing –
Its dead
No darlin breathe quickly for mummy
Its dead its dead!
Breathe!
I'll 'elp you! Look – shake you!

She shakes the child.

Take it t' the kitchen an 'old it under the tap
(*Calls to the door.*) Come back an 'elp me!
It's dead!

She cries.

EIGHT

Military Post by a Quarry

A SQUAD OF SOLDIERS *rests on the ground. The* SON *stands and looks off.*

SOLDIER 3. Used t' live for me leave
　Booze an screw
　Nice easy breakfast
　Look through the window
　Quiet start t' the day
SOLDIER 4. Nowhere t' 'ave leave
　All corpsin soldiers an corpsin civvies on corpsin bomb
　sites
PEMBERTON (*to* SON). Why dont yer sit down?
SOLDIER 1. First screw I seen on 'er own with a kid
SOLDIER 3. 'E's off
SOLDIER 4. Different version each time
SOLDIER 1. No, straight. All the previous there was people
　about. Go up. Bin shoppin. Thinks I wanna see 'er
　permit. Poke me barrel in the pram. After this lamp-
　post looks like its bin painted for a carnival. 'Wet
　Paint.' Ain the way I'd run the world but I wasnt
　asked.
SOLDIER 4. 'E fished one out the lavatory pan
SOLDIER 1. Dont 'ave lavatories round ours, we do it under
　the table
SOLDIER 2. 'E does it on the table
PEMBERTON. You run the world it'd go backwards
SOLDIER 3. Come before yer got 'ard
SOLDIER 1. Tart chases me down the street. Pram's goin
　the other way. I shout stop it. Silly cow turns round
　an runs after it. Screechin like a skeleton in a spin-
　drier.

PEMBERTON (*to* SON). Give me the creeps stood there

SOLDIER 2. They see yer can still stand they'll 'ave us chuckin bricks from one 'eap t' another

Wanna looked shagged out like corpse after its bin tryin t' wank

SOLDIER 3. Leave 'im – off 'is rocker –

SOLDIER 4. Corpsed 'is own kid while its mother's out the room

SOLDIER 3. Couldnt 'e find no one else?

SOLDIER 2. You couldnt find a fly up a corpse's ars'ole if it 'ad an amplified buzzer

SOLDIER 4. Know why 'e's stood there: see in t' the quarry

CORPORAL *comes in.*

CORPORAL. Sent a truck for the ammo

SOLDIER 1. What a corpsin army – runs out of ammo!

SOLDIER 4. Way we're stuck out 'ere they'll run out of corpsin soldiers

Ought t' be in bunkers

SOLDIER 1. Rather be out 'ere – bunkers direct 'its – corpsin live-meat in a concrete sandwich

CORPORAL. There wont be no more missiles – the war's over

SOLDIER 2. Go an give yerself a post-mortem

CORPORAL. They've 'ad a taste of what they'd get next time

You think you 'ad it rough

We blew that lot so far apart some of 'em are goin round with some one else's guts inside 'em digestin their food

SOLDIER 2 (*looking at the* SON). 'E's stood there like a corpse at the wrong funeral

PEMBERTON. 'E dont like leavin em waitin like cattle

Wants t' finish it off

CORPORAL (*lights a cigarette*). O I'd finish em off if I 'ad the ammo son

PEMBERTON. We got a box

CORPORAL. Keep your thievers off that
That's reserve
They dont mind waitin – you ask em

He throws away his empty cigarette packet.

SOLDIER 4. Wanna get em all in one place an drop a rocket
All this pop-pop

SOLDIER 2. They're waitin like the rest of us
Soon's we start gettin back t' normal they'll 'ammer us
so 'ard the corpses'll 'ave diarrhoea

CORPORAL. Dont start 'im off
Where's my fag packet?
(*To the* SON.) Oi pick that up
The war's over an we won

SOLDIER 4. Next time there wont be a warnin, they
cremated the warnin system

CORPORAL (*to* SOLDIER 2). I warned you
(*To* SOLDIER 4.) Listen corpse-crap any more shit out of
you an you'll look like a skeleton with no bones
(*To the* SON.) Pick that packet up
Oi cloth ears, my officer's comin round: pick it up
Wassa matter with 'im?

PEMBERTON. 'E wants t' get on with it

SOLDIER 1. 'E's corpse-'appy

CORPORAL. Wassa matter? (*To the* SON.) Wassa matter
wanna see the MO?

PEMBERTON *goes towards the cigarette packet.*

(*To* PEMBERTON.) What you doin?

PEMBERTON. Pick the packet up

CORPORAL. Leave it – I told 'im – that's 'is privilege
(*To the* SON.) You 'ear me?

SOLDIER 4. You threw it

CORPORAL. O–ho

I threw it an 'e can pick it up

(*To* SON.) Wanna psychiatrist report t' see if yer can bend yer back?

SOLDIER 2. If they cant organise ammo they wanna get someone 'oo can

CORPORAL. You tell 'em mate

Now pick that corpsin packet up like a good lad

SOLDIER 1. Cant they organise a refuse collector?

CORPORAL (*To* SON). Dont play the 'ard man with me

I watched bigger soldiers than you crawl out of empty bags

PEMBERTON. Lay off 'im corp

SOLDIER 1. If 'e ain droppin corpses 'e thinks the world's come to a stop

CORPORAL. My officer'll be round in a minute

That packet's army issue – you leave it there an 'e'll know we dropped it

You read company orders: sanitary discipline – no litter – spreads infection

SOLDIER 2. Get anthrax off your packet

CORPORAL. Conduct yer get off apes – they drop litter

I only dropped it cause 'e was rabbitin on about rockets

SOLDIER 4. Dont bring me into it

CORPORAL. You'll all be in it

(*To the* SON.) Now you pick it up or I'll get serious

SOLDIER 2. Corpse-in arse'oles its a fag packet

CORPORAL. No it aint –

PEMBERTON. If yer was that fond of it why did yer drop it?

CORPORAL. – its an order soldier

Im orderin you t' pick that packet up

Ain far – you've only got a walk the length of your own corpse

SOLDIER 2. 'E'd make a skeleton's flesh creep

CORPORAL. Right you soldiers witness this: I give 'im an order an 'e wouldnt take it

PEMBERTON. For corpse-sake pick it up

You'll drop us all in the corpse-shit

If they dumped you in a mass grave the others'd leave

Yer know that lot're screwed up as tight as a miser's coffin

We're the ones 'oo'll get it in the corpsin neck

Pick it up an let's 'ave a bit of sense

CORPORAL. I'll give yer arf a minute

Then you're in vintage shit

If I order yer t' fart in time with the national anthem yer fart – it dont 'ave t' be musical

SOLDIER 2. For corpse-sake you're goin looney

CORPORAL. 'Arf a minute

PEMBERTON. Shittin-corpses we get enough corpse-crap droppin bodies all day without this

(*To the* CORPORAL.) 'E dont wanna pick it up, 'e's entitled t' a bit of freedom

(*To the* SON.) Yer mad bugger pick it up: yer know 'e'd order a skeleton t' scratch its bollocks

(*To the* CORPORAL.) I 'ope that fag rots your lungs

CORPORAL. Fifteen seconds

As a matter of fact its very agreeable . . .

'E aint goin t' pick it up – 'e aint goin t' do it

I'll squeeze yer so corpsin 'ard yer bones'll try t' get out

Pause.

Right I dont know what your trouble is lad but they'll find out at the inquest

(*To* SOLDIER 2.) Ask captain 'Arris t' step this way – you'll find 'im at the rendezvous waggon

SOLDIER 2. For corpsin-shit-sake I aint –

CORPORAL. That's an order

SOLDIER 2 *goes out.*

PEMBERTON. Bin shootin corpses for lootin tellies – kids up there, dead for lootin gear – didnt live long enough t' see if it fits!

Its an empty packet – ain even full!

If 'e asked yer for a full one yer'd give it to 'im!

SON. Why dont 'e live on a rubbish tip?

CORPORAL. Captain 'Arris'll sort 'im out

PEMBERTON. Bugger's mad

CORPORAL. Too 'ard t' pick up a packet?

Dont stare at me corpse! – I'll 'ave you starin up from the bottom end of a pit!

SOLDIER 4 (*looks off and rubs his hands with glee*). This 'd make a skeleton swallow its false teeth

CAPTAIN HARRIS *and* SOLDIER 2 *come on.*

CORPORAL. Squad shun!

SOLDIERS *stand to attention.*

CAPTAIN HARRIS *and the* CORPORAL *salute.*

CAPTAIN. Thank you corporal

At ease men

The SOLDIERS *at ease.*

Spot of trouble . . .

CORPORAL. Soldier refused order sir

CAPTAIN. Dear me why's that?

CORPORAL (*points to the packet*). Declined t' pick up an article of refuse when so ordered sir

CAPTAIN. Well it looks easy enough

(*Inspects the packet.*) Can you see the packet soldier? – of course you can

Pick it up

Pause.

What seems to be the matter?

When your NCO called you to attention you were kind
enough to oblige

Is it an ordinary packet corporal?

No special history attached, not a booby trap?

CORPORAL. No sir

It's a packet which was thrown away on bein found t' be
empty

CAPTAIN (*picks up the packet and examines it*). He'd pick it
up if it was full

Drops the packet where it was.

Well it seems a feasible order

You've refused your NCO

Now Im ordering you

SOLDIER 1. Corpsin arse-oles

CAPTAIN (*to* SOLDIER 1). Have you an opinion you wish to
share with us soldier?

Silence.

(*To the* SON.) Did you hear the order?

SON. Yessir

CAPTAIN. Has this man refused orders before corporal?

CORPORAL. No sir

CAPTAIN. Not the job at the quarry?

CORPORAL. No sir

CAPTAIN. Well we cant leave the packet there

Its a small thing – but its an army-issue packet and those
civilians who can read would know it'd been dropped
by a soldier and that would encourage further acts of
obstruction

There's enough lawlessness and general mayhem without
that

You realise that anyone who infringes military discipline
puts their comrades at risk?

I cant overlook it

PEMBERTON. Permission t'speak sir

CAPTAIN. No

PEMBERTON. With all this rubble sir – the 'ole city's a shit'eap – no one'll notice one packet

CAPTAIN. Thank you for that observation

(*To the* SON.) You see how one act of disobedience incites others?

For all I know this is a stratagem to distract my attention from some terrorist manoeuvre

I have a quarry full of prisoners waiting to be shot

We cant do what we have to do – and come through it decent – without the utmost discipline

D'you want to change ends in the quarry?

We're all under strain

As an officer Im privileged – honoured – to share the comradeship of arms with men I admire

I depend on their courage and loyalty to perform their duties even when they go against our first inclinations

After what our people've suffered at the hands of the enemy any demand they make on us is too little

I'd like you to consider my own feelings soldier

Dont make me go any further down this road

Is there some reason for this insubordination I dont understand?

Has the corporal mistreated you? Have you a complaint against me?

CORPORAL. Per'aps I've bin over-'asty – Im sorry I dragged yer down sir – the lad's 'ad 'is lesson an I'd be 'appy t' –

CAPTAIN. Please dont apologise for your exemplary military conduct corporal – it isnt the moment

Soldier Im ordering you to march to that packet

Not to pick it up

Soldier by the right quick march!

After a lightning pause the SON *marches to the packet.*

Soldier mark time!

The SON *marks time by the packet.*

You see how easy I can make it for you
The packet's by your feet
What? – an arm's length away
Soldier halt!

The SON *halts.*

Now kneel
That's very little to ask
I havent asked you to pick it up
If you cant do that for me I take it amiss

The SON *kneels by the cigarette packet.*

Now its almost yours
If I could ask it to jump into your hand I would
I cant help you anymore
We're living in the aftermath of a nuclear bombardment
I dont know what will happen next or what we'll be
      ordered to do
War makes that little packet very big
All you have to do is reach out and pick it up
CORPORAL. Squad shun!

The SOLDIERS *have already stiffened to attention:*
now they become rigid.

Get those backs straight!

CAPTAIN. Corporal shoot that soldier
PEMBERTON. I dont believe –
CAPTAIN. Silence!

The CORPORAL *shoots the* SON. *The* SOLDIERS *waver.*

Still!
Who told you to move?
He's the only one to move!
CORPORAL. Squad shun!

The SQUAD *stiffens.*

CAPTAIN. We cannot carry liabilities
    I could've sent him back to the quarry and your corporal
        would've arranged an accident
    Security would've been restored and any rumours
        could've been dismissed as tittle-tattle
    My military honour forbids me to deceive men when I
        may have to ask anyone of them for his life
    We're in a war to defend the standards of our society and
        I refuse to betray them to the very men who're waging
        that war
CORPORAL. Sir permission t' leave 'im in the quarry sir?
CAPTAIN. Take him back to the bunker
    He was a soldier and he did good work
    The ammunition will be here shortly
    You'd better get your men back in the quarry
CORPORAL. Yessir
    (*To* SOLDIER 2 *and* 4.) You an you – get 'is legs – you 'is
        arms

SOLDIERS 2 *and* 4 *pick up the* SON.

CAPTAIN. Corporal put the packet in his pocket before it
    becomes a tourist attraction

The CORPORAL *puts the packet in the* SON's *pocket.*

SOLDIER 2. Best thing too sir – bloody nutter
SOLDIER 4. Corpse-'appy –
CAPTAIN. Quiet!
    Anyone who abuses a soldier from my company will go
    on orders!

CORPORAL. Squad back to the quarry at the double-march!
  Hup

  The SOLDIERS *trot out with the body.*

CAPTAIN. That should've been foreseen corporal
  Its up to you to know the state of your men
CORPORAL. Sir I –
CAPTAIN. Well it was a useful demonstration for the others
  And it got rid of a weak element
  God knows he gave us warning – shot – his brother or
    sister was it?
  I was on the qui vive for the next stage
  No place for mavericks in the army
  We mustnt lose the benefit of this: every chance to
    exercise command helps to fit us for leadership

NINE

Wilderness

Seventeen years later.
The WOMAN *comes on. She carries a bundle and has a satchel
slung on her back from a rope.*

WOMAN. What about this?
  (*She looks round.*) Watch out when it looks empty
  This'll do
  (*She drops the satchel on the ground.*)
  Legs say no

  *She takes a plastic food container and a spoon from the
  satchel.*

  Dont bother t' 'eat it up
  Taste just as good cold

She nurses the bundle and spoon feeds it.

There: that's what we wanted
Mmmmm
Taste good
Dont 'og it give mummy some

She feeds the bundle and eats some herself.

Mmmm
Mummy race darlin'

WOMAN 1 *comes on. She is pregnant and has a bundle on
her back.*

WOMAN 1. Help me
WOMAN. Woman – uh – woman!
WOMAN 1. Help me please!
WOMAN. Spoke – uh – s'woman – uh – stick –
WOMAN 1. No no I wont hurt you
WOMAN. Uh – friends – uh – friends – with sticks – all
    sticks!
WOMAN 1. No you're on your own – I followed you!
WOMAN. Uh – follow –
WOMAN 1. For days!
WOMAN. Days? – uh – s'woman –
    Off – off!
WOMAN 1. Im going to have a child!
WOMAN. Uh – child? – off – off
    'S'woman – child – uh!
WOMAN 1. I followed you along the river bed – I hid in the rocks
WOMAN (*dazed*) Uh child – follow – child – uh – no no no
    – go!
    Where am I?
WOMAN 1. Help me have the child – I cant manage it alone!
WOMAN. 'S' woman – out the ground – uh
WOMAN 1. Please help me

WOMAN. No – no place – my food – no – go!

WOMAN 1. Im on my own!

WOMAN. Uh – child – child – child – 'ow can – uh –

WOMAN 1. I dont now how to have it!

WOMAN. Uh uh uh uh uh uh!

WOMAN 1. Please help me

WOMAN. Uh – 's'woman – says she's got a –

WOMAN 1. I think my time will be soon!

WOMAN. No no no place – go – no food!

WOMAN 1. Help me – Im sorry I –

WOMAN. She says she's got a – uh –

WOMAN 1. I cant hurt you! Please!

WOMAN. A child –

WOMAN 1. I felt it move –

WOMAN. Is she dead?

WOMAN 1. No – I followed you till I was sure I –

WOMAN. No 'elp 'ere! – a child – so close – 'er eyes – movin

WOMAN 1 (*sits*). I cant go any further

Let me rest

I watched you washing and cooking and talking to
yourself – you were always so busy – I thought my
baby'd have a chance –

WOMAN. No one for years – your eyes –

A child? Can that still – ?

WOMAN 1. Yes

WOMAN. I thought all that was dead – all that was passed
on –

WOMAN 1. Im sorry I upset you – I should've shouted from
up there

I didnt want you to run away

WOMAN. Uh run

Yer cant stay 'ere – no food – I search all day for scraps

WOMAN 1. Help me to have the child – then I'll manage on
my own

Or you might think – ?

Let me have the child – I've brought it so far

WOMAN. The child

When I saw your eye – remember a stone movin – beetle
    rockin it – underneath – years ago

'Ave you 'ad a child before?

WOMAN 1. No

I've never seen a baby

I was too little to remember before the bombs

WOMAN. Never seen a baby

(*She points at herself.*) Mother

WOMAN 1. You've given birth? (*The* WOMAN *nods.*) You
    know what to do?

WOMAN (*points at herself*). Twice

(*She points to the bundle.*) There's one

WOMAN 1. I thought you were feeding it . . . !

. . . It looks like a bundle

WOMAN. Wrapped up t' keep the cold out

WOMAN 1. Its like . . . a piece of cloth

WOMAN. That's what they look like wrapped up

WOMAN 1. That came out of you . . . ?

WOMAN. O yes

Its a good child – not always cryin

Tries t' comfort me

Its older than its years

Uh – if yours is as good you'll be lucky

Some children cry

Mine knows I've 'ad a lot t' bear – it doesnt burden me

WOMAN 1 (*stares at the bundle*). Is that inside me?

WOMAN. Of course

You're scared of it! – uh! – yer mustnt let 'em scare yer!

Mothers must love their babies

(*To the bundle.*) Did the lady stare at my precious?

(*To* WOMAN 1.) Stare at yours like that an it'll be a
    grizzler

WOMAN 1 (*to herself in dismay*). Nothing works – they

    pulled it all to pieces – how can I have a child
here . . .?

WOMAN. D'you find them ugly?

  Not all women are meant t' be mothers

  Per'aps they think we're ugly

  Stare at the strangers 'oo've brought them into the world

  I stared at you

WOMAN 1. Its a nice child

  How old is it?

WOMAN. I've 'ad it a long time – out the war

  The 'ouses shook as if they was cryin for the people
    inside

WOMAN 1. You've been on your own all this time?

WOMAN. If I saw people I ran off – for the kid's sake

  There's no one outside these arms I'd trust it to

  Then the others died as if they 'ad t' be dead by the end
    of the year

  The sky was red for a long time – then fluffy white clouds
    floated over – it was a wound makin its own dressins

  Then they got as mucky as old bandages

  And then it was winter: it lasted for years

  I lived in a cave over a lake – sat in the mouth an watched
    the water

  My 'air was long an as grey as the sky

  No birds – the wind 'issed, didnt rise or fall

  Then I began t' walk

  That was before the rubble was buried

  Gardens were like ruined factories

  Green wires an fruit an veg like bits of plastic machinery

  Yer 'ad t' chew it

  I found a greengrocer's stall that'd run wild – some of
    the seeds'd took

  Marrows – not big but they cooked up – wizened spuds
    – there was even an apple tree

Next year I went back an it was all rotted: tree covered
    in mildew

Then I walked in a mist so long I didnt know if my eyes
    worked

When it settled it covered everythin in a white scum:
    that's the origin of the dust

When it was new yer sank in up t' your knees

The top of trees came through like roots

There are 'ouses under our feet – people sittin in cars –
    in lifts

Yer could look at the sun: like an empty plate on the
    table

Later the green seaweed came out the dust – grew
    everywhere

Scoop it up an ate it or made stew

Then it died out: now yer 'ave t' scrounge crumbs out
    the rocks

When its cold or the kid's poorly I might live in a ruin

Even 'ang up a picture

In winter I boil the stones for salt

That's 'ow we live: this dust is barren

Never seen a child before . . .

WOMAN 1. I couldnt even find a photo of one in the houses

WOMAN. The mothers took 'em down in the shelters

    Dont let your kid rule you: they've got fists like
    bulldozers

WOMAN 1. We had warehouses full of tins but we burned
    them

WOMAN. Uh? – people do

WOMAN 1. There were fifteen of us but no children – the
    men were sterile

    Then a stranger turned up

    Its his child

    We suddenly started to die

    It was terrifying – there were so few of us

We panicked and burned the stores

There were no tins left but the disease stopped

We started to work – built a factory

We were holding our breath

One morning one of us was dead – and two more died the same day

It killed so quickly!

We split up and lived apart

I stayed with the man: I had the child so we said its too late to split up – and we didnt want to

But one night I walked out with the child

I lived on a hill where I could see the houses

There was no smoke – they'd stopped cooking

Sometimes the sun shone on their windows as if they were giving parties

The machinery was lying on the slopes – we'd been dragging it to the factory

The field died – no one watered it

I went as close as I could risk an shouted

They were all dead – I hope the man died before he knew I'd left him

I thought: go as far as possible – there may be other people

I waited for days after I saw you: if I'd felt I couldnt trust you with my child I'd've gone off in the opposite direction

WOMAN. Per'aps it'd think it was best not t' be born?

We didnt ask that when I 'ad mine – but now its different

WOMAN 1. No – we were fools but we were learning how to live together and not kill each other

If my friends hadnt died we'd've built a good place for my child

I saw the beginning: now it'll have to build it for itself

If it can find other people they'll make a home out of this dust

WOMAN. If that's what they want
   Take my child
WOMAN 1. No
WOMAN. You – flinched! You're scared!
WOMAN 1. No
WOMAN. My poor girl you'll 'ave t' get used t' 'olding your
     baby!
   That's 'ow you show you love it!
WOMAN 1. I will when –
WOMAN. What nonsense!
   I shouldnt bother t' bring it into the world if that's the
     treatment it gets!
   Take my child

WOMAN 1 *takes the bundle from the* WOMAN.

   There – that's easy isnt it?
   Careful – mind you support the 'ead – that's right
WOMAN 1. Like this?
WOMAN. Yes – you make a good mother
   Rock it a little – mmm-mm – that's what they like
   Look it feels safe in your arms – its goin' t' sleep
WOMAN 1. How d'you know?
WOMAN. They shut their eyes like us of course!
   An a look of peace comes in their face
   I'll take it back
   If it suddenly woke up it might 'ave a shock – its not
     used t' you yet

WOMAN *takes the bundle from* WOMAN 1.

   Did you enjoy it?
WOMAN 1. Yes – thank you
WOMAN. Give me your pack
WOMAN 1. Its all right
WOMAN. No you dont in your condition!
   You must think of the young one!

Give it t' me (*She takes* WOMAN 1's *pack*.)
We'll find somewhere good for the lyin in

She picks up her satchel.

We need water an wood for a fire
They make a mess the mucky things
If you was my daughter you'd be makin me a
    grandmother
(*Bundle*.) What's in this?
WOMAN 1. A shawl and a hat – and other bits
WOMAN. You 'ave bin thoughtful
When there's two kids we'll share the nursin

WOMAN *and* WOMAN 1 *go out.*

TEN

Wilderness

A week later.
The WOMAN *holds her bundle. On the ground are her satchel
and a baby. She looks down at the baby. It is wrapped in a
sheet and shawl and wears a hat.*

WOMAN. Fine baby
    Surprised me – full of life – real fizzer
    My baby's got some catchin up t' do
    You're still livin off your mother's fat
    Now you 'ave t' do your own growin you'll feel the
        difference!
    Take you back a bit till you toughen up

*She talks to the baby and herself and walks up and down.
The bundle accidentally unfastens and slowly unwinds –*

unconsciously she gathers it and drapes it on her arms and shoulders in simple shapes.

When a kid's in you yer dont know what you're carryin
Could be a monster or so strange it'll never know yer
The pains of 'avin it might be the easiest pains it gives yer
One day it might 'ate yer
Yer could be carrying the knife that kills yer: or generations that'll never know your name
Yer cant tell
When you were born you 'eard 'er yell an she 'eard you 'oller
You were arrivin but yer seemed t' be sufferin all the pains of partin

I forgot 'ow mothers shout
So used t' the shouts of the wounded – they die like babies crying for their mothers
Your mother gave a good shout: like the whack of fish on the water or the thump of wet concrete on stones
Mine slept through it all
Its a bit jealous: it screws up its face when it sees yer

What are kids for?
T' comfort the smart they give yer?
Mine feels my face with its 'ands an I see the world through its fingers
Too many 'ands wear your face out – feet wear out stone steps an yer see the rain in the 'ollows
I'll tell you the oldest story: the mother goes into a burnin 'ouse t' bring out 'er child
I lived in the burnin 'ouse: the street outside was 'otter
With one 'and I beat out the flames on my dress an nursed me kid with the other

It got used t' the stink of scorchin and charrin: it
developed a little cough from the smoke
That's 'ow we nurse kids now

All the time your mother followed me not one pebble
rolled down the 'ill
She didnt step on one twig t' give me a warnin
When she looked over the rocks she covered 'er 'air so
the wind wouldnt shake it an tell me
Respect your mother
Im sorry she's dead
I laid 'er out with 'er face t' the sky an covered 'er with
old doors – I weighed 'em down with stone —
She saw you – stared as if she'd bin woken up – she was
too tired t' smile – or too busy lookin
Well a starvin man doesnt smile at food
You 'ad a taste of 'er milk – didnt you guzzle! – I bet it
was good

She never gave me your name
Per'aps you'd be better off as an animal?
A rabbit 'as fur – that's more use than a name
Birds fly out of danger
A fox 'as four legs an a mouth that's as good as an 'and
There used t' be foxes t' eat birds an birds t' fly out of
foxes' mouths
The wind still sometimes uncovers trash a fox could live
on

I cant take yer with me
I 'ave t' feed my kid an provide meself with enough t'
keep goin
The world cant cope with another mouth
There are 'ole cities with one blade of grass
My kid needs more than one blade of grass

Once kids 'ad as much grass as they wanted even when
 they was dead

The WOMAN *has gathered up the sheet and made it into a*
bundle again.

I dont 'elp none of us 'angin on 'ere – you're tough – got
 yourself born an chucked your mother away like an
 empty sack – look at yer smothered in gear – my baby
 'asnt got an 'at – that grime on its face comes from the
 cold – that's permanent, it wont grow out – yer could
 spare it that 'at – it didnt ask – I asked for it – its good
 t' give – start as yer mean t' go on – there's a good kid
 (*She takes the hat from the baby.*) – thank you – no keep
 the shawl – that's a souvenir of your mother, she was
 fond of that pattern – O look what its give us! (*She*
 takes the shawl.) – say thanks t' your friend – my baby
 says there wont ever be one mark on this shawl!

The WOMAN *picks up her satchel and hides the hat and*
shawl in it.

We'll take good care of our presents

The WOMAN *picks up her bundle and goes out. After a*
moment she returns.

'Alf a blade of grass – my kid cant live on that
It'd be best if you was an animal in all this space
I didnt take all the clothes – I'll pay for what I took

She draws with her stick on the ground.

There's a 'ouse – with two doors – an' a pond – a tree –
 these dots are the apples – a sun with a cloud – a car –
 an a boat on the lake – all ready for when you're big –
 an a matchstick lady in an apron t' feed you an teach
 yer lessons

The WOMAN *goes out. A moment later the baby raises a
hand and gives one short cry that is lower than would be
expected.*

ELEVEN

Wilderness

Two months later.
The WOMAN *pushes on a little handcart. It is made of a
wooden box on an axle with two pram wheels and there is a
long wooden handle. The bundle is propped up in the handcart.
It is wrapped in the shawl and wears the hat.*
The WOMAN *stops.*

WOMAN. Far enough t'day
  (*She looks round.*) Might as well do
  Was it a nice ride?

  She takes a water bottle from the cart and drinks.

  Would you like some of this water?
  'S better than bein squashed against me – see a lot more
    from there
  Mum cant carry yer all the time
  In a sulk are we?
  (*She takes the bundle from the cart.*) Give you a cuddle
    t'night

  Shouldnt tell yer but we 'ave t' be a bit naughty to stay
    sane
  What day's t'morrow?
  Your birthday!
  There! – yer cant sulk on the day before your birthday
  Got you a present – crep off when you was asleep
  Look: wrapped up like all the kids 'ave

Shall we be really naughty an open it?
Lets!
(*Unwrapping.*) Look at its greedy little eyes
What can it be?
A book! With letters an pictures!
Didnt mummy give us a surprise?
Now we'll learn our alphabet
Children used t' learn their books in school
A is for apple – that's an apple
B is for bat – that's a thing yer play with
A picture book of the world
You thought I was lyin when I told you all the things
    there used t' be
This book proves Im not a liar
We'll put it away till your birthday

She gives the bundle her breast.

Never too sulky for the milk
You grow up an be big an strong an 'elp mummy
She gets tired pushing
One day it'll be your turn t' push me
That's 'ow it goes – you'll read that in the book
We'll 'ave some fun t' look back on
When the world changed I was too old t' understand
Need to grow up with that t' see it properly
When you're older you'll tell me what it was all for
Then I shant worry – I'll know yer can take care of
    yourself
I dont want t' die while you're a child
Watch you lyin on the ground wonderin why I cant get up
You grow quick – an be smart

There its gettin sleepy
In the night you burrow into me an breathe on my face
    an press my cheeks with your rough little 'ands

If you touched a wall with those 'ands it'd bend down an
 pick you up
I wish I could 'ear your voice
Im a good mother, I know your moods
I've learned t' understand the sounds yer make with your
 clothes
But one day I'll 'ear your voice in all this silence
That'll be my reward for all these years
Will yer sound like me?
I'll teach yer t' use good words that make sense: then yer
 can think
We'll 'ave such talks
That's enough
Sleep
Mummy's too tired t' sing

The WOMAN *holds the bundle and sleeps.*

TWELVE

Wilderness

Two years later.
PEMBERTON *and* SOLDIERS 1 *and* 3.
*They wear a mixture of filthy uniform and civvie rags. The
ammo box, rifles and other gear are stacked on a ground sheet.*
SOLDIER 3 *stirs food in a bucket over a fire.*

SOLDIER 1. Shouldnt send them two t'gether
 Always come back late with rubbish
 Spend the time kippin

 SOLDIER 3 *picks up a water bottle.*

 That dont need more liquid

SOLDIER 3 *puts down the water bottle.*
The WOMAN *charges in with her bundle. She is dirtier and very weak. She goes straight to the bucket, scoops out food with her hand and eats with desperation but efficiency.*

WOMAN. No food since days
  (*Gestures round.*) 'S dead – no rain

The SOLDIERS *stare at her.*

PEMBERTON. Where did you come from?

WOMAN *gestures vaguely.*

WOMAN. There – 's'dead
SOLDIER 1. You on your own? 'S there anymore?
WOMAN (*shakes her head and eats*). No – terrible – nothin
SOLDIER 3. She'll scald 'er 'and
PEMBERTON. Put some in a mug

  SOLDIER 3 *puts food in a mug.*
  SOLDIER 1 *takes the mug, then he takes the* WOMAN's *hand and empties it over the bucket. He gives her the mug.*

WOMAN. Thank you thank you – my baby – share it
PEMBERTON. D'yer stay 'ere?
WOMAN (*eats and shakes her head*). Walk – keep on the
    move
  Sorry I came an – kid's 'ungry

She dips her finger in the mug and offers it to the bundle.

  There – eat
  So 'ungry – thought this time gone too far – never get
    out – this'll be the end
PEMBERTON. You're welcome t' the grub – there's not
    much but we survive
WOMAN. Soldiers?
PEMBERTON. We dont fight – you're all right

WOMAN. Sky grey – no rain – months

PEMBERTON. Poor woman

WOMAN. Didnt feel 'ungry but knew I 'ad t' eat for the kid

SOLDIER 1. Give 'er some more

WOMAN. No – stomach's shrunk
  (*To the bundle.*) Lick the finger

SOLDIER 1. That a baby?

WOMAN. Barged in – stupid – take more care – not let meself get desperate – soldiers (*Vague gesture.*) – you might've – shot us

PEMBERTON. Its all right we dont kill anymore or break things
  We're dead
  You're safe with us

WOMAN. Dead? 'E thinks 'e's dead – uh!

SOLDIER 3. She dont understand

PEMBERTON. Poor woman thinks she's alive
  (*To* WOMAN.) You're dead

WOMAN. Dead?

SOLDIER 1. That's why yer dont feel 'ungry

WOMAN. When did I die?

PEMBERTON. I dont know

WOMAN. Im not dead . . . When? . . . I dont remember dyin

PEMBERTON. Yer dont remember bein born

WOMAN. Am I with the dead?

PEMBERTON. Yes

WOMAN. No – there ain enough of yer – too few, too few –
  I saw the people dyin, all of 'em
  We're not the dead we're the ones 'oo didn't die
  I felt the warm inside me when I ate

PEMBERTON. Let 'er be – she'll sort it out

WOMAN. Dont you say you're dead
  Poor things, look at your poor bodies – you've suffered but you're not dead

PEMBERTON. We've been dead a long time

WOMAN (*to herself*). Per'aps the 'unger did this

  I met these people 'oo were kind t' me but its upset me
    'ead because I was weak

  They say one thing but I 'ear 'em say somethin else

*SOLDIERS 2 and 4 come in. They are dressed like the other
SOLDIERS. SOLDIER 4 carries a large, full sack on his
back. They have already seen the WOMAN and are staring at
her as they come on.*

SOLDIER 1 (*to* SOLDIERS 2 *and* 4). Come out of nowhere –
    thinks she's alive

As SOLDIER 4 *stares at the* WOMAN, *the sack on his back
opens at the neck and bones fall out. They make a heap at
his feet.*

WOMAN (*points to* SOLDIERS 2 *and* 4). Are they more dead?

PEMBERTON. Everyone's dead

WOMAN. God knows there ain much difference – that went
    long ago

  But I 'ave t' live for the kid's sake

  It cant fend for itself

PEMBERTON. That's dead too – you must've died t'gether

WOMAN. Thanks for the food

  If I cant – its for the kid: if I cant feed it – can we come
    an eat again?

PEMBERTON. Dont be scared of us

WOMAN. Im not – you were very kind

PEMBERTON. We dont like t' see you in that state

  Surely the dead can 'elp each other?

  Stay an rest while we eat

WOMAN. The dead dont eat

PEMBERTON. Its odd: a lot of the time we still do what we
    used t' do

  That's why it ain easy t' know when you're dead

(*To* SOLDIER 4.) This place is like a sty – you ain eatin till yer cleaned that up

SOLDIER 4 *collects the spilt bones.*
SOLDIER 3 *fills the other* SOLDIERS' *mess tins with food.*

SOLDIER 2. Did 'e put in too much liquid?
SOLDIER 1. Just caught 'im
SOLDIER 3. Give us 'is tin

SOLDIER 2 *gives* SOLDIER 4's *mess tin to* SOLDIER 3. *He fills it with food. The* SOLDIERS *eat.*

PEMBERTON. If you'd saw what we saw you'd 'ave an excuse for not noticin you're dead
We was corpsin civvies in a quarry – ran out of ammo – (*Points.*) just that one box left
We was going back t' the quarry: then it 'appened: the end of the world they talked about
No explosion, just the wind
We was down in a gully, a sort of defile
All the bodies – livin an dead, army an civvie – shot up in the sky
It was full of bodies whirlin round in circles like a painted ceilin
The wind blew em up there
Whirlin round over our 'eads – looked like a dance
SOLDIER 3. Some of em was still alive
PEMBERTON. An chairs an tables – they went up with 'em
SOLDIER 2. One woman tried t' steady 'erself on a table up in the air
SOLDIER 3. We could see more of the circles whirrin in the sky – dotted all over
PEMBERTON. Some of the people were on fire – whirrin round like torches
The woman with the table ended up goin round an round in a burnin chair

Some of the other groups burned out

SOLDIER 1. Just puffs of ashes an smoke driftin where
they'd bin

SOLDIER 3. Like thumb prints on the sky

PEMBERTON. Some of the people fell down on fire
The wind was all over the place
There was one line of people goin round one way an
other lines goin round outside em other ways – like a
barn dance
An lines goin over the top

SOLDIER 2. They 'ad their arms out as if they was tryin t'
'old each other's hands

PEMBERTON. That was the wind – they was all dead by
then

SOLDIER 2. The people we shot were dancin up in the air

SOLDIER 3 takes the food bucket to the WOMAN *and pours
the dregs into her mug.*

SOLDIER 3. Last drop – you 'ave it

PEMBERTON. No ammo no bodies – they was up there
(*Shrugs.*) So we deserted
'Id in a cave

SOLDIER 4. Should've gone back t' the bunker

SOLDIER 3. Standin orders: loss of physical contact –
communications blackout – make your own way back
t' the bunker

PEMBERTON. I was the senior soldier so I took charge

SOLDIER 4. Standin orders
If we was deserters we'd need the discipline or we'd get
in a state
So we stuck t' orders

The SOLDIERS *finish eating.* SOLDIER 3 *collects the mess
tins.*

PEMBERTON. Stayed in the cave two days

If there was any army left they'd've come searchin: chop!

SOLDIER 3 (*to* SOLDIER 2 – *mess tin*). Pass us that

PEMBERTON. Last night we was in the cave we 'eard this rushin an thumpin

Didnt get light in the mornin so I switched on the torch

SOLDIER 1. 'Ad t' go careful with the battery

PEMBERTON. The mouth of the cave was full of bodies

The wind'd been chuckin em at us all night

We dug our way up till we come t' the open

Not one breath of wind: dead still

Grey sky with black chips an black lines in it – dead straight – like cracked enamel

Didnt move – a lid

(*Bones.*) Get that lot sorted

The SOLDIERS *sort through the bones.*
They methodically put the smaller bones in one heap and break the larger bones into smaller pieces.

PEMBERTON. There was solid waves of rubble a 'undred feet 'igh – like gums with big red 'oles gouged out where the teeth'd bin

People strung up with placards round their necks – said they was prime minister

SOLDIER 2. Lots a' them

SOLDIER 4. An army chiefs

SOLDIER 1. They lynched the postmen for carryin government mail

PEMBERTON. After a few months there were no more survivors

Their bombs blew up our stores of chemical weapons

SOLDIER 2. There was the tower block

PEMBERTON. One of them glass jobs

SOLDIER 2. One wall left

PEMBERTON. All the rest – walls an floors – ripped away

SOLDIER 2. One sheet of glass twenty stories 'igh

SOLDIER 3. Straight up in the air
SOLDIER 2. An all the people 'oo was in the offices squashed
    flat on the glass
SOLDIER 4. 'Uman blobs
SOLDIER 2. Squashed flat
SOLDIER 1. Like specimens
SOLDIER 4. Flat blobs
SOLDIER 1. On the glass
SOLDIER 2. Like specimens on a microscope slide

The SOLDIERS *go into a dry hard hysteria. Each stays shut
in himself. They rock their bodies and cry into the ground –
they glance at each other only once or twice.* SOLDIER 4 *taps
with a bone. The hysteria rises and fades away quickly.*

Seein 'er 'old the kid reminds me of the woman
SOLDIER 4. Woman with a dead nipper
SOLDIER 2. Patted its 'ead
SOLDIER 1. I saw that
SOLDIER 3. The nipper was fallin t' pieces
SOLDIER 2. Arms twisted the wrong way round
SOLDIER 3. She kep tryin t' twist 'em back
SOLDIER 2. But they wouldnt stay
SOLDIER 1. Too loose
PEMBERTON. I saw it
SOLDIER 3. Kep twistin back
SOLDIER 1. Danglin an 'angin
SOLDIER 2. Like the 'ands on a broken watch
SOLDIER 1. The 'ole kid was fallin t' pieces
SOLDIER 4. An the old man
SOLDIERS 1, 2, 3. The old man
SOLDIER 3. Tryin t' kill 'is son
SOLDIER 2. The son was in pain
SOLDIER 3. The old man
SOLDIERS 1, 2, 4. The old man
SOLDIER 2. Tryin t' kill 'im with 'is crutch

SOLDIERS 2, 4. T' 'elp 'im
SOLDIER 1. Jabbed the end of 'is crutch in 'is mouth
SOLDIER 4. Only the mouth was left
SOLDIER 1. That's all yer could see
SOLDIER 3. It was floatin in a puddle of blood
SOLDIER 4. A mouth in a puddle of blood
SOLDIER 3. The mouth was sayin – not shoutin –
SOLDIER 1. It was in pain
SOLDIER 3. Sayin
SOLDIER 4. I thought the mouth came out of the ground
PEMBERTON. No
SOLDIER 4. It belonged t' the ground
SOLDIER 2. The mouth was in a puddle of blood
PEMBERTON. There was an 'ead under the mouth
SOLDIER 1. A 'ead in the puddle
SOLDIER 3. The old man was jabbin
SOLDIER 2. The end of the crutch kep slippin
PEMBERTON. It slipped off 'is mouth
SOLDIER 3. The old man was jabbin
PEMBERTON. Off the side of 'is 'ead
SOLDIER 2. The mouth wasnt screamin
SOLDIERS 3, 4. Just sayin
SOLDIER 1. That it was in pain
SOLDIER 2. The old man 'it –
SOLDIER 4. Jabbed
SOLDIER 2. – it while it spoke
SOLDIER 1. Jabbed
PEMBERTON. The 'ead was bobbin about under the puddle
SOLDIER 2. The blood was bubblin out of its mouth
SOLDIERS 3, 4. The old man jabbed at it with 'is crutch
PEMBERTON. 'Is son's 'ead
SOLDIERS 1, 2. 'E wanted t' kill it
SOLDIER 4. A mouth in the ground
SOLDIERS 1, 3, 4. I saw it
SOLDIER 2. I saw it

SOLDIER 1. The woman who tried t' crawl in the crack
SOLDIER 2. A flat bit of rock with a crack
SOLDIER 4. A flat bit of rock on a curve with a crack
SOLDIER 3. She was black with soot
SOLDIER 2. Oil burn-out
SOLDIER 1. Crawled along the crack
SOLDIERS 2, 3, 4. Crawled crawled crawled
PEMBERTON. Like a spider
SOLDIERS 3, 4. With one leg
SOLDIER 4. Like a spider with one leg
SOLDIERS 2, 3. Crawled crawled
SOLDIER 1. She tried t' get into the crack
SOLDIERS 2, 3. In the crack
SOLDIER 4. 'Er dress caught under 'er knee

Silence

PEMBERTON. When yer realise you're dead its like droppin
    a 'od-load of bricks off yer back
  Or losin a sack of clay
  Yer grow tall with relief
WOMAN. When did you die?
PEMBERTON. One afternoon we come down a slope –
    covered with grey rubble
  It was either part of an old mountain or debris thrown up
    by a bomb
  I thought there was a river at the bottom but it was a
    shadow
  We think it was on that slope
SOLDIER 1. Our bodies must still be there
WOMAN. Per'aps I am dead – it'd be nice – god knows
  I've 'ad worse times when I was alive
  Let me stay with you
  I'll work for what I eat
  I dont mind bein dead as long as the child's alive
PEMBERTON. We're all dead

WOMAN. Yes but not the child
  It nearly died more than once but I saved it
  It'd take a lot t' kill it now
SOLDIER 4. Chuck 'er out – we're dead – we 'ad enough
    rows before we settled that
  We dont wanna go through that again
WOMAN. Keep your 'air on
  Its only a kid – what's it matter t' you if its alive?
  Yer wont even notice it
PEMBERTON. Let's 'ave a look
WOMAN. No
PEMBERTON. Well you look at it
WOMAN. What?
PEMBERTON. Look at it
WOMAN. I am
PEMBERTON. No you ain – 'ave a good look
  . . . You cryin?
WOMAN. No
PEMBERTON. Then yer can see straight
WOMAN. Its asleep
PEMBERTON. Wake it
WOMAN. Yeh wake it!
  A typical soldier!
  It 'as enough t' put up with bein dragged round this 'ole
    – let it sleep while it can!
PEMBERTON. It dont talk
WOMAN. No – that's my fault – go round broodin stead of
    teachin it – then *I* complain it dont talk!
  I dont need someone 'oo's dead t' tell me if my kid's alive
    or not!
  Dead – not born – never thought of – that'd be best!
  No kids to anyone!
  But it was born – !
  There now I've got angry an woke it up

(*She pinches the bundle*.) Is my precious wrinklin its little
    face an they say its not alive?
Look at it smile at its mother!
(*She laughs*.) You make the soldiers eat their words!
Fall over that age, crack their 'eads: jump up an crack
    em even 'arder!
Drop out a window an sleep through it!
No – I ain showin my kid a lot of dead people!
Might do 'im no end of 'arm
It'll 'ave t' get used to yer slowly
I've got its sleepin things in the cart

The WOMAN *goes out*.

PEMBERTON. Yer stupid corpses!
    That thing in 'er 'ands is a bunch of rags in a woolly 'at!
    Stinks more 'n you – an you've been dead longer than
        yer were alive
    Poor cow's mad
SOLDIER 1. Why's she say its a kid?
PEMBERTON. After our war yer can say what yer like
SOLDIER 4. She reckons it smiles
PEMBERTON. Sticks 'er finger in its gob an makes a dent –
    that's its smile
    Bet she can do what she likes with that rag: make it cry –
        wink – stick its tongue out
    She gets more pleasure out of the creases in that mucky
        scrap of rag than most mothers get out of their real
        kids
    If you tried t' take that off 'er she'd struggle so 'ard she'd
        bring 'erself back t' life
SOLDIER 1. What we goin t' do?
PEMBERTON. Cant chuck 'er out in 'er state
    Wait till she finds its dead – she'll 'oller then
    Let 'er stay
    Oo's on sentry?

SOLDIER 1. Me

PEMBERTON. Lucky its someone with a bit of nous

PEMBERTON *gives* SOLDIER 1 *a loaded magazine.*

Five rounds – check it

SOLDIER 1. Five rounds checked

The WOMAN *wheels on her handcart.*

WOMAN. Why d'yer go out findin bones?

SOLDIER 2. Put em in the soup

PEMBERTON. When its dry or winter – otherwise we
  manage
  Dead livin off the dead
  We sleep on the ground
  'E's the sentry: we keep up military discipline

They settle down for the night. Quiet.

WOMAN. . . . Did it 'ave an excitin day then? . . . Yes it
  did . . .
  All the brave soldiers t' keep us from 'arm . . .
  In the mornin when they go marchin out for their bones
  we'll go (*Drum.*) tum-ti-titty-tum-tum an wave our
  'ands
  She sings:
  The snow will melt in Iceland
  The grass will grow in China
  And you shall sail the sea

Night. SOLDIER 1 *stands sentry.*

SOLDIER 3 (*whisper*). Soldier

SOLDIER 1. Quiet!

SOLDIER 3. Where she put the kid?

SOLDIER 1. No talkin!

SOLDIER 3. She got it with 'er? See what it –

SOLDIER 1. I'll call the officer!

Silence.

SOLDIER 3. She wont let us look t'morrow
She'll scarper while we're out foragin

SOLDIER 1. Why?

SOLDIER 3. 'Er kid's alive. That's why it looks different
from us

SOLDIER 1. Yer'll land us all in the corpse-shit!

SOLDIER 3. If you're caught say yer was goin your rounds
Look at it!

SOLDIER 1 *hesitates and then starts to try to find the*
WOMAN. *He stops.*

SOLDIER 1. Im scared

SOLDIER 3 (*stands*). I'll come with yer

SOLDIER 1. Get down! – 'e'll 'ave us all on orders!

SOLDIER 3. We 'eard a noise an went t' look!

SOLDIER 1. Corpse-shit-'ouse

SOLDIER 3 (*searching*). Where . . . ? I cant . . . ?

SOLDIER 1. There!

SOLDIER 3. 'Ead – arm – clutchin it – uh!

SOLDIER 1. What?

SOLDIER 3. Moved

SOLDIER 1. 'Er – breathin – that moved it –
Footprint! – she's 'oldin a foot!

SOLDIER 3. That's the face!

SOLDIER 3 *goes to* SOLDIER 2.

SOLDIER 1. What – ?

SOLDIER 3. Quiet – (*To* SOLDIER 2.) she's got a kid –
alive –

SOLDIER 2. Alive?

SOLDIER 3. Look

SOLDIER 2 *stands and goes to* SOLDIER 1. SOLDIER 3
wakes SOLDIER 4.

SOLDIER 1. Its knee's movin
SOLDIER 2. Its the moonlight
SOLDIER 3 (*to* SOLDIER 4). Quiet – it ain a bundle its alive
    – we seen it
SOLDIER 1. What'll we do?
SOLDIER 4. I knew it was alive

The SOLDIERS *stand in a group.*

SOLDIER 3. She showed 'im the rag – the real kid was in
    the cart – took it out in the dark –
SOLDIER 4. Corpse-shit!
SOLDIER 1. Sh!

> SOLDIER 1 *gestures the other* SOLDIERS *to follow him. They
> go.*
> *Morning.*
> PEMBERTON *sits brooding on the ground. The* WOMAN
> *takes a wash bowl, flannel and water bottle from her
> handcart.*

WOMAN. 'Avent slept so well in a long time
    Most nights I sleep like a dog with one eye open
    'Ave a look round: they cant be far
    Gettin extra grub for me an the kid
    I'll be all right on me own

She goes to the bundle.

Shall we give the world a nice clean face?

She pours water into a bowl and washes the bundle.

Shut those eyes so we dont get the water in
This one slept too – knew I felt safe, kids can tell
Every mornin its grown a bit, even this whisp of nothin
Dont like 'avin its ears done
'Ave t' take care of my precious
All these ruins are for you

That's what they said: fight for the kids' future
No trouble too great – they spoiled yer
Yer'll 'ave t' grow up t' be grateful – show yer deserved
   it
Thank the soldier for a start

PEMBERTON (*brooding as he worries about the missing
   soldiers*). I didnt press any buttons – not bright enough
Saw it through the glass panel – on guard duty
Machines dont tell me nothin – just lights an computers
Knew somethin was up
They 'ad these easy chairs but they was pantin
Mouths pulled back like dogs that'd bin runnin – showed
   all their gums and teeth

WOMAN. There

PEMBERTON. That was the first exchange

WOMAN (*puts bundle in the handcart*). You sit still till
   breakfast

*She empties the bowl, drapes the flannel to dry on the handle
of the cart and tidies her things.*

Gets filthy when its carried – wait till it crawls!
Mucky little pup

PEMBERTON. Must've bin shittin themselves – couldnt tell,
   the glass shut the stink in

The SOLDIERS *come in.*

(*To* SOLDIER 1.) No sentry permitted t' leave post
   without alertin senior soldier
Absent on duty!
You're on company orders – you wont eat for a week!

SOLDIER 1. We 'ad a look at the kid

PEMBERTON. What kid? Its not a –

SOLDIER 1. Let me finish
We saw it last night

Yesterday we didnt know the difference between that an
a bundle of rags

What does that make us?

We dont know what state we're supposed t' be in!

Are we dead or alive?

PEMBERTON. If that was a kid why's she –

SOLDIER 2. Let 'im finish!

SOLDIER 1. When I look at me 'and I'd like t' know
whether its real – then I know what t'do with it!

What we marchin for? What we eatin for?

If we're dead why dont we put ourselves in the ground!

(*To the* WOMAN.) Where's that kid?

SOLDIER 2. She's 'id it in the cart!

SOLDIER 4. Get it out!

SOLDIER 1. Show 'im!

The SOLDIERS *stare at the* WOMAN.

WOMAN. Yer didnt see people dancin in the air

That dont 'appen even in this world

Yer saw somethin yer dont like t' remember an that's 'ow
yer forget

Look at your poor faces

I dont know what you've been through or what yer got
up to – things yer shouldnt

But you're good people

When I came 'ere I was confused but that kid knew
where it was

At that age they ask all the questions that matter

Yer fed us an made us welcome

I slept as if I was younger than the baby I carried

I've 'ad every reason t' die an one reason t' live: 'oo else'd
take care of the kid?

I kept walkin for its sake

But you could settle down – build permanent shelters –
if yer looked after the soil things might grow

Yer could still do your foragin
Yer'd be comfortable in winter – take care of each other
  when you're ill
Yer wont want t' march when you're old
Per'aps other people'll find yer – there might be children
  my child could grow up with
I felt all that last night – didnt dream it – it was the first
  time the ground'd stopped tremblin since the
  explosions
We ought t' be with people
I met a woman 'oo'd bin with people – they died out –
  but *you'd* stand a chance – you're as tough as this kid
Is it so terrible t' be alive?
When my kid's sick I 'old it so its warm an it gets well
Its in rags but it never cries for the cold
I dont know where I'll get our next meal but it trusts me
It doesnt know all this is ruins – this is what it expects
Be like my kid – dont be ashamed t' learn from it
You're alive

She holds the bundle out to them.

Im sorry I wouldnt let it see you
(*To the bundle.*) Look at these poor men
Look 'ow they suffer
We'll go away – but you stay 'ere an take care of yourselves
There's water by the stones
Put up the shelter – it dont 'ave t' be a palace or a
  barracks –
PEMBERTON. That's not a kid its a bundle of rags!
WOMAN. I know that's what it looks like – a bundle of rags
  like its mother!
That's just what its wrapped in!
PEMBERTON (*to the* SOLDIERS). Take it an look at your
  kid!
SOLDIER 2. Let 'er keep it – it dont matter –

PEMBERTON. Take it! – that's an order soldier!

WOMAN tries to wheel the handcart out. PEMBERTON *goes to her.*

WOMAN. No dont 'urt the kid!

PEMBERTON *takes the bundle.*

No no!

PEMBERTON *throws the bundle to* SOLDIER 4.

PEMBERTON. Catch!
WOMAN. Arent there any bombs t' kill them!

SOLDIER 4 *catches the bundle.*

PEMBERTON. Undo it!
WOMAN. No no its alive!
SOLDIER 4 (*fumbling with the bundle*). She's tied it –
WOMAN. A bomb that didnt explode underground!
PEMBERTON. Undo it!
SOLDIER 4. I cant – the cunnin' – she's – corpseshit – its warm!
PEMBERTON. That's where she 'eld it!

SOLDIER 4 *fumbles and drops the bundle on the ground.*

WOMAN. No no please I carried to so long – I pressed it against my side so its 'ardly bin born!

SOLDIER 4 *is on the ground fumbling with the bundle.*

PEMBERTON. Spread it!
SOLDIER 4. I cant! – its movin!
PEMBERTON (*to the* SOLDIERS). 'Elp 'im!
WOMAN. They're spreadin it on the ground

PEMBERTON *helps to spread the bundle with his foot.*

PEMBERTON. 'Old it still!

The WOMAN *walks away and covers her face.* PEMBERTON *goes to her.*

Look – its a sheet
WOMAN. My child with the soldiers
PEMBERTON (*to* SOLDIER 2). You – 'elp 'im – 'old it up –
    'old it up!

SOLDIERS 2 *and* 4 *hold up the open sheet as if it were on a clothesline. There is a round stain towards one end.* PEMBERTON *turns the* WOMAN *to face the sheet.*

'Igher! Straighter!
Look at it!
What is it? An empty sheet!
What's that dirt? – that face? – its the stain where it was
    open t' the air! – grease where your fingers mauled it!
    – is that your kid? – a *spoil* mark!
WOMAN. My poor baby
PEMBERTON. Is it a conjurin trick? – a kid on the other
    side?

PEMBERTON *goes to the sheet and slides his hand behind it like a conjuror. He shows his empty hand.*

No rabbit?
WOMAN. It wont last – think of 'ow I 'old you –
PEMBERTON. Now rip it!
WOMAN. No no

SOLDIERS 2 *and* 4 *tear the sheet into two pieces.*

It screamed!
PEMBERTON. A sheet bein torn!
    There's nothin emptier than that sheet! – its got a 'ole in
    it!
    'Er? – that was the local looney
Went round with a sheet long before the bombs!

I reckon she was always barren!

SOLDIER 3 *picks up the two pieces of sheet and takes them to the* WOMAN. *He tries to knot them together.*

SOLDIER 3. 'Ere's your kid – take it back
  We didnt 'arm it – fell over – an cut its knee

The WOMAN *helps him as he fumbles with the knots. They tie the sheet.*

It wants its – mummy
You'll soon get it better
WOMAN (*nursing the sheet*). My child I couldnt 'ide you
    from the –
  I took care of you so long
  Forgiveness
  It was a violation

She tries to join the pieces together.

I sit 'ere – they bring my kid back – I look for the
    wounds

She half-drops the sheet and gathers it up.

Mothers sittin – 'oldin torn pieces –
Its finished – I promised you – the soldiers wont touch
    you
PEMBERTON. Yer see!
  The rag's not a kid: she was wrong!
  She says we're not dead: she's wrong!
  But she opens 'er mouth an yer believe everything that
      comes out!
  You're not ready! Not trained! Not soldiers!
  Not even decent deserters!
  We're dead! All of us!
  No one could live through what we went through – or
      want to go through it again!

Give me the gun!
I'll put a bullet in 'er!
Prove she's dead!
She wont turn a 'air!
SOLDIER 2. What if – what if she falls?
PEMBERTON. She wont!
And if she does what does it prove!
You ask too much!
We could be lookin at 'er lying there like someone's
    lookin at us on that slope!
We're all dead!
(*To* SOLDIER 1.) Give me the ammo!

SOLDIER 1 *gives* PEMBERTON *the loaded magazine.*

(*Fiddles angrily with his rifle.*) I cant even load it!
Yer see – we dont stay in trainin!
SOLDIER 1. Clips in there!

The WOMAN *kneels by her bundle and nurses it.*

WOMAN. It was my fault – I wanted t' eat – my selfishness
    drove me on – I put you at risk
Next time I'll starve
SOLDIER 4. Put the safety catch off
PEMBERTON. We got idle!
That's why we're in this corpse shit!
Now on – rifle practice – everyday!

The WOMAN *is bent over the bundle talking gently to it.*
PEMBERTON *aims at her.*

The sight's bent!
SOLDIER 1. Dirt in it!

SOLDIER 4 *flicks the sight clean.*

WOMAN. I'll soothe the pain – when my precious is at rest
    my pain will go – that's how you'll 'elp your mother

SOLDIER 3. Where's 'e aimin?
PEMBERTON. Quiet! – yer –
SOLDIER 2. Get nearer!
PEMBERTON. – put me off me stroke!

PEMBERTON *goes closer to the* WOMAN *and aims.*

SOLDIER 2. Cant miss from there even with no practice!
SOLDIER 1. Take the first pressure on the finger –

PEMBERTON *takes the first pressure.*

SOLDIER 4. We'll soon know!
SOLDIER 2. Ready – fire!

PEMBERTON *pulls the trigger: the mechanism works but the*
bullet does not fire.

PEMBERTON. Corpsin-creepin-shit'ouse! It didnt fire!
SOLDIER 4. Do it again!
PEMBERTON. There's no point!
   The shell's dead!
SOLDIER 1. Bin carried around too long!

The WOMAN *stands and takes the bundle to the handcart.*
The SOLDIERS *do not notice this.*

SOLDIER 4. Get the ammo!
PEMBERTON. That's reserve!
SOLDIER 1. One round!
PEMBERTON. If we break the seal the weather'll get in!
   We've got t' stop this!
   Its gettin out of 'and!
SOLDIER 2 (*dragging the ammo box*). We must see if she
   falls!
SOLDIER 1. Give 'im a jemmy

SOLDIER 4 *throws a tool to* SOLDIER 2. *The* WOMAN *is*

slowly wheeling out the cart. She does not notice the
SOLDIERS *and they do not notice her.*

WOMAN. No more cart till you're better
All carry
If mummy can manage
'Old tight – that gives me some 'elp

The WOMAN *goes out with the cart.* SOLDIER 1 *prises off the lid of the ammo box. All the* SOLDIERS *stare at the ammo.*

SOLDIER 2. Corpse me
SOLDIER 3. Mint condition
SOLDIER 1. I could lick the oil off that
SOLDIER 2. Perfect
SOLDIER 1. The most beautiful sight I've seen since we've
    bin in the ruins
SOLDIER 3. I want t' be shot
SOLDIER 2. Give us that lid
SOLDIER 4. No dont cover it
SOLDIER 3. I want t' be shot
I dont want t' live anymore – all this bein dead
I dont know what I am
What d'yer want of me?
Let me be dead – please
Its bin like this since we went on the run
SOLDIER 2. The shit-out-of-corpses –
PEMBERTON. Shut up!
SOLDIER 3. Im more tired than a corpse
I dont want t' go marchin for bones anymore

SOLDIER 3 *takes* PEMBERTON'*s gun. He loads it from the ammo box.*

PEMBERTON. Leave those shells! – army property!
SOLDIER 3. T'morrow: 'the kid was rags but she's got a
    real one in the ruins'

I aint goin t' change
Im dead – or I soon will be

He gives the gun to PEMBERTON.

Its loaded – I done the 'ard bit
'Ow I 'ate you officers

SOLDIER 3 *walks away and turns to face the others.*

Corpse knows I shot my share – they went down in waves
I 'elped t' blow up the world
SOLDIER 1. Its 'is carcass 'e can do what 'e likes with it!
PEMBERTON. Shut up!
SOLDIER 3 (*touches his chest*). Shoot 'ere
   I'll take a breath – bigger target
SOLDIER 1. Corpse 'im! Corpse 'im! Corpse 'im!
PEMBERTON. No grub for a week!
   The lot of yer on orders!
SOLDIER 1. Corpse 'im! Corpse 'im! – an me!
   (*He joins* SOLDIER 3.) Corpse me! Corpse me!
   (*He dances.*) I'll be dead!
   I'll send yer a sign!
   Corpse me! Corpse me! I'll be the dancin lad!
   I'll speak when Im dead! I'll shout! I'll 'oller!
SOLDIER 2 (*joins* SOLDIERS 1 *and* 3). Yeah! Let's be dead
   an enjoy it!
   Dead an free!
SOLDIER 1 Dead an dance!

SOLDIERS 1 *and* 2 *dance together.*

SOLDIERS 1, 2. Corpse me! Corpse me! I wanna be dead!
SOLDIER 3. I wanna be corpsed!
SOLDIERS 1, 2. I wanna be corpsed!
   Me mates is waiting!
   I want t' dance again!
   The dead've a right t' be corpsed!

We'll dance with our mates!
Get the ground over your 'ead!
SOLDIER 2. An 'im! An 'im!

SOLDIER 2 points at SOLDIER 4.
SOLDIER 4 runs. SOLDIERS 1 and 2 stop him and drag him back.

SOLDIER 4. No no – I dont want it! I dont want it!
SOLDIER 1. Corpse 'im with us!
SOLDIER 2. Corpse 'im! Corpse 'im!
SOLDIER 4. I dont wanna die – please – let me march – carry the bones – please –
SOLDIERS 1, 2, 3. Corpse us! Corpse us!

Silence except for SOLDIER 4's crying.

SOLDIER 1 (*to SOLDIER 4*). . . . 'S all right – brave lad – so many went there before – they go through it –
SOLDIER 2 (*suddenly points at PEMBERTON*). The soldiers! Rifles!
They've come for us!
SOLDIER 1. We're goin t' be shot!

SOLDIER 2 suddenly throws his arms up like a pope. The other SOLDIERS support each other. SOLDIER 1 makes a protective gesture over SOLDIER 4. (Goya: The Third of May 1808.)

PEMBERTON. Yer vengeful bastards! Dont you threaten me!
I'll shoot the corpse-shit off yer tongues!

PEMBERTON fires an automatic burst. The SOLDIERS fall. PEMBERTON walks away and sits.

Get control
Soldier goes too far a'ead of 'is lines, cant get back
Like this after the bombs

*He notices the ammo box is uncovered, goes to it and puts the
lid on it.*

Weather's the soldier's enemy
Every round a life

SOLDIER 1*'s leg moves.* PEMBERTON *goes to him and
shoots him. He looks at the other bodies. He sprays them with
an automatic burst.*
He walks away. He stands still.

Dont push 'em too far
Watched 'em from the back in a wood
'Eads down in case they tripped – eyes on their feet
In the evenin – found just the right time t' call 'alt
Posted the sentry
Wake up in the mornings: what's the sky doin?
Liked all that

THIRTEEN

Wilderness

Two days later.
The WOMAN *comes in carrying the bundle and pushing the
cart. She is tired.*

WOMAN. Stop 'ere an give the cart a rest
   Too late t' eat
   Should've nicked grub from the army thugs
   Pretended t' sleep – trick the sentry – easy 'elp meself
   No: slep like a kid! – kids shouldnt sleep in this world!
   I know what goes on in your 'ead: why's she keep draggin
      me round till Im sick!
   Now yer know: yer've 'ad your education – that's what
      people are: wicked or mad or in uniform

She sits and puts the bundle on her lap.

Let's see the state of yer

She probes the bundle and winces.

Did that 'urt?
Wont look too much t'night, leave it till the mornin
Mummy'll be so gentle a string of sand wouldnt break
Lump still there . . .
Mummy's worried the soldiers 'urt er precious so much
    it . . .
You will get better? Mummy couldnt manage without
    yer
If I lost you an 'ad t' find another one in the ruins, it
    wouldnt be the same
I could never bury yer: cry so much I'd wash the earth
    off, keep puttin it back an washin it off, we'd wash the
    mountains away
You're so 'ot – your face burns me fingers
When you get better you'll still 'ave a limp
Sometimes I pretend you're playin in the street – I call
    you up an yer bring the cold air in the room
Stupid woman keepin you awake tellin yer t' get better:
    'ow can yer get better if I dont let yer rest?
Goodnight, we'll go t' sleep

The WOMAN *lies down with the bundle.*
Silence. The bundle cries.

You cried!
I 'eard your voice
I waited so long
Thank you, thank you
Your precious voice – so beautiful – now it'll be all right,
    now I'll live
But dont cry, dont cry – it breaks my 'eart

BUNDLE. Mummy

WOMAN. My precious spoke!

   It spoke! What is it? Tell me!

   I can feel you tryin to speak, I can feel the words!

   What is it my precious?

BUNDLE. Sol – sol –

WOMAN. Soldiers?

   No more soldiers – we're safe now

   Dont speak about them – speak about yourself – you,
      you – all the things in your 'ead – what yer feel – what
      yer think all day! Such 'appiness, such joy!

BUNDLE. Sol – soldiers put baby on gr – ground

WOMAN. Yes my precious but dont talk about them

BUNDLE. Baby is so thin mummy

WOMAN. Dont waste your voice – there's so much you can
   tell me!

BUNDLE. So thin

WOMAN. Hush hush

BUNDLE. Why do the – the sol – sol – soldiers – spread
   babies on the – the ground?

WOMAN. That's what soldiers do

BUNDLE. So thin

   The wind blew under me an I rip – rip – rippled on the
      ground

   I didnt know I was so thin

WOMAN. My poor child

BUNDLE. As – as thin as a piece of cloth

WOMAN. No no hush

BUNDLE. I could see the four corners – rip – rippled in the
   wind

   Why did I have t' lie on the ground? – is the ground
      cold?

   Im too – too small t' warm it

WOMAN. Its finished, finished

BUNDLE. One sheet t' cover the hill – was that why I was
   born?
  Too small t' cover the wind – the wind went under me

The WOMAN *cries.*

  Dont cry
  I could've spoken a long time ago
  But then if I died you'd miss my voice
  So I didnt speak
WOMAN. My precious thought all that for me
  'Ow good, 'ow kind
  You understand me so well
BUNDLE. I could've grown big
  I was afraid you'd leave me
WOMAN. Never
BUNDLE. Im heavy t' carry
WOMAN. No no
BUNDLE. I make mummy tired
WOMAN. T'night all the walkin an pain is worth it
  You tell me such wonderful things
  We'll talk all the time – you'll tell me what you see from
    the cart
  You know more than me
BUNDLE. Sh . . . we must go to sleep
WOMAN. Yes talk my precious an all the world can sleep
BUNDLE. Sh . . .
  I watch you sleep
  Your poor face
  In the mornin your bones have t' breathe on you to wake
    you up

FOURTEEN

Wilderness

Some years later.
The WOMAN *alone with her cart and bundle. She offers the bundle a mug of food.*

WOMAN. Try!
 If yer dont eat you'll be ill!

She walks about nursing the bundle.

What can I do? What more?
 Yer wicked child yer dont want t' 'elp yer mother!
 You're not ill!
 Yer do this t' frighten me!
 One day! – that's all yer spoke! One day!
 I carried you for years!
 I made a mistake an showed I was 'appy!
 Now Im t' be punished for that?
 What d'yer do with yer words? Pass 'em out in your shit?
 Oh dont try my patience!
 If what I feel ever turns t' 'ate you'll be sorry!
 You think they 'ated when they dropped the bombs?
 Baby's piss!
 When I 'ate one spit dilutes the rivers! It curdles oceans!
 Watch out for me yer little bastard!

Pause

Nothin wrong with its tongue . . . looked . . . not its
 teeth

The WOMAN *puts the bundle on the ground and walks away.*

Im goin!
Look me feet are moving!
I shant 'ear when yer call I'll be too far off!
I've got friends I can go to – seen their ashes in the
    fireplaces – shit in corners!
Im sick t' death of carryin yer!
I'll be glad t' get rid of yer!

The WOMAN *hits the bundle.*

Soddin little bastard!
Dont stare at me!
I'll black your eyes for yer!
Yer 'ad your warnin!
Thought I wouldnt do it!
'Ad me twisted round your finger!
(*She shakes the bundle.*) Fingers can break!
Im not lettin this go t' waste!
Slavin after you!
(*She eats food from the mug.*) Ooo lovely!
Yer can beg till yer starve!

 'Ow much longer does this go on?
Round an round inside a skull!
Stirrin a spoon in an empty bowl!
Am I the ground for the rain t' piss on?
Stitch rocks with a needle an thread?
I've trod this sand small!
One 'and black an one 'and white!
I rub them t'gether – an one stays black: one white
Not one spot passes from one t' the other!
Not one spot wiped away!
I rub them t'gether!
Pitch black! Pure white!
. . . If I left I'd come back when it called – if I lost it I'd
    spend my life lookin for it

I thought I 'ad everythin: I've got nothin
Its a millstone round my neck

P'raps it cant speak – or even make a sign
I dont know 'ow bad the soldiers 'urt it
Poor creature

She picks up the bundle.

Every mornin I look at the sky – to me the light's like a
  woman shakin 'er skirts
She goes through the ruins: with all those dead, an she
  never cries
'Er children wait an she straightens their crooked arms
  an legs
So they can 'ave peace
'Ow shall I carry you?
If I carried you in a procession I wouldnt clutch you
I'd sing an 'old you over my 'ead – 'igh up t' the light,
  facin away – for the others t' see!
If you was a torch – the glare'd blind me – I'd 'old you
  up for the people on the 'ill – the procession's for them
  – let them see the light!

I wont shout at you anymore
You'll speak when its time
Look I dribbled the food on your chin

She wipes the bundle's chin.

That smack didnt 'urt – you'll get worse than that – this
  wet's worse than that smack

The WOMAN *is bent over her bundle.*
MOTHER *comes on leaning on her* DAUGHTER.

WOMAN. Who're you!
DAUGHTER. My mother needs 'elp
WOMAN. Where yer come from?

You alone?

You 'avent got soldiers?

DAUGHTER. No –

MOTHER. My daughter an me – no one else –

DAUGHTER. My mother's ill

    We was sleepin in the ruins – I 'eard talkin – we've bin sleepin all day – my mother needs rest

WOMAN (*stares at them*). . . . Two women . . .

    This is my place – nothin for you 'ere – get off!

    Is she ill? I dont want 'er 'ere!

DAUGHTER. 'Oo were yer –

WOMAN. Is she your mother? I cant 'elp yer!

DAUGHTER. You were talkin t' someone –

WOMAN. No one 'ere! Get off!

DAUGHTER. My mother's bin ill for weeks –

WOMAN. Then dont drag 'er round! Let 'er rest!

    There's no doctors 'ere!

DAUGHTER. We met an old man – 'e said there was people in the south

    Im takin 'er there

MOTHER. They'll be able t' 'elp me

DAUGHTER. She's not bleedin – she cant be very ill

WOMAN. Yer dont 'ave t' bleed t' be ill! You dont know much!

    This is my place – anythin growin 'ere's mine!

    I ain 'avin you scroungin!

    Two of yer! – an yer think yer can live off me?

    I ain 'elpin yer!

DAUGHTER. 'Ow did we know this was your place?

WOMAN. Should I put a sign up?

DAUGHTER. You werent 'ere when we come!

WOMAN. Dont cheek me yer tramp! – yer know now!

MOTHER. The old man said in the south they've got electricity

DAUGHTER. 'E saw the light in the sky

MOTHER. It didnt flicker – 'e remembered what electricity
   was like

DAUGHTER. If they can make all that light they must be
   able t' take care of the sick

WOMAN. Why should they share their electricity with you?
   What've you got t' offer?

MOTHER. We'll go an take our chance

WOMAN. Well yer wont find no electricity 'ere!
   . . . Electricity . . .
   (*Mug of food.*) Yer can finish these leftovers then clear off

DAUGHTER. Thank you
   (*To* MOTHER.) Sit down
   Yer see we've already got 'elp!
   When we get south there'll be more people t' 'elp us
   Let me steady the spoon?

The DAUGHTER *helps* MOTHER *to eat.*

This'll do 'er good

WOMAN. Its not much . . . you're welcome

The WOMAN *walks away and looks round.*

MOTHER. 'Ave some

DAUGHTER. Its for you

MOTHER. Yer must eat for the journey

DAUGHTER (*to* WOMAN). Can we finish it?

WOMAN. You're in a bad way if you're grateful for that pap

DAUGHTER. She needs t' save 'er strength
   Could I leave 'er with you while I go on south?

WOMAN. Leave 'er with me?
   No! Impossible!

DAUGHTER. The walkin's wearin 'er out
   We go less far every day an she gets more tired
   Soon she wont 'ave a chance even if we find other people

WOMAN. Dont put your burdens on me!

DAUGHTER. She's not a burden!

I dont want t' leave 'er with a stranger, I want t' take 'er with me – but she's wastin away!

WOMAN. I cant feed your invalids!

What if soldiers come? I wouldnt stay with 'er – I'd run! She'd be left on 'er own

MOTHER. If soldiers come none of us could do anythin about it

DAUGHTER. She could 'elp if she wanted – she's makin excuses

MOTHER. No yer mustnt talk about people like that – she's bound t' be scared of us

WOMAN. Im not scared – I'd 'elp if I could

MOTHER. I'll only be a burden for a few days

Let my daughter go on

After I've rested I'd provide for myself – I might even catch 'er up

My daughter found a shelter in the ruins – its out of your way

If I could sleep an not 'ave t' walk – I'm afraid t' walk anymore, its wastin my strength

Just a few days' grace – otherwise I'll drag on an then 'ave t' stop – an that'll be that

WOMAN. What if she's tryin t' get rid of yer?

'Oo could blame 'er? She'd 'ave a good excuse! – left yer in good hands

MOTHER. Children dont treat their mothers like that

WOMAN. Yer can stay a month

A day longer an Im off

Any trouble – Im off

I've got me own responsibilities

What can yer pay?

DAUGHTER. Pay?

MOTHER. She means for my food

WOMAN. I wont charge for this (*Mug.*) – left it too late t' ask, didnt think – but she'll expect t' be fed every day

There aint a market

DAUGHTER. I cant pay – we only get what we pick up an
eat – like you

WOMAN (*points to daughter's neck*). That shawl

DAUGHTER. I need this at night

WOMAN. You've got young bones – dont feel the cold like
me

DAUGHTER. You've got a blanket – I'll 'ave t' leave ours
for my mother

WOMAN. 'Ave a good journey

The DAUGHTER *gives her shawl to the* WOMAN.

A shawl for your mother – fair price
When you're cold just think you're shiverin for 'er sake
– that'll warm yer up
Your electricity people'll give yer plenty of shawls

DAUGHTER. I'd like t' stay till morning but I'd better start

MOTHER. Come an say goodbye

The WOMAN *stares at the* MOTHER *and* DAUGHTER *as
they embrace.*

There – I've 'eld you up long enough
Remember t' wash an do yer 'air an brush yer clothes
If yer dont look like a 'uman bein you'll scare people off
Dont show yerself t' anyone till you're sure they can be
trusted – wait till there's a woman if yer can
Say please when yer ask for anythin – an thank you even
if yer dont get it: it might change their mind

DAUGHTER. Dont worry, I remember all you've taught me
You rest an get well
I'll take me shoes off so I can run faster
Even if I dont find anyone you'll be rested when I get
back
We'll be as 'appy as we was before you were ill

MOTHER. Now I dont 'ave t' walk t'morrow I feel better already

MOTHER *and* DAUGHTER *kiss.*

Do go – you're wastin time
We've 'ad all this luck, we mustnt waste it

WOMAN. A month – dont try t' make it longer, it wont work

DAUGHTER. Yes – goodbye – (*To* WOMAN.) Thank you – (*To* MOTHER.) goodbye

The DAUGHTER *goes. The* WOMAN *and* MOTHER *stare after her.*

WOMAN. 'Ow old is – ?

MOTHER. Sh! – let me see 'er go

Silence. The WOMAN *goes to her bundle and picks it up.*

MOTHER. Nineteen
(*She stares after her* DAUGHTER.) Uhh . . .

WOMAN. What is it?

MOTHER. Stay there – if yer come an 'elp me she'll turn back
Let 'er go . . .

WOMAN. You're in pain

MOTHER. Let 'er go!
(*Smiles and waves.*) Be back soon!

WOMAN. Sit down – you'll fall

MOTHER. No – let 'er see me stand – if its the last time she sees me let 'er remember me well . . .

WOMAN (*waves and calls to the* DAUGHTER). 'Urry! Run! Run! – the silly cow's stopped!
'Ow can I make 'er move?
(*Waves the shawl and calls.*) Run! Be quick!

MOTHER. . . . . Poor kid

WOMAN. If you're so ill she shouldnt 'ave left yer

MOTHER. She doesnt know – I 'id it
Per'aps I could sit . . . she'll think that's natural
It'll pass, its 'appened before
I'll be all right when I can shut my eyes

She trembles violently as she sits.

It may be the last I'll see 'er – I cant stop tremblin
We 'avent been parted since she was born
WOMAN. Shall I call 'er back?
MOTHER. No let 'er run
WOMAN. She's pleased – yer can tell even from that little
    black shape
Look at 'er feet . . .
MOTHER. 'Old my 'and: it'll stop the tremblin
    (*The* WOMAN *takes* MOTHER's *hand*.) 'Arder
WOMAN. Where's the pain?
MOTHER. I wanted t' cry at every step
    I longed t' lie down an sleep
    I wanted t' be like those 'ills – lie still an let the pain run
        through me like water
    I couldnt, I darent let 'er see I was so near t' the end
    (*Waves*.) She'll need more than electricity t' see me
    (*Cries*.) Let 'er be 'appy
WOMAN (*waves the shawl and shouts*). Good luck
MOTHER. Thought of 'er alone in the ruins at night – my
    daughter'd become an animal
    She only knows this desert – *we* grew up in a proper
        world: that's where we learned t' survive
    We're so weak: she could break a leg an lie there
WOMAN. She wont abandon you
MOTHER. It doesnt matter, as long as she finds other
    people . . .
WOMAN. You're very ill
MOTHER. A moment ago I thought I was dyin
    I used too much strength tryin t' show 'er I wasnt ill

   Dont worry I wont be a nuisance
   We're too alike t' need any fuss
WOMAN. I 'ad a kid too
MOTHER. Did it survive?
WOMAN. Yes – (*Shows the bundle.*) Look
MOTHER. Is that your kid?
WOMAN. Yes
MOTHER. My dear you've 'ad your baby since the war?
WOMAN. Yes
MOTHER. Why 'asnt it grown?
WOMAN. It 'as but its slow
   The bombs stunted it or I couldnt feed it properly
   I loved it but that wasnt enough
MOTHER. Its a nice baby
   If my daughter finds 'elp she'll take care of us both
   We'll share what she –
WOMAN. Its easy t' share what yer 'avent got!
   She soon showed us 'er 'eels . . .
   'Ow did you come through the war?
MOTHER. Im too tired t' –
WOMAN. Tell me
MOTHER. A crowd of us sheltered in a cinema
   We cooked in the cafeteria
   Left when the town burned down
   I was carryin the baby – I couldnt keep up with the rest
   The army'd left some tanks on a square
   Lived in them for a while – they 'ad food an water
   One night the 'ole square tipped up an the tanks rolled
     down the slope towards the river
   Noise like chains inside yer
   The one I was in ran onto the bridge
   I walked along the bank
   Later on there werent any people
   I brought 'er up – watched 'er grow – she's my 'ole life

I taught 'er all I knew so if she 'ad t' live on 'er own I'd
    still be a 'elp to 'er

WOMAN. Did we meet before the war?

I knew a woman like you – younger of course

She 'ad a kid – she'd be your daughter's age now

They were my neighbours

MOTHER. I should go t' my place

WOMAN. Strange if we survived all these years – an the kid
    brought 'er mother t' me – an left 'er in my care

What was our street called?

The soldiers wanted t' kill the kid

The mother was clever – pulled a trick

It went through 'er ead in two seconds an it changed all
    the years since

Alderton Road – I remember!

MOTHER. Im not well – 'elp me back t' my place

WOMAN. Wait – she might come up on the slope be'ind

I'll 'elp yer in a minute

Did yer play with 'er when she was a kid?

Once I thought I 'eard laughin in the 'ills – in the mornin
    an later on

It could've bin stones fallin

*MOTHER makes a sound. She begins to hallucinate and tries
to crawl back to her place in the ruins.*

Dont! – that sounds like a dog on the whimper – didnt
    wait all these years t' be whined at by a dog

MOTHER. 'Elp me

WOMAN. Dont whine

Where did yer live?

They were number twenty-seven

The girl wouldnt know me but you would

*The WOMAN walks away and sits with the bundle. She
holds it up to look at MOTHER.*

Look at 'er face – numb with pain
A fly could lay eggs on it

She holds the bundle as if it's learning to walk.

Walk t' the lady – time you took your first steps
Ask 'er 'oo she is: kids only ask the questions that matter
See if you know 'er – you're good at noticing
When she saw you 'er face dried up
She knew 'oo you were

MOTHER. Is my daughter 'ere?

WOMAN (*with increasing menace*). That's not sufferin: I
    suffered more

A lucky woman: I thought I was lucky but she was *chosen*
    for luck!

People runnin 'er messages round the world: they'll
    bump into each other!

The world's too small to accommodate 'em

Old men announcin electricity

Me 'ere t' do 'er washin an cookin an carry the bedpan

If 'er son'd bin a soldier 'e'd've sat in 'er window an shot
    'is mates when they come down the street

Mine would've whistled 'em up: 'the sod's in its cot!'

What good did all that luck do 'er?

Landed 'er 'ere on my bit of ground

'Er or another woman – what's the difference? – one
    'ead, two arms, legs – they're all the same

With one arm they 'old a child an caress it: with the other
    they knock a child down with their fist

(*She decides to kill* MOTHER *with a stick.*)

'Er daughter comes back an she's dead?

What could she do in this place?

If justice 'erself came 'ere she'd beg me for somethin t'
    eat

She'd flog 'er sword an scales t' the rag man for a glass of
    water . . .

(*She decides to nurse* MOTHER.)
Let 'er luck 'old

The WOMAN *stands and carries her bundle back to*
MOTHER.

You're too ill t' move
Make your bed 'ere

The WOMAN *spreads the shawl on the ground and lifts*
MOTHER *onto it.*

MOTHER. Is the square slopin?
WOMAN. Makin you comfortable till your daughter gets
    back
    The ground's 'ard: did you enough damage when you
    were walkin
    You're 'ot – you frighten me – your daughter may be too
    late
    Look –
    (*To the bundle.*) Forgive me – the woman's in pain – she's
    not used t' bein without 'er daughter

The WOMAN *loosens the bundle and flattens it into a pillow.*

    (*To the bundle.*) I'll spread you a little – gently – if you
    knew what she suffered – you'd forgive me
BUNDLE. It hurts . . . gently . . .
    No mummy must I carry her head its so heavy . . . ?
WOMAN. My precious – she's so ill – she must rest or she
    wont come through
MOTHER. Who's speakin? Is that my daughter?
BUNDLE. I forgive you
WOMAN. Thank you
    (*To* MOTHER.) Lift your 'ead – there –
MOTHER. My daughter . . . ? Give me your 'and . . .
WOMAN. She's gone for a long time – you must be patient
    till she comes back

I'll stay with you

She strokes MOTHER's *head and the pillow.*

Poor creatures – forgive me – the two of you
The grey hair of my baby . . .
Look at 'er feet: you could repair shoes with the skin
The bits of my gruel round 'er mouth are like old
    woman's whiskers
'Er poor 'ands are knots: did you see 'er little fists on 'er
    daughter's cheeks?
If the earth died they'd bury it in 'er body – it 'as more
    'istory
Now *I'll* share your worries: not your daughter, a woman
    like yourself
When things are more than we can bear, we break: that's
    a kindness we're given
A coat's worn till it's old: then its a floorcloth t' mop up
    the filth: then its stuffed in a broken window t' keep
    out the draft
And when it cant be used no more – no cloth, no rags –
    it falls into shreds – an the wind blows them – an then
    the coat covers a country
(*She strokes* MOTHER's *head.*) You can forgive me
We're the fruit that grows on the tree that's bin cut down
    an carted away
Long after its gone the children reach up an pick our
    fruit: its the custom
You lie under 'er 'ead an I'll be 'er blanket
Im not as young as 'er daughter but I still give some
    warmth
I could tell from their faces they slept together
(*She lies beside* MOTHER *and holds her.*) There – an
    t'morrow we'll make our plans

FIFTEEN

Wilderness

Two months later.
The WOMAN *and* MOTHER *lie asleep in each other's arms under blankets. The* DAUGHTER *comes on with a* MAN, *a* MIDDLE-AGED MAN *and a* YOUNG MAN. *All of them carry haversacks and camping equipment. The* MIDDLE-AGED MAN *has a carpenter's tool-fold and wears a tool-belt.*

MAN. Which is your mother?
DAUGHTER. I cant tell
    (*She lifts blanket.*) This is 'er
MIDDLE-AGED MAN. They're both alive

> *The* MIDDLE-AGED MAN *and the* YOUNG MAN *double their fists, raise them shoulder high, turn them inwards and signal satisfaction by shaking them in quick jerking movements and grimacing.*

DAUGHTER. Can I wake 'er?
MAN. Gently – she mustnt be shocked
DAUGHTER. They're sleepin in each other's arms like
    sisters
    Poor things – 'ow they've suffered – yer can see it in their
    faces
    Sleep cant touch so much weariness
MAN. Let the other woman sleep
DAUGHTER. I'll ease their arms apart
MAN. Let me 'elp

> *They disentangle the two sleeping* WOMEN.

See if she can sit up – lift 'er

> *They sit* MOTHER *up.*

She's goin t' wake

YOUNG MAN. She's wore out

DAUGHTER. But she looks at peace – 'er face is changed
Mother wake up

MOTHER *opens her eyes. The* DAUGHTER *embraces her.*

MOTHER. My child – 'ere

DAUGHTER. My dear – look I've brought my friends t' 'elp
us
I've such wonderful things t' tell – so much is 'appening
in their place
Are you in pain?

MOTHER. My dear – you've changed –

DAUGHTER. I was gone two months

MOTHER. So little? – yer look ten years younger
I'd forgotten your eyes were so bright – and is your 'air
such a colour? Isnt it darker?

DAUGHTER (*laughs*). I am your daughter

MOTHER. My dear – so pretty

MAN. Try t' stand

DAUGHTER. I can see your pain's gone – your face is gentler

MOTHER. Thank you – I can stand
(*She stands.*) Everyday in the last few weeks I've taken a
few steps
She let me 'elp t' prepare the food
I 'eld the bowl in my lap an washed the plants

DAUGHTER. Yer didnt tire yourself?

MOTHER. No it was a pleasure t' watch me 'ands work
You look so young!
Im ashamed before all these people – please dont stare
I've bin mendin me clothes for when yer got back
I thought they were so smart: I've bin proud of rags!
What a miserable sight for you – your mother an ol' crow

DAUGHTER. Dont be silly – I'm so 'appy t' see your kind
face

YOUNG MAN. We've rescued a lot worse than you – some real 'ags

MIDDLE-AGED MAN. Is the other woman all right?

MOTHER. Yes – she's in a poor way, 'er 'ead's full of stories But she's as 'armless as a child

MAN. We're not doctors but we've got a nurse – she 'ad t' stay with our sick – an she gave us some drugs

An there's food – most survivors are sufferin from malnutrition

We'll take you back in easy stages an then see what we can do t' make yer well

MIDDLE-AGED MAN (*food*). We wrap our bread in cloth t' keep it fresh

An these're our apples – old crabs, not much cop – the trees run wild

We're graftin good stock

The WOMAN *wakes and stares at the others. She stands. At first they do not see her.*

DAUGHTER. Try it

MIDDLE-AGED MAN. Its a 'eavy bread that lasts in the winter

DAUGHTER. Only take a small piece

YOUNG MAN. I'll lay a bet

The MOTHER *breaks a piece of bread and eats.*

MOTHER. Well that's not 'eavy – its as light as –

MOTHER *chokes and spits the bread into her hand. The* YOUNG MAN *laughs.*

DAUGHTER. Just like me!

MOTHER. It tastes of sweets! (*She licks the inside of her mouth.*) – my mouth tastes sweet – why cant I eat it?

MIDDLE-AGED MAN. You're so used t' rubbish your body cant 'andle goodness

Yer 'ave t' learn t' eat again
Be weaned off muck

MOTHER. Im sorry – wastin your good bread –

YOUNG MAN. Yer'll soon be peckin like a lady an tellin us off for bad manners

MAN (*sees the* WOMAN). You were so sound asleep we didnt wake yer

WOMAN (*protectively pulls her clothes round herself*). So – yer found your . . .

DAUGHTER. These are the people with electricity
They light up the 'ill at night an yer see it in the sky

MIDDLE-AGED MAN. We've brought yer this gift of bread
We couldnt carry much on the long journey
We've fetched other people from the wilderness so we've got it organised
Most of em manage t' walk to us – but sometimes we 'ave t' go back for the old and sick

YOUNG MAN. At least they've got a cart
We'll convert that for the sick lady t' ride in
Mostly we 'ave t' get bits an pieces from the bomb sites an knock up a stretcher
Yer dont often find good wheels like that!

MIDDLE-AGED MAN. Try the bread
We brought enough for the two of yer
We bake every week an use the flour from our own wheat
(*To the* YOUNG MAN.) Scout round for some planks
I saw the marks of a village when we came up
Stamp on the ground till yer feel floorboards under your feet

The YOUNG MAN *goes out. The* MIDDLE-AGED MAN *lays his tool-roll on the ground and takes a hammer. He starts to rebuild the cart by knocking out the two ends of the box.*

I re-use the nails – saves me raidin my nail box

In the perfect world nails'd grow on trees an nails an wood'd come t'gether

(*Working.*) We all know its not the perfect world

DAUGHTER (*to the* WOMAN). Thanks for takin care of my mother

She says I look younger since I've bin with people: she looks younger since she was with you

You 'avent eaten your bread

MAN. Dont force 'er

Remember what you were like when yer came to us – stood at the end of the street an shouted – I thought it was a dog barkin at the 'ouses

The last time your mother an 'er friend saw so many people t'gether they were dead

We 'ave t' take them out of the wilderness gently

One old boy thought we were comin with bombs: ran off an next day we found im dead

Yer can kill people with empty 'ands . . . !

(*To the* WOMAN.) Its a great day for us when we find more people

We want t' put our arms round yer an thank yer just for bein alive!

Everyone 'oo comes out of the wildnerness knows so much!

Its amazin the knowledge your people 'ad!

Its not like findin scrolls in the sand – but findin the people 'oo wrote em!

We're lucky t' be young enough t' do the 'ard work – but we need your generation t' teach us

When we start pickin your brains yer'll think yer've bin rescued by idiots!

MIDDLE-AGED MAN. This was a cradle before it was fitted with wheels

Probably kids makin themselves a playcart

That rim on the wheels 'eld the rubber tyres – they went
    round the world a few times before they fell off
In them days they could make anythin . . . !
MOTHER (*to the* WOMAN). 'E's spoilin your cart
MAN. She wont need that old one
    She wants a cart we got plenty of better ones she can
      choose from
    (*To* WOMAN.) Its too far for your friend t' go on foot
    (*To the* DAUGHTER.) Your mother's frail
    We must get 'er back quickly an gently an then see 'ow
      gravely she's ill
    If the bombs 'adnt bin dropped she'd still be a young
      woman
    Some survivors recover overnight – yer'd think an artist'd
      made the young model 'oo'd sat for an old portrait
    We'll do what we can: nursin people like 'er is a way of
      'ealin our own wounds

The WOMAN *has picked up her bundle and walked away.*
She stands staring at the others. The YOUNG MAN *comes in*
with three planks.

YOUNG MAN. Struck lucky!
    Tell yer what we'll do: we'll nail these on top of the old
      bottom so's she can stretch out 'er legs
MIDDLE-AGED MAN. What d'yer think I sent yer t' get em
    for?
    We'll pad em over with blankets an make 'er comfortable
YOUNG MAN. Come out an old 'allway – not s'long as
    regular boards
MIDDLE-AGED MAN. Cut em down t' the same size
    Knock the nails out first: dont want me saw ripped t'
      pieces

The MIDDLE-AGED MAN *and the* YOUNG MAN *cut the*
boards and nail them into the cart.

DAUGHTER (*to* MOTHER). A 'undred people! Its so crowded
I thought they'd knock into each other in the streets!

Yer told me what cities were like but I couldnt imagine
it: now I've bin in one!

MOTHER. I'd think this was a dream: but no one could be
so kind in a dream

MIDDLE-AGED MAN. Watch 'ow yer cut the wood – yer
dont want t' splinter 'er t' death!

YOUNG MAN. Will those wheels take 'er weight?

MIDDLE-AGED MAN. 'Ave t' see

YOUNG MAN. Dont fancy carryin 'er

MIDDLE-AGED MAN. What she weighs, be like a bird
carryin the feathers on its back

MOTHER (*to her* DAUGHTER). We must be kind t' the
woman: she 'as a claim on us

Nothin was too much trouble

She walked miles t' find food when it was picked clean
round 'ere

Came back every evenin more tired than I was an cooked
an washed an took care of me like me own mother

She'd've folded me 'ands for me if she could – polished
the ends of me eyelashes

Im worried these people wont understand 'er

They mustnt ask too many questions

Just let 'er chatter then she's all right

If I can still give yer any 'appiness now you've got such
good friends –

DAUGHTER. 'Appiness? – the dirt on your face is worth
more t' me than all their lights

MOTHER. – if we can still make each other 'appy, we owe
it t' 'er

She brought us t'gether again

I wonder so much goodness can come out of this waste

DAUGHTER. You werent so ill!

MOTHER. When you ran off it was like watchin me own
    funeral
  I didnt think I'd see yer again
  I sent yer away t' find 'elp for yourself
DAUGHTER. Why didnt yer tell me?
MOTHER. Would yer 'ave gone?
  I only told yer what 'd 'elp yer t' live
  I was dyin? – out 'ere that was just another piece of
    information
DAUGHTER. I got very afraid
  She said she wouldnt wait more than a month
  When it was time t' start back I found some signs on a
    rock – so I knew I was near people
  I was runnin further away from yer so that I could get
    back t'yer
  Ridiculous! I argued all the time I was runnin, day after
    day, round an round in me 'ead till I shouted t' meself
    t' shut up
  I was so determined – if a dagger'd bin stuck in me back
    my body would've spat it out so that I could keep
    runnin!
MIDDLE-AGED MAN (*to* MOTHER). Try if its comfortable
  (*To the* YOUNG MAN.) 'Old the 'andle an I'll steady the
    side

  The MIDDLE-AGED MAN *and the* YOUNG MAN *help*
  MOTHER *into the cart.*

YOUNG MAN. Go steady on the boards – you're not a
    balancin act
MIDDLE-AGED MAN. Not a throne on wheels but it'll get
    there
  What d'yer say?
MOTHER. Its perfect!
  Will yer really push me?
YOUNG MAN. Easier than carryin yer

Lugged one old boy on a stretcher five weeks
Me arms were a foot longer
'E cursed an shouted at every jolt – I was scared t' breathe
   in case it upset 'im
The moment 'e sees our 'ouses 'e jumps off the stretcher,
   stands on 'is 'ead and yells yipeeee!
See 'im now an' the cantankerous old bugger says I'd
   rather be bombed than saved by you!
If I was carryin 'is coffin 'e'd stick 'is 'ead out an tell me
   t' bury 'im somewhere else

MIDDLE-AGED MAN. Yer'd drop 'im

YOUNG MAN. I was keepin that secret
   (*To* MOTHER.) I didnt put the 'oles in the ground: I
   wasnt alive

MIDDLE-AGED MAN. Lad if yer was a book yer wouldnt
   know what pages 're for

MAN (*to* MOTHER). All these things 'ere?

MOTHER. Yes just these

MAN (*to the* WOMAN). You got anythin else?

The WOMAN *shakes her head.*

We'll leave yer alone a minute
Its the last time you'll see this place

MOTHER 2. I've seen all I want t' see of it
   I'll carry it away in me 'ead – I wish I didnt
   We can go

MIDDLE-AGED MAN. Yer can lie flat or sit up when yer
   want t' look round
   Use your bundle as a cushion
   (*To the* WOMAN.) There's room for your things – she can
   use 'em for more cushions

The WOMAN *doesnt respond.*

She'll put them in later – she's afraid t' overload it

YOUNG MAN. Shame – its 'er cart

MAN. Lets go

MIDDLE-AGED MAN. I'll push first – get yer used t' it before the 'uman 'urricane takes over

YOUNG MAN. Couple of days we'll be challengin 'em t' races

Everyone goes out except the WOMAN. *She stands still for a moment, then looks down at the bread in her hands and eats. She chokes it out into her hand but crams it back into her mouth, forces it down her throat with her fingers and swallows violently, making a strangling sound.*

MIDDLE-AGED MAN (*off*). Come on

The MAN *comes on.*

MAN. D'yer want t' follow on be'ind till you're ready t' catch up?

The first few weeks back with people are 'ard – it soon gets easier

Yer could sleep a little way off on your own an join us in the mornin's?

No response.

They've got t' get the sick woman back as fast as they can – we can follow on slowly an I'll keep you company

Tell me what I can do?

WOMAN. Im not comin

MAN. Not at all?

No response.

Yer cant stay out 'ere!

No one does that!

(*Apologising.*) The young man makes 'is silly jokes t' cheer 'imself up in this – (*Vague gesture.*) graveyard

Please come

WOMAN. Go away

MAN. I dont know what t' do

Im not askin yer t' go back t' the old world – that'd be like an invitation t' the grave

We dont 'ave so many guns an bombs that even the livin are corpses!

Its not safe out 'ere – there could be an unexploded bomb under our feet!

Yer'll change yer mind an then 'ave t' run t' catch up

WOMAN. That'll be all right then

MAN. Yer cant stay 'ere

WOMAN. Im used t' it

MAN. Yer shouldnt get used t' it!

'Used t' it' is as bad as 'some of 'em'll survive'!

Its just pissin on the ones 'oo didnt!

WOMAN (*looks off*). Those people've stopped – you're 'oldin 'em up

That woman perked up when she saw 'er daughter – but that'll've taken a lot out of 'er – an she didnt 'ave much left

If I was you I'd 'urry if yer want t' get 'er alive t' where-ever-it-is

MAN (*calls*). She wants t' stay

(*To the* WOMAN). They wont go without yer

They'd feel they was droppin another bomb

O yes you ain the only one 'oo 'as t' struggle t' keep themself in one piece!

At least the lot 'oo dropped the bombs 'ad some excuse: they 'adnt seen what they'd do

We 'ave – we ain addin t' that misery – not even the little bits of cruelty that 'appened so often in your world they werent even noticed

If we did that we'd know we weren't 'uman!

That's *our* pain – an our good fortune

The MIDDLE-AGED MAN *and the* YOUNG MAN *come on.*

MIDDLE-AGED MAN. Dont yer believe we've got a settlement

Yer saw 'ow 'appy the girl was – would she deceive 'er mother?

WOMAN. They're nothin t' do with me – two strangers come an I 'elped 'em out – now the lot of yer clear off

YOUNG MAN. Dont mess us about: we need a strong girl like you t' 'elp with the pushin

MIDDLE-AGED MAN. Its not a joke

YOUNG MAN. I dont 'ave t' be told that

We cant go without yer

There's a party when we get back!

This time even the cantankerous old bugger'd cry!

Please come – it takes us weeks t' get the sand out of our clothes

When yer pick them up t' get dressed in the mornin they leave sand on the ground

We cant leave yer 'ere

MIDDLE-AGED MAN. We'll build yer a shelter outside the 'ouses – yer'd like that

We can dig yer a patch an give yer seed

Then we can keep an eye on yer – an yer can call when yer need 'elp

The DAUGHTER *and* MOTHER *come on.*

YOUNG MAN. She wont come

MOTHER. Yer looked after me so well

Now let me an my daughter take –

WOMAN. Bugger off the lot of yer!

I didnt ask yer t' come 'ere!

This is my place! Yer've got everywhere else!

Cant I 'ave one place t' be at peace!

MOTHER. Dont be so bloody ungrateful!

These people 've come all that way!

'Ow can I go off an get well when I know you're 'ere?

What sort of peace of mind would I 'ave?

Not even walkin, bein pushed!

You're the most selfish woman I know!

WOMAN. You 'ad your choice – yer could've died!

MAN. Its like findin a raft at sea an one of the survivors
asks t' stay!

WOMAN. Why not if that's what she wants!

MAN. Yer 'avent even got your cart!

WOMAN. That bloody cart! Take the bloody cart!

I dont need the bloody thing! – I only 'ave t' carry more
junk t' put in it!

(*To the* YOUNG MAN.) It creaks – the noise drives me
mad – that put your mind at rest?

(*To the* MAN.) Not fit t' judge?

I've bin 'ere long enough t' judge meself an earn the right
t' judge others!

What can you offer me!

If I threw one 'andful of this sand over your 'ouses I'd
bury em!

MAN (*to the* DAUGHTER). All this wranglin's bad for your
mother – we must get started – its a long journey

Talk t' 'er an bring 'er with yer

(*To* MOTHER.) Take my arm – it'll be all right

The MAN *and the* YOUNG MAN *help* MOTHER *out. The*
MIDDLE-AGED MAN *follows them.*

MOTHER (*going*). Let 'er ride in the cart

YOUNG MAN (*going*). Sh

DAUGHTER. I must go with my mother – I cant stay an live
with you –

WOMAN. Live with me? What d'yer think I am? I wouldnt
take yer away from that sick woman!

DAUGHTER. I could've stayed if I 'ad a choice

You 'elped my mother an I'd try t' 'elp you in anyway
yer asked –

WOMAN. I'm askin yer t' go!

DAUGHTER. – even if I 'ad t' stay out 'ere till yer changed your mind or died – which you'd find less of a change!

Most of these people were only on their own a few years – that boy was born in the settlement

They see the wilderness every time they look out of their first-floor windows

Everytime they go down the street they're walkin towards it

It terrifies them: one day they'll be part of it

Out 'ere they dont know if they're walkin on dirt or 'uman ash: both

WOMAN. 'Oo told you that?

DAUGHTER. You – an my mother

(*She points to the ground.*) There's a nail – they search for nails like we search for food – but they didnt see it

I see lot of things they cant

Its as if there was a rock in the road an they walk straight into it!

I know what'll 'appen t' them – I see what they'll do t' themselves

Its like watchin babies: they babble and dont know that one day their noise'll be words

They 'avent left the 'ouse but I see them comin in through the door after a long journey . . . with sad faces and gifts in their 'ands

I dont know what it means . . .

This place isn't empty is it? Its full of people you knew

Leave them – they can't 'elp you

(*Laughs.*) Yer should see that lot sittin on chairs!

Like birds perched on a wall gossipin!

When I sit on a chair I 'ave t' 'ang on with both 'ands or I'll fall off!

People 'oo can sit on chairs are very clever

They've got all the gadgets an machines – they never go cold an 'ungry!

Its a paradise: an later on they may even learn what you learned in the wilderness

Some of the people they take back die – they'd've lived longer out 'ere

My mother's illness'd come back if she went there without me

Yer can eat an starve an be cold under a blanket

If you come I'll 'ave two mothers – I need two in the world I was born in

Please – paradise would be such fun with you!

WOMAN. You said you wanted t' be my child . . . ?

You're a kind girl . . . I wish I'd known you before . . . now it's too late

I cant come

You'll think Im mad

When you dumped your mother on me – its all right, Im glad you did – I started t' remember: yer see, you gave me a new life too

I thought you an your mother'd been my neighbours when you were a kid

Then I realised you 'adnt: I'd made a mistake

But I let myself pretend you 'ad: it 'elped me t' remember things that really 'appened

And then I started t' remember things I couldnt believe could 'appen – till t'day –

And now somethin terrible's 'appened

I pretended about you an your mother – but that man *is* my son

DAUGHTER. 'E cant be

WOMAN. I dont expect yer t' believe me

T' meet after so long – everythin was against it – a world was destroyed an the rubble piled up between us – but even that couldnt keep us apart!

I've met my son!

I cant be mistaken: 'e made sure of that!

It'd be a miracle if I *didnt* know 'im!

If I'm wrong – I've confused somethin I 'ad t' keep clear

That was why I was in the wilderness – otherwise I'd've killed myself long ago – willingly!

If Im wrong about that Im mad

And if they took me back t' their place they'd 'ave t' build a mad 'ouse t' keep me in!

DAUGHTER. If 'e's your son go an tell 'im!

WOMAN. If 'e came down that road on 'is knees t' ask forgiveness I'd dig up the road t' stop 'im with my bare 'ands – yes, if it was made of rock!

DAUGHTER. 'E isnt your son – it's not possible!

WOMAN. I know 'im! – as much as you knew that was a nail!

DAUGHTER. I'll go an tell 'im you say 'e's your –

WOMAN. No!

Bombs dont wipe out what 'e did: they make a memorial to it!

I wouldnt be buried in the same earth as 'im if there was another!

I cant even look where 'e stands – if our lives depended on it I couldnt tell yer what 'e was doing!

Take that torment from my side!

That's my 'appiness – and I want it

I can live in this 'ell – not 'is paradise!

I can still talk but my mind knows I need t' be silent

I was ripped up like an execution wall – I tried t' 'old all those who died in my arms but they fell t' the ground

Take those men away – tell them the lies that'll let them go – they'll be 'appy t' get away – then let them be at peace

Im content –

DAUGHTER. No

WOMAN. – where 'e isnt

Say I'll follow in a few days – that'll put their consciences t' sleep

If they come back I'll be gone

DAUGHTER. If 'e's your son talk t' 'im – dont quarrel after all the –

WOMAN. Hu!

I let 'im go out of kindness!

The worst punishment I could inflict on 'im is tell 'im 'oo I am

'E didnt know me: let 'im enjoy 'is ignorance

We've spent eighteen years in the wilderness – so I can ask you to do something no one else would do for me

Take 'im away

Dont say another word

The WOMAN *kisses the* DAUGHTER.

The DAUGHTER *goes. The* WOMAN *watches her in silence for a moment.*

So: I cut off the last of 'uman flesh: (*To the bundle.*) – if only you'd speak . . . ?

The WOMAN *goes off with her things.*

SIXTEEN

A Room in the New Community

A table and chairs. The DAUGHTER *brings in another chair. The* MAN *brings in cutlery and two plates of food.*

DAUGHTER. Is it a disaster?

MAN. No

(*Calls.*) Bring some water

DAUGHTER. P'raps the others'll work

The MAN *puts the plates on the table. They eat.*

MAN. Not if this one doesnt – nothing mechanically wrong
  – cant get it to work without petrol
  They're portable generators they used when there was no
    cable
  We tried to start it on current – then run it on steam
  Must be like putting a saddle on a car

The YOUNG MAN *enters with a plate of food, glasses and a
jug of water. He sits at the table and eats.*

YOUNG MAN. Forget it
  People managed without electricity for centuries
DAUGHTER. This place is so busy!
  Everyone 'ammerin an carryin an measurin
  The skyline changes every day
MAN. We're lucky we dont 'ave t' go back t' the stone age
  We live over an industrial site – dig up the machines an
    try t' start 'em – or use 'em for somethin else
  We build 'ouses with the tools they used t' make bombs
  Like takin a knife out of a suicide's hand an cuttin a loaf
    with it
  What becomes of us depends on electricity – power
YOUNG MAN. Bombs were power
MAN. The more power a society has the more it changes –
    an the more people change
  That brings things to a crisis
  New power – new people: old owners – old society
  So you change the owners – or society blows itself up
  Its a law
YOUNG MAN. Stick t' candles
MAN. The person who first put an edge on flint started t'
    make H bombs
  If you get rid of electricity you get rid of the 'uman mind

DAUGHTER. Does that mean that when you've built this place someone 'as to blow it up?

MAN. No

Societies dont have to destroy themselves

People can learn

If the garden of Eden had been full of machines Adam wouldnt 'ave 'ad t' eat apples

The machines would've shown him how to make the world work

Well we've got machines coming out of the ground

We're not so ignorant we have t' invent gods t' teach us 'ow t' be 'uman

MOTHER *and the* MIDDLE-AGED MAN *come in.* MOTHER *wears clean clothes and supports herself on a stick. The* MIDDLE-AGED MAN's *hands are oily and he carries a folded oil rag in his hands.*

DAUGHTER. We didnt wait

MOTHER. Im slow

The YOUNG MAN *half stands.*

MOTHER. No no – let me

I dont get enough exercise

(*To the* MIDDLE-AGED MAN.) If you're staying wash your 'ands

(*To the three at the table.*) The crowd 'ad a disappointment

They watch machines like we watched fireworks

MOTHER *and the* MIDDLE-AGED MAN *go out.*

DAUGHTER. So you're better than the old people?

MAN. That's not the question

Yer dont save the world by being good or blow it up by being bad

All the big crimes were committed for the best reasons

What did you do when you ate our bread? – threw up

Because you were used t' eatin shit
Eatin shit is what they called culture
They were so used t' eatin shit their bodies worked
  backwards
When they spoke shit came out of their mouths
They weaned the kids on it
They died for the right t' eat it
They blew the world up t' defend it
In the end democracy was just the way the military gave
  orders to civilians
We dont 'ave t' live like that – work for their owners –
  drop their bombs – eat their shit
Why should we vomit up the ideas that'll let us live?

*MOTHER comes in with a plate of food. The YOUNG MAN
pours water into a glass for her.*

YOUNG MAN. Your room's ready
  You 'ave t' pick the furniture
  You can 'ave your own room if you change your mind
DAUGHTER. She wants t' be near me
MOTHER (*to the MAN, nodding over her shoulder*). You're in
  trouble – 'e's on the moan
YOUNG MAN (*explaining to the MAN*). You out on the 'ill
  this mornin

  MOTHER sits. They eat in silence.

MOTHER. Good

  Silence.

MOTHER. I cant eat if you stare at me love
MAN. What? . . .
DAUGHTER. Never 'ad furniture before
MOTHER. We dont need much

  The MAN leaves the table.

MOTHER. Two chairs an a bed – till you find a lad t' sleep
with

The MIDDLE-AGED MAN *comes in with a plate of food. He
sits at the table and eats.*

MIDDLE-AGED MAN. We're not beaten yet
Four generators – even more
Get one working they'll all work
MAN. The wind's started t' blow the dust on to the edge of
the fields
YOUNG MAN. Could blow the crops out the ground
Centuries before the storms die down
The wind used t' be black
MOTHER. I saw it
Night an day an no evenin between
Night came in a straight line
YOUNG MAN. Chriss . . . !
MOTHER. Dont want t' see that again
What'll we do if it gets bad?
DAUGHTER. Go in the shelters
MIDDLE-AGED MAN. Could last years – we've only got
supplies for a few months
If the generators worked it'd be different
They could be the difference between life and death
YOUNG MAN (*to* MOTHER). We'll be all right: yer'll teach
us 'ow t' survive in the wilderness
MAN. You could go through a storm with a naked flame on
your 'and
MOTHER. I wouldnt try: that's your first lesson
MIDDLE-AGED MAN. On the 'ill again this mornin?
MAN. She could be stood out in the dust tryin t' make
'erself come in
Get all the way – then panic an go back
YOUNG MAN (*to* MOTHER). If yer need anythin repaired
for the room I'll fix it

MAN. Now there's no light at night she might think we've been wiped out – disease

MIDDLE-AGED MAN. Light was a waste

Anyone 'oo wanted 'ad already seen it – the rest were too far out or *didnt* want!

MAN. Why'd she say I was 'er son?

(*Shrug.*) My age . . .

MOTHER. I read a story before the bombs

Indians – if they were being followed they walked backwards so their footprints pointed the wrong way

Anyone followin them went off in the wrong direction

There was a forest – dark – with a monster inside

If they wanted t' destroy someone they went t' the edge of the forest and walked off backwards

Their enemy came running along the footprints an straight into the dark

Simple

MIDDLE-AGED MAN. What's that supposed t' mean?

YOUNG MAN. Dont follow in anyone's footsteps

We should've pinched 'er doll – then she'd've 'ad t' come

MOTHER. Dont be so sure

She mothered it but per'aps in the back of 'er mind she knew it was a rag

If she'd brought it 'ere you'd (*The* MIDDLE-AGED MAN.) make it a cradle an you'd (*The* YOUNG MAN.) take it walkies

If yer'd kidded 'er per'aps she'd've gone on kiddin 'erself

I dont know

(*Shrugs.*) When she propped it up on the cart *I* used t' think the funny little thing was laughin at me

MIDDLE-AGED MAN. Dont understand women an dolls

(*The others laugh.*)

Look after machines – not stand on 'ills

YOUNG MAN. When I think of 'er out in the winter me stomach's sick

    Cant stand other people's sufferin's
    Its as if she 'ad t' be cruel t' 'erself

MIDDLE-AGED MAN. We're not goin lookin
    If yer cant stand other people's sufferin's 'elp me
    I'll suffer till the generators work
    An so'll you if the wind comes

YOUNG MAN. Wouldnt find 'er anyway – she'd see us
    comin an vanish

MIDDLE-AGED MAN. She knows what she's doin: not
    everyone needs a 'ouse
    Some people – throw 'em a rope when they're drownin
    an they 'ang themselves

The MIDDLE-AGED MAN *stands and goes out with his plate.*

MOTHER. Dont wait on the 'ill
    I'd like 'er t' live with us – she wont
    She's found 'er own way t' be 'appy
    Per'aps its 'arder for us than it is for 'er – its painful t'
    dig a grave not lie in it
    When a tree's burned one side can be black – all the
    branches twisted an gnarled – twigs burned off – an
    the other side's got green leaves an fruit
    The fruit doesnt taste of ash – its sweeter than if the tree
    was 'ole
    She chose 'er part of the world – let 'er mark it out an
    per'aps when you're ready – later – people'll go there
    an make it their own?
    You youngsters wash up: watchin that machine stand
    idle wore me out

The DAUGHTER *and the* YOUNG MAN *clear the table and
go out with the things.*

MAN. I said to meself she's 'oldin that bundle as if its alive
    – or she's got somethin in it she doesnt want t' crush
    I thought it just showed out there even rags 're valuable

The bundle in one 'and an the bread in the other
I looked at the end of 'er nails – they was as clear as a
    spider's legs
Each one – a perfect arc – pitch black
As if a jeweller 'd made somethin out of dirt

The DAUGHTER *comes back.* MOTHER *has fallen asleep.*

MAN. Your mother's let me talk t' meself
    Let's get 'er t' bed
DAUGHTER (*takes* MOTHER'*s arm*). You fell asleep
MOTHER. Nonsense . . . I was tellin 'im what t' put in our
    room

The DAUGHTER *and the* MAN *start to take* MOTHER *out.*

MOTHER. We dont want much – I bump into things if I
    don't concentrate
MAN (*to* DAUGHTER). I've got t' collect my kids
    You come – you're their wilderness aunt

The DAUGHTER *and the* MAN *take* MOTHER *out.*

SEVENTEEN

Wilderness

Three months later.
Bitterly cold. The WOMAN *wears black. Her things are on the*
ground. She is alone and stares intently off. The MAN *comes on*
from the direction of her stare. He wears a long grey herring-
bone coat. A length of woollen cloth is wrapped round his
shoulders and muffles his neck and half his face. On his back
there is a coat rolled up in the shape of a bedding roll. A
knapsack hangs from his shoulder.

MAN. Brought yer some tins

    You all right?

WOMAN. What yer want?

MAN. Your friends –

WOMAN. Uh?

MAN. – the woman yer nursed – yer wouldnt know 'er since
    she's 'ad good food an lived in 'er own 'ouse
    (*Sits.*) Sit down
    (*Looks round.*) Long way t' this graveyard
    Come back with me?
    Shall I open a tin?

WOMAN. Leave 'em when yer go

    The WOMAN *picks up her bundle, walks away and stops
    with her back to the* MAN.

MAN. The black storm's comin: they say it'll be as bad as
    the winter after the bombs
    Yer survived then – yer was younger
    (*Gently.*) This one'll topple yer over an cover yer
    It'll be 'ard for *us* – out '*ere* yer won't stand a chance

WOMAN (*without looking at him*). Seen winters start as bitter
    as this – then a warm wind comes out of nowhere an
    yer'd 'ave an early spring if things still grew

MAN. Why wont yer come back?
    (*No response.*)
    Yer said yer're stayin because I'm your son
    If yer die Im t' blame
    That gives me a right t' some answer
    (*No response.*)
    Im not your son

WOMAN. Yer've got the decency t' want t' deny it

MAN. I knew me mother
    I was with 'er when she died
    I wish you were 'er
    I miss 'er
    You're nothin like 'er

WOMAN. Stop it!

MAN. Im not going away

WOMAN. Yer wont last the winter 'ere

   I've lived through a winter ten years long

   Yer breath turns t' snow an falls out of yer mouth when
      yer open it t' curse

   You're used t' 'ouses an fires an nursin when yer're sick

   Yer'd curl up an cry for me blanket

   They wont send out a search party till spring

   Then they'd gossip

   Sit over their fires: lad led astray – the poor world an the
      creatures in it

   Spare them the bother

   Gossip gossip – I'd rather 'ear bones rattle on cement

   Go away

MAN. No

   If Im ill yer'll 'ave t' nurse me or abandon me – up to
      you

WOMAN. Clever little shit!

   Yer ain dumpin yerself on me again!

   I wouldnt prise yer off the ice if yer was stuck t' it!

MAN. Why d' yer 'ate me?

WOMAN. Because yer was born!

   You're not messin me about this time my lad!

   You're not my son? Good! – we dont 'ave t' speak t' each
      other!

   Clear off an let me be a 'uman mother 'oo only gave birth
      t' uman kids!

MAN. If that's 'ow yer treat your son Im glad Im not 'im!

   Yer make me responsible for 'alf the world's misery – no,
      all of it! – then tell me t' clear off!

   I pity any kid of yours!

WOMAN. Yer pity my kid?

   Get out of 'ere!

   I gave you birth – yer gave me the right t' be your death!

And I will be, late though it is!

Leave me alone! Yer're not my son!

MAN. What did 'e do?

WOMAN. Go away!

I've seen the world drip off the end of a spade!

I've seen the sea turned t' stone!

Yes – stood on the shore – the cliffs'd fallen into the sea
– the waves set as 'ard as cement

The dust on that sea'll always be dry

Stone fish stick out of the waves

People 'oo'd run into the sea out of the fire – or were
they starvin an after the fish? – stick out of the solid
waves

Some of them with their feet in the air – some trapped
from the waist down

Now they're skeletons

I thought I 'eard the sea movin under the waves

No the skeletons are smaller than the 'oles their bodies
made in the cement

The wind was rattlin the bones in the 'oles

That was the sound of that sea

Go 'ome – an leave me in peace

MAN. What did I do?

WOMAN. These 'ands took care of yer before your own
could

Washed your face an straightened your 'air

Why arent they scarred? Or stained? Or covered in hyena
'air?

No no I dont want t' remember . . . !

When I bore you the earth would've pushed you back in
my womb if it'd known what was goin t' walk on it!

Why didnt the sheets scream?

Go away!

MAN. What did I do?

WOMAN. When you came 'ome – as a soldier – whatever you did would've bin wrong

That wasnt your fault

I asked yer t' do somethin wicked – a crime – but if I could ask, you could've done it!

Everythin else was wrong: yer could've done the one wrong thing that would've put the rest right!

It'd've bin my crime too: but that day I could've bin struck by lightnin an lived!

I sat at the table an waited

When yer'd come back I'd've 'elped yer, fed yer – washed your 'ands

'Oo can wash my 'ands?

If I used the world as a towel the grass'd die in the last fields, even on the graves of infants

MAN. What did I do?

WOMAN. They wanted a dead child

MAN. You killed it?

WOMAN. I set out – went through the streets like a wolf – but I didnt

I gave birth t' the son 'oo killed my child

Killed it in the cot I'd nursed 'im in

I was so 'appy when yer was born – smiled – wiped the spit from your mouth

Then yer came back – a killer with the face of a knife

Not one of your fingers stopped when yer killed my child

No each of them twisted as if it was a 'and!

Why mine, why mine!

MAN. I dont know

WOMAN. It was killed by my own son! Its too close! Its out of nature!

MAN. If 'e was lined up with others an one 'ad t' be shot, would 'e 'ave stepped forward?

Per'aps 'e only did t' your kid what 'e'd've done t' imself?

Or was 'e shit scared an took the easiest way out?

Then 'e was a bastard!

Is that what yer want?

Tell me

If the men 'oo dropped the bombs 'd bin like your son
they'd've dropped them on their own kids

Yer dont want sons like that

Yer want your sons t' be ordinary killers so yer can be
good mothers

Tell me, Im waitin

WOMAN. I dont know, I dont know

MAN. Nor do I – I never met 'im – I cant tell yer anythin

Let me take yer 'ome

We'll walk slowly an talk – you tell me about your son an
I'll try t' say what 'e'd say

Then we'll blame 'im or forgive 'im – whatever seems
best

There are soldiers in the settlement: yer could talk t'
them

Your son might even turn up – you did!

(*No response.*)

I made as big a mess of this as your son would've

March eight weeks – worked it out on the march: give
the tins – talk calm – then offer t' find 'er son

Felt sure yer'd fall for that . . .

I wanted t' teach yer t' live in a 'ouse

Watch yer sit at table and eat like a 'uman bein: yer swill
like a pig

Listen t' yer move in the 'ouse – 'ear the click when yer
shut your door

See your face in the mornin

Is that bad for the world?

If someone came back from the dead we'd never take our
eyes off them – long after the dirt 'd fallen from their
face an bin washed out of their clothes

Why did I come 'ere?

You're not my mother
All this way for a 'eap of rags and bones that stinks an
    says no
A woman with teeth on the ends of 'er fingers
What've you got t' offer?

WOMAN. Nothin an if I did you wouldnt get it

MAN. What's in that bundle

WOMAN. My things

MAN. Why d'yer 'old it so close?

WOMAN. So's its not lost

MAN. I'll make an agreement with yer
You 'ad twenty years t' know your son: give me a few
    days
Per'aps I can work out why 'e killed the child?
Let me stay a week
Then I'll do what yer say
I wont struggle anymore

WOMAN. Your sort cant keep their word
The world'll creak on somewhere new an yer'll find that
    interestin – an then that'll be a new reason t' stay
The business between you an me's bin seen an said
This isnt your place: the tears never reach the ground 'ere
The pain's so deep they leave the eye but never rest

MAN. Yer talk t' it

WOMAN. Ah I see the old cow's bin gossipin
Everyone talks when they're on their own
Surprised a grown man takes it serious
(*No response.*)
Stay a week
Keep out of my way – talk t' yourself
When a week's up I'll tell yer t' go
Yer wont but at least yer'll see you're a liar

MAN. Then what'll yer do?

WOMAN. Yer see! . . .
What I'll do then is my affair

Why d'yer still stare? – its a cloth
(*Opens the bundle.*) Empty
Nothin in it
I kept it in case it comes in 'andy
Rags are useful out 'ere or at your place
Empty nothin
(*She drops the cloth.*)
My baby's dead
Now if I could go t' the dead an press the air out of their
    bodies
If I was as gentle as if I was standin one grain of sand on
    another
When the air passed through their mouths their tongues
    might speak
If they died with the truth in their mouths
An tell me why I suffered an 'oo its for, an why we live
    on this earth an are buried in it?
An afterwards if I'd bin gentle they'd thank me because
    I'd let them speak
MAN (*whistles once flatly through his teeth*).
Is that the question?
Let it rest – once you 'ad 'im in your belly – it was close
    enough
Let it pass
The dead cant answer
They'd ask you their questions – shout an shout an shout
    – till yer put your 'and over their mouth t' stop them –
    an they'd chew it down t' the wrist!
Live till your own time comes t' be dead
It'll be soon
Till then you answer the questions
WOMAN. 'Ave yer got tins?
MAN. Yeh
An a tin opener
We started a can factory

WOMAN. The winter'll be cold – the gossip was right
  I went through the black wind once: I turned aside but it
    caught me
  I went through the edge: soot an dust an ash – black
  It filled the 'ollow where I 'old the bundle against my
    chest
  Then I came out on the white dust – dazzled – I was 'alf
    glad t' look back at the storm
  Yer could see where it'd passed
  One 'alf of the 'ill was white an the other 'alf black as if
    it'd bin painted along a line
  I 'ad t' shake the ash off like a dog worryin itself when it
    comes out of the river

EIGHTEEN

Wilderness

Next morning.
The MAN lies asleep on the ground. He wears his coat and his
head is wound in his muffler
He wakes and immediately stands, looks round, snatches up his
things and runs out.

NINETEEN

Wilderness

An hour later.
The WOMAN walks on with her bundle. She is wrapped up
and her head is down.

MAN (*off*). Stop!

The WOMAN *goes on walking. The* MAN *runs on.*

Yer said yer'd wait! – a week!
Not one day! One day!
Liar! Liar!

The WOMAN *stops and stares at him a moment.*

WOMAN. The noise it makes
　A waste of time t' wait – went along with it t' shut yer up
MAN. Liar! Liar!

The MAN *crouches on the ground to regain his breath.*

WOMAN. Dont cling an row
　That's not the way t' conduct yerself
　People'll just say what yer want t' get rid of yer

The WOMAN *starts to go. The* MAN *gets up and stops her.*

MAN. Yer gave your word! Liar!
WOMAN. 'E understands nothin!
　That was yesterday – a 'ole day's gone – I broke me word
MAN. Yer said – could stay a – week!

The MAN *crouches in front of her to bar her way and struggles
to regain his breath.*

WOMAN. Why stay? Curiosity? – an empty crowd?
　Yer can see I wont change
　What a shame when someone cant see what they should
　　do . . .
MAN. Got your 'ouse – ready
　Quiet – warm – corner 'ouse
　Watch out the windows – get used t' people – till you're
　　ready t' join 'em
　Put furniture in

Arranged it – 'ow yer'd like

A fireplace – the windows work – a garden

WOMAN. No

MAN. There's a green cover on the bed – an a carpet on the
floor – red

WOMAN. No

MAN. I'd be your son

'Ow yer wanted 'im t' be – I'd try

WOMAN. No

MAN. It'd be better than a bundle!

Not a bundle!

WOMAN. The bundle wasnt my kid

It was the other kid

Or the kids in the ruins

I passed through cities where a 'and reached out from
every brick

I'm sorry your visit didnt work out as yer wanted

It was a good visit for me – thanks – Im glad yer came

That must be all

MAN. I didnt ask t' meet yer in this 'ell!

I didnt ask yer t' call me son!

Now keep your word!

I've got t' go back – t' work

Dont make me drag this wilderness with me!

WOMAN. Give me your 'and

The MAN *reaches his hand to her. She stoops and helps him
to his feet.*

This may be my last winter – I'll choose 'ow I live it

If I let yer yer'd take the air I drew in my mouth for your
own breath

MAN. Not just for me – for the others – its your place –
come back t' them

WOMAN. No

Go 'ome – your friends need yer – yer'll know 'ow t' 'elp
them

MAN. Yer wont come?

WOMAN. No.

MAN. I'll visit yer
(*The* WOMAN *laughs.*)
Not as your son – or ask for anythin
Yer cant live two winters 'ere
If yer changed your mind yer wouldnt 'ave the strength
t' reach us
I'll come t' see if yer need 'elp

WOMAN. A year?
Will yer still find this place?

MAN. O yes
I know the way like the back of me 'and
We've trod a road

WOMAN. A year . . .
Why does 'e bother with calendars?
I let things pass
Per'aps 'e'll be too busy t' come
Then dont bother – no need
In a year – when its cold – I'll walk on this road
If I dont speak dont talk t' me: look
I shant see if you're 'ere or not
(*Half raises her hand in farewell.*)
Its best if you go

MAN (*hands her a bundle*). Yer left your tins
(*Unrolls a coat*). A coat – padded – wintersports

The coat is long and made of light blue, padded nylon.

It was my last argument

WOMAN. Ah
Warm – padded
I dont feel the cold but I'll wrap it round my body

The MAN *goes. The* WOMAN *stares at the coat for a moment.*
Then she sits. She sleeps. Time. She wakes.

What?
'Ow long?
A man . . . gave me a coat
Must move

She gathers her things and wraps them in a blanket.

Too open winter 'ere – up there
Tins – dont touch – emergency
Padded

She picks up her unwound bundle.

A useful thing . . . is . . . useful

She drapes herself in the padded coat and starts to leave,
dragging her things along the ground behind her on the
blanket. After a few steps she stops and looks back at the
blanket.

Draggin it . . . on the ground

She stares at the blanket and gives it a short sharp jerk
towards her. It grates on the ground. She turns back to face
the way she's going and walks a few steps. She lets go of the
bundle. Without looking back she clenches her fists and walks
a few more steps. She stops. She drops dead.

TWENTY

Wilderness

A year later.
The coat has been turned over. In it are the WOMAN's *bones,*
not as a skeleton but lying roughly in the human shape. In the

stomach: tins, some open and empty. The MAN *comes on. He carries a bundle of provisions. He stops and stares at the coat. He lowers the bundle to the ground with a slight thud.*

End.

Commentary on *The War Plays*

At last the darkness thinned and dispersed like smoke or cloud. We saw real daylight and even the sun shone, but with a yellow light as in an eclipse. With terror we saw everything changed, buried in ashes as deep as snowdrifts. We went back to Misenum and looked after our bodily needs as best we could and then passed an anxious night alternating between hope and fear.

Of course these details are not important enough for history. You will read them without any idea of recording them.

> Pliny on the eruption of
> Vesuvius on 24 August AD 79
> (*Letters*)

Palermo Improvisation

I devised a scheme for improvisation by students at Palermo university. A soldier returns home with orders to choose a baby from his street and kill it. Two babies live in his street: his mother's and a neighbour's. His mother welcomes him and shows him her baby. He goes to the neighbour and she shows him her baby. He kills it and goes home. What would this show? Airmen killed children in Vietnam and were demobbed and went home to their children; soldiers train with nuclear weapons and go home on leave to their children; technicians make nuclear weapons and at the end of each shift go home to their children; and civilians give their children a home and their soldiers threaten other children with nuclear death. When the soldier in the improvisation returned to his mother and her baby we would see one of the contradictions in which we live. But as I planned the improvisation I realised how it would end. I noted the end in my notebook.

Next day the students improvised. I asked them to act honestly what the soldier would do. The soldier came home and was welcomed by his mother. She showed him her baby. He went next door. His neighbour welcomed him and gave him her baby to hold. The action became very slow. The soldier seemed to be staring into a watch as if he tried to tell the time from its workings. He gave the baby back to the neighbour. Then he went home and killed his mother's baby. In my notebook I had written that that is what he would do. He and the other students were surprised that he had done it. They were surprised when the next student to play the soldier also murdered the 'wrong' baby. All the students played the soldier and none of them could bring himself to kill the 'right' baby. It was a paradox.

Was the paradox true only on stage? In a nazi prisoner-of-war camp in Russia in 1942 prisoners were paraded every night for roll call. After all of them had responded to their number a few were killed in front of the others. They were not killed because they had committed what we would recognize as an offence, but to frighten the others into obedience. The commandant and his guards were not sadists – killing made life easier for everyone, it was an aid to discipline.

Some of the guards were Russian. Every few days new prisoners were brought in. One day it happened that one new prisoner was the brother of one of the guards. Two Russians: a nazi and a communist. Being a good administrator the commandant abhorred all waste and made the best use of every murder. That night after roll call he told the prisoners they would see a demonstration of nazi discipline. The communist brother was brought forward and the commandant ordered the nazi brother to shoot him. He pointed his pistol at his brother's head. The commandant shouted 'Fire!'. The guard lowered his pistol. He asked the commandant to let someone else shoot his brother.

The commandant probably relished the moment and approved of the request. Didn't it show the great resistance nazis overcame to do their duty? Again he ordered the guard to fire. This time the guard did not even raise his pistol. The commandant would not have relished that. It was military insubordination in front of his prisoners. It is said to be easier to kill someone at a distance than when you are face to face with them. But the nazi guard had often placed his gun as close to his victim's head as we place pen to paper or knife to bread. In those days nazis killed as other people pick their teeth – to remove a nuisance. The commandant told the guard that his refusal would not save his brother. He – the commandant – would shoot the prisoner and then the guard. He ordered the guard to shoot. He would not. A paradox! The commandant shot the guard and his brother. Surely this is one of the world's great stories?

I do not know what was in the commandant's mind as he walked from the square and the bodies – as the commandant had been upset, there would have been seven or eight at the end – were dragged to the ovens. For years he had been taught that Slavs were vermin and wasn't this one more proof? But I am sure – and this is as true of the commandant as it is of the guard – that no one willingly gives up the name of human. It takes a great deal of culture to make us human, it takes even more culture to make us beasts.

Does the paradox occur only in crises, or is it present in much or even all of what we do – creating an ambiguous struggle which determines who we are? If, as I think, that is so, then we are constantly struggling to express our humanity in ways which society, because it is still inhuman, first discourages, then forbids and then corrupts – and finally rewards, calling the corruption 'duty'. This would explain much of human suffering. It would mean that we can only be human in conflict with society – yet society demands the right to define what is 'good'. Good – after love – is the most ambiguous of words.

But the problem is even stranger. Human nature is not 'natural' but is created by society. I do not mean that society imposes a social form on an instinctual, animal nature. Except when it regulates purely physiological functions – such as stabilizing the body's temperature – the human brain works holistically. The higher, learnt cortical synapses are involved in the lower brain's functioning. It is because of this that we can be human. Whenever we act we must do so for human reasons and from human motives. Our unconscious is not more animal than our conscious, it is often even more human. The unconscious sees through us and our social corruption and sends us messages of our humanity, ingeniously and persistently trying to reconcile the divisive tensions in our lives. Our unconscious makes us sane; it is only in an insane society that our unconscious colludes in insanity.

The brain's higher – not its lower – functions are the foundations of our psyche. The infant's mind begins by learning, not being. Our instincts become active only by being connected with analytical, interpretative feelings and images, and later concepts, of the world. At first the process takes the form of malleable, corrigible identifications; later our instincts acquire explanatory motivations, and drives become ideas. We have to distinguish between feelings and emotions. Feelings are genetically formed, emotions are learned. We learn them through experience and interpretation. Emotions mediate between feelings and ideas; this is the way in which we become what we are. Pain is a feeling, sadism and masochism are the cause of emotions. The development of civilization makes our rationalizations and concepts increasingly rational. Slowly – with detours and reversals – history makes us more society's guardians and less its victims. This is part of the process which frees society from political distortions.

We need art because the brain is holistic. It cannot perform its other social functions without art. Art is reason's struggle with rationalization, the traffic between images and ideas. Attempts to reduce art or any other human activity to instinctive, biological impulses, or to give instincts priority in the mind, are a philosophical confusion. The psyche may be likened to a building whose foundations are laid as the ground floor is raised. Our psychology is formed socially.

Under the human instinct of hunger, forming and inform-
ing it, are psychological concepts which are ultimately
derived from social experience and social teaching, just as
under the food on a plate there is a pattern – Amerindian,
Etruscan, Delft, whatever – symbolic of its maker's society.
That is why it takes a great deal of culture to turn people
into killers – whether they kill in uniforms, suits or rags.

Radical Innocence

In the Palermo improvisation the soldier killed his brother
or sister. In the camp the soldier refused to kill his brother.
Both decisions came from the same paradox. The paradox
is never absent from our mind. It is the crux on which
humanness is poised, an expression of the radical innocence
which makes us human. We are born radically innocent,
and neither animal nor human; we create our humanness as
our minds begin to think our instincts. As we grow our
radical innocence becomes embroiled in the social contradictions which turn our cities into armed camps in peace
and ruins in war.

Dostoievsky and Blake understood that evil is a form of
innocence; and even the church accepted that this is so
when it taught that the Devil is a fallen angel. Radical
innocence is the state in which infants discover and interpret the world. The discoveries and interpretations structure the mind's early learning. The mind cannot lose this
structure any more than the unlesioned brain can return to
a state without language. Radical innocence is the psyche's
conviction of its right to live, and of its conviction that it is
not responsible for the suffering it finds in the world or that
such things can be. To believe that it *was* would be to
believe that it had no right to exist. The mind that believed

that could not functionally integrate itself or even intellectually discriminate – it would lose its symbolic ability and be dead. There is no other way we can lose our innocence, even when it turns into our curse. It is the innocence of evil that makes it so terrible.

Children think of the future as adults think of the past. For children the future is the place from which come determined events – events they often rage against. The child cannot escape from the future or its parents' – all authority's – secret knowledge of the future. It does not know the law yet is judged by it. It sees its offences as if they were forced on it, just as we are forced to accept the events of history. We accuse children of committing the crimes of the dead – back to the earliest generations. When they are accused of doing wrong they feel as we would if we were accused of burning Joan of Arc or causing the Black Death. That is why children cannot abandon their sense of innocence – or their knowledge of it. Because *we* bring consciousness, reason and morality into the world, we must see it as unjust and absurd. It is our primal shock.

In its innocence the child judges its judges as guilty – it is a judgement not only against people but against the fact of the world. If a child is to be persuaded that it is responsible for its own wrongs it must be persuaded of the rightness of social teaching. Before radical innocence can submit to authority the child must adopt its judges' judgements. But it cannot simply replace radical innocence with radical guilt; that would mean it had no right to be born, and a mind that attacked itself so radically would destroy itself. So innocence protects itself by becoming corrupt. It accepts that authority's right to be is like the right of pain and evil to be – greater than its own right to be. And as the child passes from being the subject of parental control to being the political subject of the state, radical innocence adopts the political injustice of class society. Education prepares it to be corrupted in this way. We inculcate morality as part of the child's social learning; but the morality is a social teaching based on society's structure, with its practical necessities but also its unjust social distortions. In this way we are corrupted by being made good, consenting, dutiful, law-abiding citizens. The individual gives to his corruption all the force of his innocence. The great social injustices, the class divisions, economic exploitation, wars of conquest and greed, the charade of law-and-order, the prisons and punishments – all these barbarities are sanctioned in the name of the highest good and carried out in the conviction of innocence. We ruin the world by our honest efforts to make it better.

The human mind's strength is that it is not determined by instincts but generates culture; its weakness is not that we inherit animality but that we inherit history and the culture of the past. Reaction and class politics are made plausible because they create the very society they condemn. People who live under threat do become enemies and are devious, aggressive or timid as occasion demands or opportunity provides. Society's interpretation of the world is the model on which it is built. Its illusions become realities, it casts its errors in concrete. And the illusions are passed on – society's survival depends on the cultural socialization of each generation. It is because it is founded on illusions that society endures and is adaptable but difficult to fundamentally change. Illusions are tenacious and subtle in adapting reality to their needs. There is a time when people sleep and a time when they wake; but that is not so of society – for society, sleeping and waking, dream and reality, are the same thing.

The paradox creates social tensions which society uses to strengthen its distorted social relations. Society, which

creates us, deforms us. That is why often, to be good
citizens, it requires us to live lives of violence and colossal
indifference. This is achieved, and innocence turned to
righteousness and reaction, by the creation of guilt. The
mind panics and flees to the protection of its accusers. Guilt
enables society to manipulate people without coercing them
with open force. Indeed guilt is society's way of making
people agents of its force. The innocence in guilt makes
social power, for the guilty, effective and distorting; and by
turning the guilty into agents of social force, innocence is
the cause of social violence. Righteousness is guilt wearing
a uniform. Society cannot deal justly with its problems
because it is founded on misinterpreting them.

The will becomes the state's agent, and if the state is a
class-society – which means that it is morally and intellectually corrupt – then the individual will is corrupt. The
corrupt do not act with the solidarity of the group but the
sweeping conviction of the mob. And this is true of their
leaders, however stately their processions and elevated their
language. Yet when political circumstances change – when
reality can no longer bear any more of our illusions – how
quickly it all changes! The great convictions and causes are
swept aside, though not even all their ruins are enough to
bury their crimes. Almost always soldiers who have massa-
cred the innocent say they did it because authority must be
obeyed. The nazis said it, so did the Americans in Vietnam
and the British in their colonies – and in the Falklands
(however farcical a war the dead are tragic). They – and
often we – do not notice that their excuse is a boast that
they would commit their crimes again. That is how closely
guilt is bound to innocence.

Radical innocence is not a natural state, an aspect of human
nature existing outside history and society. The need for
moral discrimination precedes any particular moral code. A

child's 'why' questions cannot be answered by scientific cause-and-effect answers. Like a judge, the child seeks motives, and it judges the world. As it subjectively develops a living relationship with its home, society and state it cannot resolve all the tensions in the relationship. The unresolved tensions may be corrupted if the unjust state subordinates them to its needs. The will has only to accept that its radical right to *be* is represented and expressed by the state. The proposition is plausible. Even unjust states pass good laws and perform good deeds – society's mere practical existence depends on it. Even corrupt radical innocence must act from good motives. If the morally corrupt were not motivated by innocence they could not commit their crimes and brutalities. That is why human conflicts are so intransigent and destructive. Himmler said 'We gas the Jews out of love'. That is terrible, but it is true. It is the most important remark of the twentieth century – it is its sermon on the mount. If we do not understand it we are left with cynicism, apathy, or the illusions of religion – and what is theology but frozen despair? If it could have been possible for any nazi leader to tell his killers that they were corrupt and that what they did was wrong, then it would have been ontologically impossible for the Third Reich to have come into the world. Instead, the corrupt go to great lengths to do good. Even lonely psychopaths – who have no flashy uniforms or nuclear bombs to encourage their self-esteem – justify their crimes by claiming to be moral agents ('a higher power possessed me') or innocent ('a lower power possessed me') and prove it to their satisfaction – and their judges' bewilderment – by acts of innocent kindness.

When radical innocence is not corrupt it is a force of reason. History is the slow removal of social injustices and distortions and the slow creation of democracy, not only formally but in freedom of the mind. Uncorrupted radical innocence learns from society just as corrupted radical innocence does. Corruption, not innocence, nurtures the child in grown people; if anything of the child survives in adult innocence it is a very old child. Nor do we retain radical innocence by being in the right social class at the right historical time – as if, for example, the industrial revolution made a place in the working class into a holy niche. If democratization is to continue, the working class – the lower class of consumers – must have not merely formal democratic rights, freedom from physical coercion and freedom to choose possessions and goods – it must gain freedom of mind, which is freedom of self and freedom to choose the future.

There are two reasons why society becomes increasingly democratic. The first is its increasing technological and economic complexity, which forces authority to concede more responsibility to its subjects, and ironically even to its victims (states usually accuse their enemies not only of stupidity but also of cleverness). The second reason follows from the first. Our mind cannot functionally integrate itself without an interpretation of the world, and the interpretation must change to accommodate the increasing technological and economic complexity. Our capacity for thought is greater than we need it to be to survive. That endangers us. Ancient peoples had practical uses for the stars but asked *philosophical* questions about them, and their philosophical answers became part of their practical life. A child's questions seem practical but are philosophical – it interprets its instincts in the way the ancients interpreted the stars. A child seeks to understand things in terms of the world: a culture wants to do this but is forced – to be practical – to do it the other way round. So dissatisfaction is built into our species. We could call our dissatisfaction divine if it were not so often devilish. Corrupt radical innocence may turn us into monsters.

But as radical innocence cannot be totally corrupted, cannot be changed in nature (otherwise our intellect would cease to be able to apprehend anything) but merely socially misappropriated and misused, then even the corrupt may sometimes face a contradiction that presents the paradox – as it did to the Russian guard. The paradox does not create mere acts of compassion; these, when they are made by corrupt individuals or corrupt societies, are only justifying tokens of humanity. Did the paradox free the Russian prisoner to ask his brother to shoot him so that at least one of them would live? No. The prisoner's fellow prisoners, though not his kin, were also his brothers. Had the guard lived he would have killed many of them. When the prisoner was shot he knew his death would kill his brother, and that there would be one guard less to kill prisoners – and in the Palermo improvisation it is not the kin but the neighbour who is saved. Nor was the guard's refusal to kill his brother an act of true kindness. A corrupt aggressor's kindness or clemency is no more than the humane gesture that licenses brutality – the kindness is like the alcohol given to troops to make them vicious. Society is made more just – and in the end this is true of individuals, too – only when political change lessens social divisions. The guard's refusal to shoot his brother was meaningless. The brothers died as enemies. Surely the guard had never hated his brother more than when he died for him? It is only that he could not kill him to please the commandant or change the commandant's mind.

The paradox confronts, publically or clandestinely, unjust authority's agents or teachings – and puts at risk those who alone or together act out the consequences of radical innocence. The risk may be taken for much or little, but it puts everything at stake because the action is philosophical. That it *is* philosophical is of great importance to theatre.

Paradoxical actions alone cannot change society but they are part of the forces of change. They show people making history rational and the community moral. Even when the actions are as 'meaningless' as the guard's refusal to murder his brother, they show the irrepressible insubordination that forces reaction to become what it is. Radical innocence must retain its autonomy and self-justification in order to persuade itself of the rightness of the social teaching it adopts; if it did not, the teaching would have no force. Ironically, tyrants govern by consent: a thing is not good because God does it but God does it because it is good – and that, for the faithful, is as true of the leader as it is of God. The leader knows best. This ensnares even people of good will. It is not only why the gaoler handed Socrates the hemlock, it is why Socrates took it: the form of the state was good. It is why the nazis murdered and why we make bombs. Our humanity is not given by the state's answers, but by our questions.

To reaction, all signs – however slight – of radical innocence, would be astounding and inexplicable, if they could not be seen as proof of original sin or our evolutionary encumbrance. But radical innocence is part of history's rational development. In the past many religious martyrs were part of this development, though they saw themselves as part of a theocratic world. The paradox is the sudden, dramatic assertion of radical innocence when it is confronted by a conflict between itself and social teaching, which social teaching cannot reconcile or conjure away. Radical innocence puts the strategic in place of the tactical, and this gives it sweeping dramatic force. It shows, intensely and simply, the whole in the part. It is an emotional ability, but also an intellectual faculty. If it were not so, human beings would not be concerned with values.

We are Sent to the Theatre

In the early world of jungles and deserts, and in the classical world of fifth-century Athens, the whole community went to the drama. If slaves, convicts, the mad and women were sometimes excluded that is because they were not fully members of society. Society sent people to the drama just as it sent them to the fields, the hunt and the well. It seems that now we are not sent to the theatre but choose to go. This is an illusion. We are still sent there by society. It must send us to the theatre even when it can only send representatives. It needs theatre as much as it needs its other institutions – its prisons, universities, parliaments and so on. But just as democratic society wrongly assumes that everyone in it, and not merely the ruling class, has power, so it wrongly assumes that when society sends representatives to the theatre it is sending the community there. Unjust society not only manipulates force by disguising violence as law and order, it also manipulates the rest of culture. Just as it usually sends the wrong people to prison and parliament, so it usually sends the wrong people to theatre. The others it sends to the petrified drama of most film and television – and their frenetic activity is a sign of their moribund state: giving electric shock treatment to a skeleton does not bring it to life.

When theatre is commercially exploited it corrupts society because the product it exploits – it is the only one it has – is the human image. To exploit that causes more apathy and pain, and in the end more destruction, than chaining and exploiting human bodies. It is the same with modern religion. Religion is a form of drama, an off-shoot of the human psyche – but it cannot develop because it cannot forget its gods when its machines no longer need them. When a society which creates a religion is technologically superceded, what was progressive becomes regressive. The modern church's excited agitation is really the empty obverse of its weariness. It trivializes morality and by this brutalizes its believers, and so becomes the servant of commercial secularism and waste. The church is now a force for social profanity.

Society needs drama (even in debased commercial forms) because in it it seeks the human image. It must do this even when theatre degrades the human image. Great national institutions – national theatres, national galleries and so on – promote culture but also control and repress it. They make the whole of society a ghetto. Theatre is comparatively free of technology. A few people in a room can make a play. This is a strength because often it frees it from political control, in both its police and commerical forms. But it is also a weakness. Our times are too fast and chaotic for the stages in attics and cellars, on their own, to be able to study and recreate the human image. We also need to show how the whole of modern technology belongs to our creative psyche. But there is a conflict between financial resources and creative forces. In unjust society creative forces can no longer come from the state, because it no longer represents a progressive class that flourishes on human reason: it represents only an exploiting class and its ability to exploit. Now the creative forces of art come from the street. There is no more folk art, it has become the kitsch of commercialism. But street art is creative. We should not romanticize the street – as much garbage and cruelty are found there as in the cultural institutions. But street skills and disciplines are as astringent and liberating as those of academies. And more important, it is in the street – though we may wish it did not have to be so – that radical innocence is most potent. Authority in unjust society must lie, the street may lie but need not. Academies and national theatres cannot develop the skills of art because they no longer *need* art. The street *needs* art.

We think art has its source in truth, but its source is in lies. A child asks what, why, how – the questions of the great philosophers. It asks these questions because its brain is over-capacious and holistic. A child asks the profoundest philosophical questions, but it asks them about its room because that is its world. And as it grows it seeks a reason even for the stars. In that they have meaning, the questions – how, what and why – are truthful, but the answers are confusions and lies. The child gives the first answers itself. They are imagistic – the images 'see' its feelings. This early language expresses more than it describes, but it is intellectual and discriminates and analyses; even the first images are symbolic because they point to the nothingness that surrounds them. Lear tells his child 'nothing will come of nothing', but everything comes of nothing. This is the infant's first encounter with truth, and from it comes the dependance on art. Later it will be taught answers – but these will be lies or full of error. Primitive societies mix error and truth in order to exist; they dig wells but worship the rain God. Authority uses phenomena still beyond its understanding to coerce and stimulate society – it surrounds it in mystery. The sacred is a way of keeping the world in thrall. The priests' function is to be so possessed by illusions that they become real – that is, people act on them – and when this is not possible, to lie. Dostoievsky's inquisitors lie to everyone except God, whom they offend with the truth.

A society that uses a hydraulics technology may still demand belief in the rain God and found its institutions on his existence. The society that does this is constantly torn apart. To preserve the 'great social truth' – what society believes in order to maintain its structure – the 'truths of society' – the knowledge it needs to exist in the world – are constantly denied. So the 'great social truth' is a lie. Society equates the world with its culture just as the child equates the world with its room. The child cannot escape from the life of its room and society cannot escape from its rain God. As the child grows it puts the world into its room, not the other way round – its mind can never leave the room because that is its psyche's foundatioh. As it grows up into its parents' world they answer its truthful questions with the 'great social truth' – the mixture of confusions and lies. A child cannot understand the science of hydraulics or the shibboleths of economics but it can understand and live with the illusions of fairy tales and rain Gods. Children are lied to so that they may learn to honour the truth.

A child interprets its later knowledge in terms of its earlier knowledge – of the assurance or vertigo and suspicion it gave it. It is not that it doubts new facts, but that all its knowledge must build on its first, early 'symbolic against nothingness' – which is not merely expressive but discriminatory and analytic. New knowledge cannot transcend the earlier mind, the mind that is created in radical innocence. Children's questions can never be answered. They could not be answered even in a life after death – even God could not answer them. God is the last person qualified to know the meaning of life, he could only make excuses. Why justify X when you need not have created X? Why give an answer when there need have been no question? Even if some creator could ordain the whole sequence of evolution he could not give it meaning. Meaning comes from experience within evolution. Even if evolution had a preconceived, determined end, this could still only be its 'meaning' for a worm – not for a cognitive, sensate being. Even if such a being conceived the same determined end, it would do so within its limitations – it would then be the limited creature's end, not the Pantocrator's. God could not even create his own meaning. He could exist only because we knew him. And to love is to be in need. So the gap between Gods and human beings cannot be closed. Christianity tries to close it by claiming that God became every man and every woman, but clearly this is not so. To be of use religion must always claim too much – and when circumstances change, the too much inevitably becomes grotesquely too little.

The profoundest religion is nirvana, but because it asks the unanswerable question most honestly it is also the most fatuous. Why should nothingness hide itself in the veil of illusion? The religion of nirvana, like all religions, depends on illusions; it cannot tell why something should come of nothing, and certainly not why Himmler should preach the sermon on the mount. The philosophical riddle is that there should be any questions. God would have to ask the child the questions, and one would be as ignorant as the other. So the child must accept responsibility for the world. What else can it do? When it asks what and why it cannot withdraw from the world to the side like God. Children cry because they are philosophers.

Children ask what and why but must learn to ask how much, how often and when? As the first questions cannot be silenced but persist, they are given the answers to the second questions. And so radical innocence creates tension and, when it is confronted, the paradox. It is said that the child is father to the man. But it is the man's duty to murder the child. He does this by his answers and – because he also was a child – his anger. We cannot look into a human face that is not the face of a murderer and his victim – and both these things many times.

Art is a language without grammar, because the child

questions in one language and is answered in another; and innocence is a way of being that has no secure action. Yet all communication seeks grammar and all being seeks action. The child's instinctual, reasoning psyche is founded on a world of illusions which are also truths – the answers of the small room. Because parents wish to protect their child and nurture its emotions they lie to it in stories, gestures, behaviour and reports. If they wish to enter the child's world to be its guide, they must lie to it. Yes, they lie to it out of love – but that is the reason Himmler gassed Jews. Only those who hate or fear children tell them the truth – it would destroy a child if it could have any meaning for it.

Society takes up residence in the child's brain at its first consciousness, not as visitor but as living-in builder. If animal instincts caused our problems they would be less dangerous, and we would be less cruel and less credulous. Confronted by the cognitive mind, instincts are like matchwood in a hurricane. We relate to our instincts as cultures relate to the stars, they become the meaning we give them. Meaning and feeling are structured in emotion, and the way we achieve this gives us our character. Character is not unchangeable because it is constantly questioned by radical innocence. If its questions are given answers that turn it into guilt, then it corrupts us. But the corruption will question us, just as innocence would have done. It is in creating a pattern of responses to these questions that, as our life passes, we become what we are. Radical innocence is not corrupted by the lies it is told, but the lies make art necessary to the brain's working. Corruption comes from society and depends on the world's traffic with the small room. Art translates two languages into each other: the language of the small room – what, why, how – and the language of the world – how much, how often and when.

Radical innocence is radical because only philosophical

answers can satisfy the questions of what, why, how – the questions of the oracle. We are morally sane when our radical innocence is not turned into a mirror image of the distorted relations of unjust society. Even when it is, the motive for action and ground of belief is innocence. Radical innocence is as impregnable and absolute as death. The double-absolute of nothingness and death, and innocence and meaning, faces us when we are born. The way we come to terms with innocence is the way we become what we are and the meaning we give to life. If this were not so human beings would not make laws.

Machines and Art

In evolution species die or evolve into new species. When a species evolves it is cut off from its past by the closing of the reproductive door. Humanity is an evolved species, but one which breeds with its dead. We pay court to the dead and they inseminate our society, our bodies and our minds with their culture. We all inherit from the dead but the poorer among us inherit most because they inherit the norms and skills of submission. The poorer class are taught to carry the dead on their back.

Society evolves as a relationship between, on the one hand, past cultures and their forms of ownership, and on the other, modern technology and the changes it brings to subjectivity and culture. From time to time the changes are so radical, caused either by some sudden technical innovation, or by the accumulation of many small innovations until they reach a point of crisis – that it is as if machines created a new species of human being. In this way we are a species that constantly evolves into new species. If we understand this we have a better understanding of our problems. Unlike other species, we breed with our ancestor species, though they could no more live with us than dogs can fly – they would starve at our supermarket doors. It is because the things we need to live – food, shelter, sex, recreation – remain the same, but the technology which supplies the needs changes, that historically our behaviour and psyche change. Even seemingly stable activities such as eating change because their structural role in society changes. Society socializes the biological. When the way we meet our needs changes, this changes the mind that needs, the social mind. A thing changes when its meaning changes – its meaning is its context. But the mind is the meaning it gives to things. The mouth that eats from God's hand is not the mouth that eats from the capitalist supermarket; the meaning of what it says would change even if the words were unchanged.

It almost seems as if the only limits to change are physical, but the subjective human image is also a limit. The human image joins us to society and stands between it and our needs. We not only interiorize the human image, we exteriorize it and perform it. It is the way we apprehend the external world and behave in it. When the old society and its institutions can no longer manage the social relations needed by the new technology, in such a way that it gives us more autonomy and the freedom to create a new species of subjectivity which is practical (so that we may live with the machines) and human (so that we may live with each other) – then reaction corrupts the human image. Consumption is not possession and so it is not autonomy – on the contrary we are often possessed by what we consume. Society puts on a mask when it looks at the human face, and only the continuing democratization of society makes the mask more human. In reactionary societies the human image becomes so corrupt that it destroys society.

Art is one means by which we develop subjectivity so that we can live with new technology and its social demands. In finding our limitations we achieve the totality open to us in a continually changing world. I write in a provocative way about our relation to machines; it could be put less provocatively but I want to stress our vulnerability in the world our machines create. Now we think in terms of deconstruction, relativity and even absurdity. But the old Gods and certainties are dead only because they no longer meet a human need. We confuse the meaning of life with the nature of existence; as if, if we could find its nature, we would know the purpose. Religion tries to join the two but one does not follow from the other. To find human meaning we must combine two things. The first is our machines. The machines ontologically alter the human mind's nature because they make it a symbolizing function: one thing stands for another and so the mental and physical are made manipulable, and the nature of mind and, for us, reality are changed. For example, if God existed it would change his meaning, though not his might. The ancient conflict between might and right would be provoked. God could be a practical adviser – a scientist, sociologist or, say, an insurance agent – but he could have no special moral standing or understanding: this is an inevitable consequence of the symbolization of the human mind. The ontological scepticism – and the social scepticism which must follow – have always been vaguely sensed. That is why authority insisted on spiritual obedience.

Machines do not change only the mind's ontological nature. Machines themselves change, and their use changes the society which owns them. We do not change society so that we can devise and use new machines – that would require an inventive dictatorship (but, for structural psychological reasons, dictatorships only imitate and enlarge – they are dwarfs on stilts posing as giants) or an unheard of political sophistication; instead we devise and use new machines and *they* change society and its members' subjectivity. Natural evolution is the development between an environment and its creatures. In historical change the technosphere is the environment and the only creature is the human mind.

In this way machines are, ontologically and historically, one of the two basic determinants of human life. The other may be described as radical innocence – and involves, for example, our awareness of mortality and loss. The latter might seem a philosopher's existential luxury. But the awareness is not a mere attitude or response, or an emotion. It is intellectual because it is inherent in the elementary ability to consciously discern and discriminate. These things are necessarily in the gift of free will. Our physical existence does not require free will – it would not be possible if it did. But we must be free to see and apprehend – otherwise we would (as it were) physically see things when they were not there (as it is we can only do this in fantasy, at the prompting of madness or ideology). The mind's perceptive function is free. But society is *invented* by seeing, believing etc – by ideology. If it were not, we could not live in societies. The problem arises: how do we discriminate between social 'fantasy' and social 'reality', when society must be partly imaginary and there is no God or external meaning to guide us? In evolution the environment is its creatures' reality. If it changes the creatures must change or perish. In history, the technosphere – the machines and the way they are owned – is the environment and the human mind is the creature. Ultimately machines are our reality – because we are consciously mortal and innocent or corrupt. There is meaning only if innocence and mortality concern us (which is not a free matter of choice; the basic function of perception and apprehension requires innocence or corruption) – and only in relation to machines. Society snares and seduces the mind into fantasy: machines are the realm of necessity – the ancient Fatum of the Gods – and ultimately they impose reality. Armaggedon is a time of machines.

Children play so as to learn to live in their parents' world, but when they are older that world has already passed away. We learn to speak a dead language or one that is rapidly dying. Yet language is not only a means of communicating with others but also a way of knowing, of being, ourself. Because we speak a dying language we die; but while it is still spoken a language has enough vitality to kill the speaker so that a new language may speak. Children, like adults, lie and speak the truth in one and the same utterance. Technological change is so rapid that adults are as unskilled as children in living in their society. Technology gives us a giant's strength but a child's impotence. We approach machines as children approach toys – that is why we make bombs.

Weapons are machines that will always be toys, they belong to the childhood of humankind. War and violence are games played by adults. Only people at play could ever kill each other. Like children we reverse reality and find meaning in games – we play at being human and kill in earnest. We have not yet outgrown our toys; but if we know they are toys and that killing is our game, then instead of being in awe of armies we will merely fear them. We must learn to make machines fit for people to live with; and so close is the symbiosis between us and them that that means making a world fit for our machines – otherwise all machines turn into weapons. Drama is one of the most useful arts because it uses language and shows people in society. It teaches us how to live with machines, and how to survive our machines' mistakes and our weapons' triumphs.

Sociobiologists do not understand that we are more closely related to machines than to animals. Animals have no language; innately they have a few calls and signs and may learn a few more. But machines have language – not in the sense that they may mechanically reproduce the human voice, but in the sense that all machines incorporate the human, symbolic mind and replicate its analytical and even its grammatical structures. We speak and create machines in our image. Animals have no language because we do not make them; their being precedes our mind. All the things we make are signs of culture and so they speak to us. Intensely culturized objects – those which are powerfully symbolic, such as uniforms and national flags – speak to us as intensely as machines do; but ultimately even their power comes, by way of cultural learning, from machines. Their symbolic imagery sums up the relationship between us and machines – soldiers wear the livery of their weapons. The difference between a natural object used as a tool and a man-made tool or machine, is that the latter make greater demands on us. They are manufactured to be of intense, ingenious use and so they use the users – change them and their society – more than natural tools do.

The differences between us and machines are so obvious, their limitations so gross, that we miss the vital kinship: they share our minds and culture. Indeed, in a real sense human beings are industrial by-products of machines. They create us by creating the society in which they can function, they form our subjectivity to meet their needs and fit us into their culture. They do this in relation to specific forms of ownership. As they are owned by a small class, they become the means by which the larger class is owned. Most people are owned by machines, but all people are enslaved by them. This is because machines are the structural Gods of our society: they ordain fate. Naturally in a conflict between the needs of people and the needs of machines, machines give themselves priority.

In simple terms of evolution, machines live in our future. They cannot breed with us but they inherit our mind: and so – by way of the future – we must inherit our mind from them. It is a circle. The machines create our mind's foundations by controlling our culture and the way ownership is inherited. Or so at least it seems – and if it were really so, if machines *always* dictated the forms of ownership, society would never change but would settle into political stasis. But machines are not loyal to their owners – they betray them by speaking directly to the machine-users, in work-places and wherever technology ramifies in society. Working, living and being with machines changes us and our behaviour. It is as if the machines speak to us behind the owners' backs. This happens because the ownership of machines, and so the ownership of society and its culture and institutions, is based on old machines, but the old institutions cannot control the use of new machines in such a way that the users can live in the old culture. Inevitably, in our world machines play the role God played in the ancient world, and both God and machines are the fathers of heretics.

If we want animals to work or do tricks for us we must train them – they have no language in which they could be taught. We do not need to train machines to work because they speak our language and already understand us. But it is a dead language. Machines, like children, outgrow their makers; but unlike children they do not grow up – they cannot experience themselves and so they cannot 'kill the speaker' and create a new language. The effects of that are more fundamental than the machines' other limitations.

Although a machine may be a force so vital that it radically changes its users and their society, it is dead. But because machines are dead they are always probating their will and we are always inheriting under it. A truly human culture would understand that we live by being spoken to by dead machines, that machines are ghosts that give birth to us, their living children; and we would let them work in peace in their graves. Instead we believe in machines as once people believed in ghosts. But *their* ghosts came from the past, from their ruling class and its superstitions, traditions and bureaucracy. The grip of our machines is harder – they come from the future and turn it into the past. We relate to machines as though they were our dead children and so we become their living children. That is all we ever can or need be, but there is a bad and a better way of being it. We give machines undemocratic power over our inner life. Machines cast the block vote of capitalist democracy. The one reason for that is that they are owned undemocratically. We cannot become more human by changing our attitudes – humanity is a question of social structure. Machines know only necessity.

The problem is not a technological one of limiting the machines' ecological damage. The problem is cultural, psychological and political. Machines create society and through society – and in conflict with it – our culture. Our future depends on the ownership of machines because whoever owns them owns culture and our species's fate. All social relationships are forms of ownership, and in the modern world all forms of ownership are based on the ownership of technology: our culture is the means that enable us to live within these relationships. But, I repeat, machines do not only create the owning-and-ruling class – they disturb it. In an unjust – undemocratic – society there are, as in all prisons, two uniforms, the warders' and the prisoners'; and if cultural jiggery abolishes the warders' uniform the machines will still make two smiles.

If machines always dictated forms of ownership we would always be (as now) culturally owned. The machines would always bring fate from the future and decide who we kill and how we die. But the daily use of machines works against that and sends shudders through the stone colossus. Even more important, because machines give rise to culture – and the great problems of law, morality and identity – they create the confrontations between radical innocence and the paradox. Socially, subjectively, we inherit the future from our machines; but radical innocence cannot enter the future, it is in the present. Machines live in our future and our past but we live alone in the present. That is why there are always two smiles – and why we may accept responsibility for the world. Machines change us and the stage on which radical innocence acts. They are radical innocence's secret ally – the reactionary parents of revolutionary children. History is produced by machines, but radical innocence uses history against the machines – and so the future always stabs history in the back. It means that democracy must develop into socialism. The development would stop only if machines were abolished – which is not the ambition of capitalism – or the elite ownership were stabilized – which is not possible. In effect, the machines stab the owners in the back. The only alternative is barbarism.

The machine is Laius who does not meet Oedipus, and so radical innocence escapes from the determination that comes from the future. Socialism recovers the past, brings it to birth again and saves it from the death of the future. Laius is dead before Oedipus is born and Oedipus has only to learn to lay his ghost. This is difficult but not impossible. The clash between inherited future and reborn past is revolution, and there will be a time when revolution is peaceful and does not have to devour its children.

Art is permanent. An artistic statement is like a mathematical statement, always recognisable. But a mathematical statement may be wrong, and in a sense art too may be wrong. Art is not culturally dependent but it is culturally relative. We still watch plays our ancestors wrote, and we would recognize as what they are the unwritten rituals of even earlier ages. But though we recognize early cave paintings as art, we do not live or think in the way their painters did; and so we do not use art, theirs or ours, in the way they did. Subjectively a work of art changes as the objective world changes, because socially we are part of objectivity and our subjectivity changes with it. What is permanent in art is the articulation of human mind; it is this articulation which we always recognize. And the image of that is not in what is depicted but in the manner of its depiction – as if we saw the letters not the words. Art reproduces the human mind; the material object presents the art. Art is the material production of the perceiving, analytical, symbolic mind. This is true, also, of the creation of machines; the difference between them (and all utilitarian objects) and art is that art skilfully embodies the artist's symbolic *attention* in the art object. The mind's presence is visible. Art is the mind reading the mind, recognizing itself in the material world. An *objet trouvé* may be seen as art, but a culture which knew only *objets trouvés* could not recognize as art the Mona Lisa if it found it – it would not know art. We use art even to recognize its absence in a 'bad' work of art.

The language of art must be translated twice to communicate: object or event – artist's mind – art object – receiver's mind. If the receiver does not share the artist's culture, because it is dead or alien, more transactions take place.

What is heard is not what is said, what is seen is not what is shown: only the presence of the symbolic mind is permanent. It is not like inferring an animal from its spoor; in art, mind *is* what is shown, whether it is the embodiment of an extreme mental abstraction or of an ideational instinct. Perhaps ultimately art is the mind's ability – and need – to produce the symbolic against nothingness. This is not a metaphysical understanding of art, because art comes from an active relation with the world.

Relations within a work of art are not natural, automatic or stochastic – and when they appear to be they achieve the appearance parasitically by invoking what is absent. Over chaos the mind throws an invisible grid of the symbolic and recognizes human intention. In the same way, ruins evoke the pathos of the history of architecture.

We do not recognize *our* mind in art but the *human* mind – this is at the basic level of presentation; at the level of organization, the level of the subject, we recognize the *public* mind. Differences in artistic value cannot be reduced to differences in artists' skills of transmission. The mind cannot reproduce without reproducing its philosophy, and this is implicit even in the mechanics of apprehension. At any time there are progressive and reactionary philosophies. The philosophy controls the skill – the borders between philosophy, perception and skill are blurred. As art depends on philosophy it means, at its crudest, that what one person calls art another may call trash – not bad art but not art at all: the presence of the symbolic mind is not seen. Ultimately the machines decide what counts as good art – they create culture and make it necessary for us to express it. Other effects – institutions, fashions, exhaustion of styles and of structural possibilities, the availability of raw materials and so on – ultimately depend on technology and its culture.

Works of art show objects and events from human situations, but a work of art changes historically. We see cave paintings as our art, but for their creators they were closer to what we know and use as machines. Perhaps their creators spoke or sang to them and gave them gifts. If so, they did it in the spirit in which we work machines. When ancient people sacrificed animals or human beings to their Gods they did what we do when we put petrol in our car. And when we pray to icons and Gods it is as if we prayed to our machines or offered them a meal. In liberated Poland police cars are sprinkled with holy water. It would make as much sense to think that when a police car ran over someone it had been offered a human sacrifice. History changes the meaning of things.

We recognize Greek drama and understand its characters and their relations. But we use Greek drama in our own way, because we are a different species of subjectivity in a different world. The first people who saw *Hamlet* and *Macbeth* believed in the reality of ghosts, and many of them would have seen witches burned for conjuring the dead. If a production psychoanalyses Hamlet and his ghost it does not make the play useful to us. First we need to know why Shakespeare's society *needed* ghosts in its politics and art – otherwise we use their machine as our picture. History makes only temporary repairs to our lives, and Shakespeare's solutions become our problems. We should treat Hamlet's ghost as if it were our machine. I do not mean we should put it on stage as a teleprinter. Changing surface images is like putting Zeus in carpet slippers, it merely reifies the past and trivializes the present. Instead we should approach the play politically. Hamlet's problem is not that he does not know how to kill but how to live. How could he? Shakespeare is creating a new species of subjectivity. Who owns the machine? Who sends it with its message?

Whose need of the king's death is greater than Hamlet's? Hamlet kills all old men because they own machines but cannot live with them; but the young men – Fortinbras and Laertes – cannot live with Hamlet. Hamlet's subjectivity must be reformed – the new industrial bureaucracy needs it – but repressed – the forms of ownership need it. Fortinbras, the owner of soldiers, graveyards and machines, sends Hamlet his ghost on behalf of the new owners. Fortinbras does not know this, Shakespeare partly knew it, and we should know it well. Fortinbras will administer industrialism; and Horatio is Hamlet curtailed – he is left holding the body and with the role of representing bourgeois sensibility.

If our machines talk our langauge we must talk theirs. Our mother tongue is the language of our machines. Perhaps until now technology could not initiate change before we were able to survive it and prosper: our machines were not strangers to us then, they knew us so well that they could teach us how to live with them. But we are agents of the change, and art is a means of making the change human. Society sends us to the theatre in order to teach the machines to talk to us more kindly. Or to put it less provocatively, we are sent to the theatre to learn how to live with our machines and each other. Čapek's panic over robots was unnecessary. Machines will not take our place, they will sooner bury us. Machines have always made our species and its history – as humans and human history. The first tools made the first humans, and made the first human psyche by giving us free will. Perhaps the first tool was part of our body: perhaps to the first humans the opposable thumb was as mysterious as an object without a shadow, was the symbolic that pointed to nothingness.

Our symbiosis with machines is not genetically inherited. Genes cannot be coded with instructions to use a hammer or paint a picture. If they could we would have a use for the hammer but not the picture. Technology would be monolithic, history catatonic and art a set of instructions – time would be dead and we would lie in its embrace. If we imagine ourselves as machines made by machines, we are machines that are changed by what they produce. But the process is chaotic – as if a ship were built by throwing its pieces into the sea. The abstract intellect is the ability to discriminate not to assemble, to particularize not to know. To *know* we need machines and the culture they provoke. We see the direction of autonomy running from us to machines because we make and operate them, but they make us spiritually and emotionally. They are the phylogenetic and biographical foundations of our consciousness; and we owe to them the achievement of our higher faculties – the illusions of soul, our moral law, our visionary art.

It is not easy to acknowledge that machines make society and its relations, and even harder to acknowledge that these relations make our mind. Yet the mind's evolution has made precisely those relations necessary to being human. Machines stand irremovably between us and our animal origin. But they are not society's lynchpin – *that* is our creative subjectivity. The human image is formed not by some ideal inspiration or spiritual essence but – ultimately – by machines and their ownership. But the human image must be not only immediate and practical but also utopian and ideal. Otherwise it causes such pain and violence that society's self-justifications become too reactionary and license so much repression that society is destroyed. The human image forms and guides subjectivity, and yet for most people the information and art on which the image is based come more and more from a gutter press and television. Modern cities have newspapers and television in the way Treblinka had a string quartet.

A work of art is like a machine which does not grow

obsolete because it changes what it produces. It does this by changing its relation with its consumers. It is like a machine which learns new languages. We do not see through a slit in our heads and then, in a cerebral darkroom, examine what we have seen and make what we will of it. The mind comes to see and perceive in one – it looks out. We cannot choose to use the art of the past as the past used it. Either we adapt it, by adding time to it, or abuse it by letting it make the gesture – it cannot be more – of taking time away from the present.

So we sit in armchairs to listen to work-chants; we use Hamlet's ghost as a machine; a picture painted in a garret hangs on a millionaire's wall; a figure carved for an altar stands in a stockbroker's lobby; images once so terrifying they had to be hidden in sanctuaries away from all but initiates, are displayed in museums to be seen by the curious and indifferent; and portraits that once rationalized power over life and death are printed on T-shirts. Even more revealing is what happens when we try to appropriate the past's social authority by imitating its cultural images. The nazis used the Greek sculptural forms of Gods and Goddesses, but they could only turn them into statues of proletarian slaves gesturing in effete bombast. The Greeks used stone to make the human image live, the nazis used the human image to mummify stone. Spiritual and aesthetic retreats – like political retreats – into the past produce monsters. The spiritual is derived from the material, not the other way round.

In *Red Black and Ignorant* the father praises his son for killing him. This seems to break the laws of psychological determinism, as if the commandant had praised the Russian guard for not shooting his brother. Like solipsism, determinism is a riddle that cannot be disproved. The mind is formed materially but is not determined. It is as if time were separated from space so that matter might exist, but that time 'precedes' space and matter, temporally and ontologically, so that mind exists in time but not in matter; it is as if time creates space, and not the other way round. Then although the brain and its working are material they cannot be reduced to physical, determined laws. And so we are free to change the physical position of matter but not space or the direction of time; because the direction of time is determined, what is in it is free – as matter would be in space if it were not also in time. Certainly if mind were strictly determined it would not be materialistic but part of an idealist world.

Really determinism is a theory of chaos. If the whole of reality is determined time has no significant direction and there is no significant difference between chance and cause-and-effect. Indeed some mystics believe it is as true to say that the teacup empties itself into the teapot as that the teapot empties itself into the teacup. The theatre of the absurd, though it does not know it, depends on a theory of determinism, and holds that intentional actions are ineffective because the course of events cannot be altered. And so wars, disease and famine are determined in all their details. The theory allows no distinction between chaos, chance or cause. But if all action is meaningless this includes art – even in the limited sense of skill. There can be no art where everything is necessary chaos. Ironically, the aesthete's theatre of the absurd is based on the premise that there is no art – only science, and even this is empty. But to say that war, disease and famine are determined in all respects is not to make a scientific statement but a moral one. This did not trouble the Greeks: if you have enough Gods and slaves it does not matter which way the flies walk on the corpses on your battlefields. What is surprising is that it does not worry the dramatists of the absurd, they are content to tell the starving man the story of the teapot and the teacup. It is because the Greeks were so *ignorant* that they were able to confuse science and morality, be undemocratic and submit to fate – and yet still create sublime art and recreate their humanity. But if we are as confused we will destroy ourselves – we know too much.

Because we are free we have a use for fiction. Fiction is a specific reality that combines real and possible events. If anything determined us it would be the paradox, in which we take responsibility for the world. That sounds grandiose till we think of Hiroshima and Auschwitz and then it seems the minimum condition for being human. The paradox determines only in the loose sense that it lies in our path and cannot be avoided. The answers we give the Sphinx determine who we are. But even when the Sphinx is dead it haunts us and we are free to change our answers. We expect the stone to fall, human behaviour is often unexpected, above all when it is faced with the paradox. If innocence accepts the paradox's imperative, it does so freely. Our will is free till it is corrupted; the corruption is social and political, not metaphysical – or natural – determination. Machines free us and radical innocence stops freedom turning into chaos; and so we are left with our free will, anxiety and moral sanity – or political madness.

Art has the authority of social institutions yet its creative power – its energy, precision and purpose – comes from outside the cultural institutions: from streets, ordinary homes, neglected schools, prisons, courtrooms, crowded hospitals, refuges – from the city we share with machines. Time and again bad art turns schools into prisons, and good art turns even prisons into schools.

Because good art comes from the street, from ordinary lives, it cannot be limited to propaganda. The problems must be faced whole, because that is how they are experienced. If we were not created by machines – or even if we *were* machines – art could *only* be propaganda; it would be to us what instructions for use are to machines. But when machines use us they change us and they have no instructions how to do that – they have only art. Machines cannot listen to propaganda because they cannot lie; in the end they can only listen to art – which is why history is tumultuous and we have to struggle to be human.

When art is limited to propaganda its political role is limited. It would be vicious spiritualism to deny that there are times when to be human we must be at one with our machines. At those times propaganda may be instruction in being human. But even good propaganda changes its meaning when the circumstances in which it was created have passed. Time turns good propaganda into art and bad propaganda into silly or sadistic chatter. Good propaganda is like an SOS and no useful poem, novel, play or picture is not also an SOS. If someone sat in an armchair and read every poem that had been written he would still not have a literary education if he had not learned to read the SOS in art. In a democracy, the under-privileged are second-class citizens but the over-privileged are tenth-class citizens.

Society needs theatre because we live with machines. Society must examine its moral teachings in each new machine-world, and demonstrate an ethics that the new species of subjectivity can accept as normative. In the past this was done by political and moral experts. Priests read stars, sages divined truth and kings and warrior castes governed. But in a democracy there should be no second-class or tenth-class citizens – they are a danger not so much by what they do as by what is done to them to gain their 'willing' consent. Our democratic credo is freedom, but our practice is reactionary in prosperity and fascistic in depression. Unresisted, the political and cultural cycle is as inevitable as the trade cycle.

We cannot get rid of technology. If you abolished machines you would abolish the human mind. We must live with potentially dangerous technology. Nuclear weapons are not the most dangerous weapons we will invent. We cannot survive long with a technology of terror. It creates hate and a society that cannot function without hate needs enemies – it even seeks its own destruction so that its social-psyche may know it was right to hate its enemies. Once people slept with a sword under their pillow; while we have nuclear weapons we are trying to live with a sword in our heart. If we understood how society was created and changed we would not make nuclear weapons; we would know that even if they served a political end, they were culturally destructive even when they were not fired. The human image is wounded by the gun in its hand even before it is fired.

Not everyone confronted by the paradox would act with the innocence of the Russian guard. Perhaps we may be so corrupt that we lose the name of human to everyone except ourselves – forfeit it to those who lead us into inhumanity and who, under their show of sentimentality, despise us for being led. But throughout history not only has the paradox produced acts of goodness and bravery that lessen our suffering, but which in an unjust society are like funeral flowers we throw at those being taken out to die – it has also ensured that authority cannot rest till everyone has, as far as they can, the chance to be human; what limitations are then left, we could call tragic – till then they are political. When radical innocence is corrupted and commits political crimes which are monstrous because they have been dragged out of history's grave, we are responsible for them if we have not fought against them. Society's crimes are far worse than any personal sins, and if we help society to commit them we would do better if instead of hanging our heads in remorse we hanged ourselves in shame. Radical innocence is meaningless and inexplicable, but that is part of its authority. We can explain our crimes and kindness, we cannot explain radical innocence. Its one meaning is that it seeks meaning. Perhaps society's profoundest reason for sending us to the theatre is to see how the meaningless paradox can give meaning to our life.

When I devised the Palermo improvisation a new range of nuclear weapons was being installed in Sicily, with the agreement of most Italians. They knew the weapons could kill the children of other nations. The improvisation showed that rather than this they would even kill their own brothers or sisters or – like the Russian guard – themselves. Surely to avoid such a monstrous choice they would refuse to have the weapons in their country? There is a great moral power hidden in the paradox which we could use to make all of us more human. If social corruption makes it possible for us to avoid the paradox, we must make it unavoidable. That is the purpose of art. This was made clear to me when I was attacked by a politician who had helped to found a party to represent 'moderation' but wanted to keep nuclear weapons as bargaining counters. In a newspaper article I asked him to appear on television and with a penknife demonstrate on a plastic doll (he was a medical man) how a child would be blinded and eviscerated in nuclear war. He said it was wrong to write and talk in this way because it disturbed people. Reality was to be fiction and had no use for art. I had pointed to the paradox.

It is said that since the second world war nuclear weapons have kept the world at peace. Really they increased the nuclear powers' fear of each other, and this lead to wars in Asia, South America and Africa. It is as if nuclear weapons are so monstrous that they hire their own killers: nuclear weapons kill by bullets, torpedoes, chemicals, high explosives, napalm . . . and if necessary they would kill by slings and arrows. Nor do they kill only third-world people so that the rest of us can live in comfort. They kill us in our community. It is not so much that we spend on them money we need for welfare – they cause the fear that eats into our morality, trivializes our emotions and narrows our mind. One day out of sheer stupidity, vanity and petulance we will wander into the final confrontation and lash out with the final terror. We will destroy the world out of apathy.

Nuclear weapons confront everyone with the paradox. They offend the understanding that comes from radical innocence, and which we can deny only by an effort which is an act of violence against ourselves. Peace based on terror leads to fear and hate, and then to the irrationality and disorder that masquerades as discipline. To live our daily lives we have to share with others the common rights of our community – and that is already in itself the love of peace. Yet we go on playing the role of the nazi commandant instead of the Russian guard or the Palermo students. In the end we will be like the pack of lost soldiers in *Great Peace*. When the Greeks submitted to their Gods they gained their humanity. When we submit to the protection of nuclear weapons we lose ours.

Theatre

Fate is a fiction made real when people are persuaded that they are politically powerless. Then they are afraid and hate, and this leads to the conviction that fate rules life – it is the process in which religions create Gods. In Greek theatre the Gods determined fate and people submitted to it. But the submission was defiance. By submitting to the Gods the heroes and heroines convicted them of cruelty, arbitrariness, triviality and other faults beneath human dignity – the judgement is passed by the act of submission. Submission to the Gods makes them less than human and the humans more than Gods. This is the way in which the Greeks transcended the Gods and gained their humanity.

To preserve the doctrine of fate the Greeks kept comedy and tragedy apart. Only the Gods may laugh in tragedy, otherwise they would be laughable and the hero's submission would have no grandeur. It would be absurd or grotesque – gothic not classical. By submitting to the Gods the hero gives value even to their cruelty and arbitrariness. The Gods' titanic frivolity and the hero's strength (which allows him to will his submission) are part of the same scheme of values and are measured in the same violence. The Greeks used their Gods as scapegoats to bear their weaknesses, and later the christians used their God to bear their sins. In this way both turned the psyche-energy, which all authorities repress to maintain political control, into creative, productive energy which added to the human-ization of society. Whenever this is done repression is experienced as freedom. The Greeks' and christians' scape-goats were stronger than themselves, and so they turned the victim into a covert aggressor and gained his power; and this released psyche-energy in ways that were even more humanizing.

Religion claims to be concerned with the soul and the other world, but really it is one of the ways psyche-energy is repressed and released by the societies of this world. The Greek separation of comedy and tragedy was part of a wider, general development away from the religions of animal Gods. In societies which practised such religions, the grotesque gave comedy the implacable power of fate.

The grotesque, macabre imagery released energy in simple, unadaptable forms – the human image was restricted by the animal image. It was as if the energy were bound in closed circles, but this was enough to sustain static societies with limited (however subtle) economic, administrative and political systems. When the Greeks separated comedy and tragedy they repressed and released energy in more adaptable, socially productive ways. For example, the *Oresteia* uses the antisocial forces of unjust society to make society more just, to change revenge into justice and the furies into guardians of law. Of course, the *Oresteia*'s reformed society was still a slave-owning, pseudo-democracy and so the compromise could not last.

Oedipus answers the Sphinx's riddle, kills it and rules the city. But the Sphinx has many secrets and it takes them to the grave – the victims always outlive their murderers; if they did not we would not need to make laws. When Oedipus kills the Sphinx he puts himself in its power. The Sphinx lives in the grave as long as it has secrets, and the grave's secrets are harder to learn than the secrets of the public highway. The Sphinx haunts Oedipus and he must learn to live with it or it will kill him. Oedipus is an innocent, the all-knower who knows too little. He is the audience at his own play. In fact the play shows the situation of all audiences – all audiences are Oedipus. The most important thing the play tells is not a traumatic family secret that became a foundation of civilization, but that Oedipus could not murder the Sphinx. The play is a classical portrayal of radical innocence.

Even when the Sphinx is dead Oedipus is chained to it, just as as a child he was chained to Prometheus's mountain. So even before he was blind he stumbled on crippled feet – they are the mark of his innocence. It is only later at Colonnus that he is corrupted. Society was unjust and so it

needed a play that took away his innocence. Oedipus suffers
and sets out on his pilgrimage, to crawl back to the
mountain. When he finally gets there it splits and engulfs
him. What does this mean? Of course it is presented as a
demi-deification, but really it is a corruption. Men do not
make miracles. Miracles are God's sins – he commits them
when he cannot bear any more reality. But men must learn
to bear reality or change it themselves. Because the mountain will not come to Oedipus, Oedipus will go to the
mountain – that is the corrupt solution of holy men. It will
not do for the practical audience. They cannot live with the
solution of their stage shadow. Oedipus is their scapegoat –
but they are wiser than he. They say if the mountain will
not come to us we will meet it half way.

It may seem we could wait a lifetime and the mountain
would not move an inch, any more than when we are dead
we can reach up out of the grave and change the dates on
our tombstone. But not only does the mountain move, the
world moves. That is our daily transaction with it, and it
involves both Psyche and Techne, and fiction and fact. The
history of theatre shows that neither fact nor fiction can be
itself without the other. Facts need fiction in order to be
facts. The relation between fact and fiction changes
throughout history. When it is good (which means, as I will
explain, when the machines can approve of it) we add to
our humanness; when it is not, society is corrupt and
destroys the human image. The relation between Techne
and Psyche, fact and fiction, is the way we create cities and
the sort of people who live in them, or the wilderness and
the human-beasts who rampage and parade in it.

The Bacchae is the last great Greek play. In it Euripides
(searching for the social truth) brings comedy back into
tragedy. Two old men, Cadmus and Teiresias, dress in drag
and dance. Their ludicrous shuffle stamps on the Greek

world. It is a comic parody of the tragic chorus and it destroys the structure of tragic drama. The dance is followed by the destruction of the 'recognition' scene. Recognition scenes were important because they were Greek tragedy's way of transposing politically repressed energy into democratic, humane forms. The device worked only because comedy was divided from tragedy. Two strangers meet, often in out-of-the-way places: it is the meeting of two social tensions, and of the two corresponding tensions in the psyche. The strangers recognize their kinship – or some other involvement in the past – and then co-operate for a common end. In the confrontation and recognition, society's existing divisions – and the tensions in the psyche that maintained them – are developed into new, more humane divisions, which are new forms of repression and release. In Oedipus's investigation of his past there are many meetings between strangers, who come from many levels of society: workers and owners, citizens and leaders, Gods and humans, and parents and children – who are more strange to each other than Jocasta and Oedipus? He traces his steps from meeting to meeting till he recognizes himself: and then the man with wounded feet wounds his head and begins to grope his way to death. The meetings are Thebes's solutions to its problems.

Such meetings seem the image of fate, but they happen when fate changes its mind. A society founded on belief in fate has to have ways of accomodating free will. The strangers recognize each other and share in an undertaking which the ruling class must achieve, but which it can achieve only by allowing or arranging the confrontation of forces which previously it had to keep apart at all costs – if it were to continue to rule. The device combined politics and psyche in one action, and this was one of Greek drama's strengths. Later, when Hamlet meets the ghost, he and it remain strangers – it is not a meeting between two equal psyches but between a man and authority. The ghost is supernatural and represents the Gods. This makes them more intimate (Hamlet is their kin) but also more distant (they are dead). What has happened is that machines are taking over from the Gods, and machines are far more demanding than Gods. Hamlet cannot gain his humanity by defiant submission, he must consent in his very soul – but the machines will pay him for it.

The meeting of tensions leads to partial recognition of the nature of the tensions, the social division which was a negative co-operation. It is the process in which the Oresteia changes persecutors to protectors. But Euripides's search for social truth made him a political sceptic and he saw through the device. Many of the meetings in his plays are polemical fantasies; in his version of Orestes's story he ridicules the way Sophocles used the device in his version. And after the dance of the two old men there is a meeting so strange that it can never lead to creative readjustment – Thebes can no longer reform itself, the state cannot live with its own social-psyche and Greek culture will begin to wander the world looking for a home. The meeting is between Agave and her son's head. She has torn it from his body. She cradles it in her lap – and does not recognize it. When at last she does she is sent out of the city. The only co-operation the meeting could have led to would have been between the living and the dead, and that is not needed till Hamlet meets Laius's ghost. The Greeks had little use for ghosts because they had Gods instead of machines.

Tragedy cannot admit the grotesque. When Agave nurses her son's fake head she prepares the way for the theatre where real heads will be thrown in the sand and real emperors will dress as women and dance. Rome managed its repressed energy in the arena, where conflict could not create meaning; instead licence joined with law and order to create discipline and an empire. Greek theatre was over and drama once again declined into religion.

Like all religions, christianity attempted to turn theatre into reality – fiction into fact, and fact into fiction. Religion combines the stage and the arena. The drama of the crucifixion removed the paradox from this world to the next. Rock opened to let Oedipus in; it opened to let Christ out. Oedipus's world is ancient, closer to nature; Christ's rock is handled by angels *and* human beings. As the world became more mechanical and human, Christ (acting for the state) spoke of another kingdom. This limited the paradox's power to influence social change. Radical innocence had acted – and been saved by a miracle. If only! Religion fatally confuses the guard and the commandant; it always undoes what drama can do. It releases repressed energy in ways which strengthen repression. The intellectual cost of religion is always greater than its social value. Of course its repression cannot succeed. The machines work against it, and even its own form of repression provokes resistance – in all societies the boundaries between social forces are frayed, the geometry is psychic not objective. The fulfilment of religion is atheism. But the astute use christianity made of dramatic fiction stabilized society for centuries. The paradox produced martyrs in various arenas, but their chief function was not to change this world but to lead a pilgrimage to the next.

Renaissance society turned from the other world to this world, and so it needed a new drama. For the most part this was created in England, where the industrial revolution began. Science discovered the real world's natural energy and technology and industry put it to work. Not only did the energy come from the ground, but its use caused such economic and social havoc that the political stability of christianity was shaken – so the new force must be the Devil. The Devil is to renaissance theatre what the Gods are to Greek theatre. As the fundamental social relations were changing, all the themes of the new drama became available together, at once, to the first of the new dramatists, Marlowe: money (*The Jew of Malta*); expansion and imperialism (*Tamburlaine*); and energy, industry and science (*Dr Faustus*). *Dr Faustus* was the most important because it created the new industrial theology.

Technology needed a new Promethean psychology, but the owners of society needed to curb it. Faust makes a contract with the Devil that Christ had no need to make, because it offered him what in the christian drama was already his: this world. This world was contained in the next, and so God could rule without the compromises of politics and the Devil. Capitalism cannot, it needs the Devil: the Devil frees people from God but puts them in chains.

Like the Greeks (and for the same reason) Shakespeare rewrote stories from the past. He did not rewrite *Dr Faustus*, though he must have wanted to. All his plays are versions of *Dr Faustus*, it is the unwritten subtitle of all of them. But Marlowe had said about *Dr Faustus* all that the times needed to be said – or all that the form of ownership, and its religion and politics, allowed to be said or could even imagine. Shakespeare could have only embellished the play with aesthetics and he was too analytical a writer to be content with that. But someone had to write *Dr Faustus* before Hamlet could meet his ghost.

Dr Faustus combines tragedy and comedy. A version of *Dr Faustus* without comedy ignores the social process it is meant to be about. The Satanic force is dynamic, destructive, irreverent, industrial and rides over corpses. The Devil is even part animal. He makes the grotesque of primitive religion useful once more (the theatre of the absurd will trivialize it again). Industrial, Satanic energy subverts judgement and enslaves people but provokes a seething discontent and confused understanding which are our hope of freedom. Renaissance society could not have been created and administered without the Devil. The machines were laughing at our stupidities.

Shakespeare needed ghosts and witches. His patron King James wrote a book confirming their existence. It is a common device of ruling class ideology – and also a symptom of hysteria – to appropriate folktales and turn them into journalism. And so the witch-hunt ravaged Europe. Witches were scotched out of copses, heaths, rural byways, village hovels – but really the tittle-tattlers and theologians were speaking the language of the new machines: witches were made in factories. Greek democracy sought order and needed Gods, capitalist society seeks profit and needs the Devil.

Later when capitalism was consolidated, the enlightenment threw the Devil out of the front door and romanticism brought him in at the back. Milton and Blake made Satan a hero, but in romanticism he is tainted with bad habits. A malaise lingers in the romantic soul like smoke over cities. The smoke of witches' fires blows away, but working class stench must be lived with. Romanticism desocialized Satanic energy and made it hedonistic and anarchic – this also relieved the tedium of bourgeois respectability, which was another consequence of capitalist consolidation. As the *nouveaux riches* went up in the world the Devil even became an aristocrat, and mill owners would have happily married their daughters to him. Well, he was a prince. Still later, romanticism became a bridge between the witch-hunt and American psychoanalysis (a castrated McCarthyism). Science still retains much Satanic theology – sociobiology puts

Satan in our genes and science fiction puts him in outer space. Nuclear weapons are a recent form of the witch-hunt – they are used to threaten Empires of Darkness. Capitalism could not survive without the Devil and his works.

As machines became more complex they took over more of society. A new social discipline was needed to allow machines to work in peace. The social violence of capitalism was interiorized. The effects are seen in nineteenth-century theatre: psychology determines fate and imprisons philosophy in character. The theatre held, as emphatically as ever, that our lives are not in our control; but in place of Gods and Devils it made the unconscious our fate. When the Greeks submitted to their Gods they discovered their humanity, but we can only submit to ourselves, and create values and understand the world in the image of our own anger and triviality. In this submission we do not gain tragic status but are merely criminals with the wounded pride of victims. God is Father, Satan is Son and psychology is Holy Ghost.

Ibsen's Master Builder falls like Satan, but not to escape from the theological tomb of heaven – he falls to his death. Drama was at a turning point. Soon dramatists would clutch at mysticism like naked men clutching at shrouds. Ibsen was a revolutionary-conservative. He increasingly turned social relations (using the tensions that disturbed social order) into mysticism or the frankly occult. The Master Builder is tempted not by Satan but by the trolls he hears deep in the mountain. The rock will not become a holy door as it did for Oedipus and Christ. And it is not Antigone's stone room. She shut out the Gods and hung alone – and there were only the stone walls, stone roof, stone floor, the rope and her body which turned to rags and bones and fell to a little heap on the ground under the hook beside the untouched food in a bowl which might have been a tin can. No one entered her room for two thousand years till the Devil came and led her out as a witch.

But Ibsen entombs the demiurges in the mountain for ever. The trolls are not dead so they cannot be reborn. They are miniature men. And there is a race of even smaller men manipulating them – the puppet-masters are smaller than the puppets – and there is still another race of even smaller puppet-puppet-masters . . . the regression is infinite. Outside the characters gaze at the mountain, and Oedipus is a dead child in chains on the mountainside. When the frozen river splits suicides throw themselves into the water and violate nature. The mountain is a pit stood on end, as you climb you descend into Satan's ice-kingdom. The witches said Satan's semen was cold, here it is a glacier crawling into the valley to inseminate it with loathing and disgust. Hamlet is killed, Hedda Gabler kills herself.

The scenic display of terror domesticates the Devil. He does not come through the floor but through the drawing-room door and sits in an armchair. The grotesque imagery (he cannot appear without it) can be confined, most of the time, to windows or a conservatory. Explanation replaces action; the trolls are far enough away to be turned into symptoms, and so middle-class neuroses can be invented. The Devil does not leave soot on the carpet or ink stains on the walls, but occasionally – to prove he is real – he leaves blood on the piano keys.

The Master Builder is also tempted by Hilde Wangel. She is a witch and combines sex and industry. She tempts him to climb his tower. He falls to his death among dolls and little white coffins – witches' toys. Another age would have burned Hilde Wangel – and the Master Builder's wife. Ibsen merely treats his wife as mad, in the spirit in which Stalinists put dissidents into madhouses. As Ibsen aged he dreamt of turning the mountain into industrial ore – but he would not accept political responsibility and it remained a magic mountain. Ibsen wrote at the end of humanist romanticism; afterwards his romanticism became fascism – and the fascists entered the mountain and brought out the trolls. Ibsen's ability to serve bourgeois democracy by taking the pulse of the dead was uncanny. The famous stage as a room with the fourth wall missing is really a coffin with the lid off.

In Ibsen the conflicts of heresy and orthodoxy in which witches were burned alive, are reduced to scandalizing local opinion and upsetting smalltown propriety. Ibsen brought the Devil into the drawing-room so that he could be an immediate, psychological force free of social mediation. His plays have become the mainstay of 'method' acting, which is also concerned with the abstractly psychological and ignores the social and political.

Beckett's *Waiting for Godot* is a rewriting of *Hamlet*. Shakespeare's play releases political energy, his ghost switches on the machines of industrialism. Beckett trivializes the play by petrifying its politics. His gift to reaction is to disguise it with sentimentality, mysticism and ritual games. Shakespeare distributed the elements of the problem among his characters, Beckett redistributes them. He splits Hamlet into two tramps – doubles can postpone meaning. Hamlet seeks himself, the tramps wait to be told who they are. The enquiry into meaning is turned into charades of misunderstanding and the soliloquies into chatter. Hamlet cannot wish away the world's cutting edge, but in *Godot* even the tree does tricks.

Lucky combines the roles of ghost and gravediggers. Shakespeare gave the gravediggers practical, working language with a wider cultural reference. But his feudalism represses their authority – they dig graves and converse with gentry but are folk-like and outside time. Since Shakespeare's age cultural initiative has passed from princes and even entrepreneurs to worker-consumers. Neither Shakespeare nor Beckett trust worker-consumers, but Beckett cannot even pay them Shakespeare's feudal respect. He scorns them, and as usual sanctifies his reactionary judgement with reactionary pity. Lucky-the-Gravedigger talks partly as a machine – say a mechanical digger – and partly as what is dug up – Yorick's skull. He does not control the machine, he is haunted by it – it is the process in which machines dictate reactionary forms of ownership. His speech might have come from a malfunctioning tape-recorder. He cannot understand what machines say though he is the only one they could talk to. The tablets are smashed on the mountain and the mosaic of debris presented as the oracle. I do not need to describe all Beckett's elisions, condensations and substitutions; the point is that Shakespeare released history, Beckett tried to stop it.

Lucky might have been a contemporary image of radical innocence. Instead this is represented by a child seen from its nanny's point of view. And so radical innocence is disarmed and authority is not confronted; the paradox is taken out of history and immured in art. The child merely runs messages – but unlike Greek messengers he brings no news. Instead he has a nimbus of interpretation – 'my halo speaks for me'. To stall all action the messenger must be corrupt, and so what the child says has the literary style of Christmas card verses and the determinist philosophy of the gutter press and the Sunday supplements. You can almost hear God bellow 'Gotcha!'

But we must be fair to Beckett: he does not try to psychoanalyse Hamlet. He is after bigger fish, behind his rearrangements is the ambition to psychoanalyse God. But to do that you must understand history and for Beckett history is bunk.

Determinism cannot energize us socially and morally, as it once did; it diminishes our political autonomy and increases repression. Democratic ideology makes worker-consumers repress one another in retaliation for being repressed. The psyche is cordoned off so that it can be politically dominated and not seek understanding. Greek and renaissance sub-mission to fate made society more human, our submission to psychobiological determinism makes it less human. Now when we submit to fate we submit to market forces and finance, even when we call it our soul.

Technology turns our life into what our ancestors would describe as a dream. We reproduce aborigine dream-time in steel, electricity and concrete, and so our dream-work must be political not occult. We do not relate naturally to the seasons; events are filmed and edited into confused images, and we are shown pictures but do not know what they mean; our social reality is a heap of luxury goods floating in space; the starving watch us eat, the wounded watch us make weapons; it is an age of killing and consum-ing. We need a new relationship to the world, so that we may keep death out of it till its due time. A new drama would help us to do this.

Theatre Events (TEs)

Every society has its own use for theatre. The means of theatre are structurally limited and every society uses them in its own way. Its drama helps to teach audiences a new species of subjectivity appropriate to its changed world. To create the people of industrial society Shakespeare freed his characters from many feudal restrictions and added to their autonomy. Social roles changed and people had to work, think and live differently – be different. But as the new social relations were still unjust, new forms of repression were needed. Entrepreneurs could only free themselves by making prisons for others and giving them reasons – pleasant or unpleasant – to enter. Instead of social position being ordained by God it was decided by a new combination of money, reward and violence. The autonomous psyche had to accept guilt and then it would act but be constrained. Only the diabolic princes of industry and commerce could rise above guilt because they sought grandeur and damnation; later when accountancy replaced adventure, this changed to affluence and bankruptcy.

Capitalism's rationale was the free man; this meant giving determinism a Calvinist twist. Capitalism needed people who were free to act and demand (it depends on a simmering discontent) but who are also unfree: the psyche must condemn itself. The Shakespearian psyche modelled such people. We live at a turning point. People on and off stage need a new freedom. The old freedom of licence and limitation becomes daily more imprisoning. The answer is always to ask 'What are human beings creating?', and the response is always 'Society'. But there are historically different ways of doing this because different technologies need different subjectivities.

We have to bring to light what in Shakespeare and Ibsen is obscure. We have more understanding of how society and psyche produce themselves and each other. Instead of stories being quasi-Biblical, or mythical or psychoanalytical wholes, or absurd, answerless riddles, they must be told as 'opportunities of interpretation'. Absurd theatre denies meaning to events. The denial indicates the desire for what is absent. Desire *is* meaning, if only because we do not have to wait for it. Godot does not come because *waiting* keeps meaning away. Because we desire we cannot describe anything without meaning, and the clash of meanings provokes judgement. But we have to abandon idealist distinctions between mind and body, emotion and intellect. Absurdity is the meaning given to chaotic lives.

The social meaning of the past has become chaotic because we now try to make it the private meaning of the present. We used the ideology that once suppressed the psyche, as a means of self-expression. It is as if we were trying to convert God to religion. The market is never free; the market forces of finance and technology drive out free will and substitute choice. Desire is replaced by appetite. The consumer is standardized by ideology and technological imperatives. And so in an age of consumerism the customers impose ideology on the rulers: entrepreneurs are the slaves of capitalism. The market, churches and prisons now serve the same purpose. Authority has lost its moral aura and justification. We apply our hand as witness to our own warrant of servitude or even death. And yet it is easier to give meaning to life in times of chaos than in times of rigid discipline. In the end absurdity is failure of desire.

Drama is not about what happens but about the meaning of what happens. We use values to judge. If an accident happens in real life we may try to establish the facts. But a judge, juror and witness will each have a different version of the accident, based on their social attitude to accidents and all other events. Even non-trivial facts cannot be established without value judgements. Judging is as complex on stage as it is off it. Before theatre can distance itself from an event to examine it, it must change the story that 'contains' it.

A stage event is chosen to question, confirm or change the values underlying social judgement. Drama is a complex intervention in reality to get at truths society obscures or denies. Theatre never slavishly serves an establishment, for the same reason that a society that knew no sickness would not build hospitals.

The ideologies dominating our stage remove the stigma of 'ritual' from it (because bourgeois theatre must above all be entertaining) but secretly try to reintroduce the immediate, self-authenticating reality of ritual by their use of psychology: stage psychology is to be real in the way street psychology is real. This is not possible. It would mean, at the least, that murderers, for example, would have to play murderers. But even then stage psychology would not be 'real'. If a war hero re-enacts his deeds on stage it is carnival not theatre. So the theory is modified: stage psychology is based on resemblance not replication. This destroys the theory since, apart from anything else, it cannot be tested: a performance may convince but there is no way of telling whether it is true in the sense of the theory. Inevitably a gap always opens between psychology and performance. A *trompe-l'oeil* painter whose apples were so life-like you tried to eat one would be neither a good artist nor a good greengrocer.

In truth everyone *is* a murderer and a victim. Not 'I was so angry I could have killed him', but 'I was angry and I killed him'. That is the experience of metaphorical imagination. It stems from the dramatization of the child's psyche. No one could commit a real murder if they had not been murdered, and if the psyche had not dwelt on murder. In fact the unpremeditated murder is often the one the psyche has lived with longest – that is just part of the plight of being human. The extremity of our psyche allows us to put reality on stage. But stage reality must be based on social realism, not fantasy, because the mind is social. To show a murder we have to place it in social determinants as they are now, not reconstruct the psyche's metaphorical reality. This does not mean documenting the specific circumstances that led to a real murder. We have to show what general circumstances lead to specific events. This is how the imagination uses art. It allows statistics to be used to describe what escapes statistics. It is why the St Petersburg streets are mapped on Raskolnikov's face. Dostoievsky's statement that two and two are sometimes five would be meaningless if it could not be shown that two and two are always four. That – the two-and-two-are-four – educates our imagination as well as our reason. When art reproduces the psyche's sediments directly it does not (*pace* Julia Kristeva) create profundity but empty fantasy; what gives dreams their importance is their origin in hard, mundane facts – in the drama of this world.

The stage should always be concerned with process not product. It should not reproduce psychology but show how psychology is produced. Ironically, if we pretend stage psychology is 'real', drama both ceases to be art *and* falls out of the real psyche-social processes of life. The pretence comes from a fear of the stage's real power.

A story no longer contains a meaning because there is no external authority. Meaning is now in the analysis of the story. A modern play should prepare the analysis and performance should develop it. It is often assumed that the actor should act the character and the director should help him to do this. But society sends the audience to the theatre to see what judgement the actor passes on the character, what meaning he gives it. The character also imposes itself on the actor, of course, and gives its opinion of him. The character contains a description of itself which the audience will be as much – or even more – aware of as they are of what the actor does with it. The audience wishes to see what actor and character make of each other. Art is plastic, and so the paper-character becomes the flesh-and-blood actor as much as the other way round. But the actor cannot surrender to blind possession or inspiration. The character is an investigator who demands from the actor the truth about them both. That is what happens in the Palermo improvisation.

Improvisation is not performance. Performance must show more clearly how the actor and the character 'use' one another. 'Use' is not a relationship limited to those two, it is part of a triangle which includes the audience. The triangle of 'use' is the area of Theatre Events (TEs). Acting is what the actor does, not what he is. 'Use' is necessary because psychology *cannot* be acted. Only philosophy can be acted. When a comedian imitates someone it is comic, if a medium makes the same imitation it is serious: the philosophy of the performance has changed. Acting is performance, that is why in all interpretation philosophy gets in between the actor and his character. Interpretation depends on meaning, and in drama that must be a philosophy of nature, society and self. So the triangle of actor, character and audience forms a gap that *only* philosophy can fill; and society sends the audience to the theatre to see which philosophy fills it. This is true of all theatre which is not ritual. In ritual there is no direct interpretation, and the direct experience is interpreted by external authority. But ritual is not possible in modern theatre because comedy has deconstructed the grotesque. The grotesque has become Grand Guignol – we do not honour the sublimity of nature but are possessed by beasts. Dracula and Frankenstein's monster are the fag ends of ritual.

The stage itself symbolizes the gap and imposes philosophy on character and action. An act is not performed on stage as it is done in real life – *there* it takes a different time and is often done in a way meant to conceal it or its meaning.

The stage introduces its own social dimension. This is not accidental. The stage is a social space to which the audience brings, from real life, its own space. Off stage, acts occupy space, but on stage space occupies acts: they are occupied by real life social space. The stage should be called not a space but a gap. It is a physical space but a social gap. The gap invokes social space; and even when the stage is empty, when the action on it is only potential, it is not abstract action. The reason for this is that all space is owned. This means that we cannot see any space without seeing the dynamics of the gap – but this becomes critical when we watch the stage because it is a void that is intended to present action. In this an empty stage is like an empty boxing ring. The empty stage invokes social meaning, it is a blank page that is read, it is the Sphinx's eye. Because space is owned the gap is filled with the invisible presence of ownership: occupation, passage, class, politics, morality, responsibility . . . The actor's philosophy must encompass these things or he is like a fish out of its element which presents its death throes as a dance. It might seem that the stage is one gap that we could fill with fantasy. But because the stage is a social gap it has the decorum of a law court and we are the murderers and victims, plaintiffs and defendants. So the stage is crowded with invisible furniture, weapons, monuments, uniforms, utensils, coins, documents, architecture . . . which social realism ignores and fantasy merely rummages in. TEs point to the stage's invisible furnishings.

Modern playwrighting should expose the gap so that psychology cannot hide it. The actor must act the analysis he gets from philosophy. Because acting is physical it does not follow that it has immediate access to emotions – that they fill it as rain fills a hollow. The mind does not speak to itself directly but only through inconsistent concepts, which is why there is no 'point' of the mind which could be called self or soul. The psyche is more like an echo-chamber. Because the inconsistent-self is formed ideologically (and is incomplete, because society is not stable), the actor should not surrender to it – either in himself or in his character. The actor should create the character in the way society creates the actor, but the actor should do it consciously and coherently. The actor's philosophy, not the character's psychology, gives the performance's meaning. The actor must be true to the character, as the Palermo students were – but that does not decide performance. Understanding this is essential to the use of TEs.

Confusion may be made worse by the role of the director. He may believe an 'interpretation' does the work of philosophy – and of course there will be some philosophy floating in it. But it will not have been developed into a consistent theatre practice (otherwise psychology would not be seen as outside or prior to philosophy). The director takes responsibility for 'interpretation' and more or less confines the actor to psychology – which leaves the actor like a fish swimming in a fishbowl that has no water in it. The interpretation then fills the gap with empty theatricalization, effects, aesthetics and style (or, worst of all, good taste – which is always worse than bad taste). Theatricalization is often derived (with decreasing return) from circus and fake ritual. Circus, sport and murder are the only rituals left in modern society and none of them is theatre.

The nazis played Bach in Auschwitz but did not have clowns there. Playing Bach as background music to murder silences culture by making it insane, a gesture the nazis had to make to protect their own rationale. To nazis the music of Auschwitz was as important as the corpses, which is saying much. But clowns do not have to be silenced. They cannot lie and so they understand everything and can change nothing. The circus is an arena for human beings as well as animals, it is its own world of sadness and tinsel where clowns nod at death. Murder is a ritual because society still needs an arena, a theatre of death – and the media can turn murder into it. Sport is a ritual because society needs to make something triumphant and does not know what – it finds nothing in the rest of its life that could lead to triumph.

What a chalice, a paper hoop, a football and a murderer's knife have in common is emptiness. Each opens an emptiness, a gap, and fills it with a false authority which is taken to be reality. The priest fills it with a dead God; sport fills it with a meaningless victory – the game matters only because we need it to; the murderer fills it with the Devil – but the Devil, like God, is dead; and the clown fills it with the child's lost dreams – but the Russian guard's pistol is not a water pistol. Some of these rituals have other values – aesthetic ones, for example. The point is that they are not theatre.

It is said that in the mass the host becomes literally flesh. A similar though profane claim is made when it is said that the actor becomes the character. Both claims come from an intense need and depend on a serious misunderstanding of theatre. The 'method' wants to fill the gap with a 'ritual of psychology'. But the psychology becomes increasingly devalued as capitalism devalues people. The method has degenerated into the 'treatment'. Excesses of energy, hysteria and pathos are pumped into performance to create significance, as if by using larger print you added to the meaning of what was said. Many film-makers encourage the treatment because its wash of emotion is like film-music and animates the screen when the images are valueless.

Finally there are forms of theatre – the theatre of the

absurd, happenings, silence and so on – which are derived from occult Maeterlinckism. This pretends reality is meaningless, reduces it to a dream and reifies the dream as meaning. It is reactionary – finance-totalitarianism cannot be resisted by the occult. Godot's messenger is pushed on stage by Maeterlinck . . .

The actor can only cross the gap to the audience by using philosophy. This cannot be a vague attitude to the world. The ramifying complications of drama will strain its details and nuances, and they become monstrous if the philosophy is inconsistent. The philosophy must be clear – the reality of the stage is that the actor wipes his knife on the audience's shirt and they should not be trifled with or needlessly offended. We are afraid of the gap and need to fill it. The problem is that many of the false ways of filling it work. But anything *works*: if you bang your fist everyone jumps. When you do it in a restaurant it is rudeness, why is it art when you do it on stage?

The Elizabethan and Jacobean theatres filled the gap with the supernatural. But their devils and ghosts had the hardest and most practical objectification in the real world – in iron, steel, concrete, industrial finance, workers' lives and witches' deaths. We need to fill the gap by showing how the existing ownership of machines (and therefore of society and psyche – of our reality) limits our humanness and freedom, and how nevertheless we may make ourselves and society freer and more human.

The gap can be filled with TEs. The name distinguishes stage events from those which it is wrongly claimed are real. All stage events are TEs, though this is denied; but unintended TEs are usually negative and destructive. I was made conscious of TEs by a real life incident. Till then I had used them without theorizing about them; they were natural to a writer of my background and origins. Because the incident comes from real life it makes the point that TEs make the stage useful again by bringing it closer to the audience's world.

This is the incident. It takes place in a Middle-Eastern city during war. A bomb explodes in a street. There is chaos – screams, sirens, smoke from the explosion and the fires it has started. Bodies on stretchers are carried through the crowd. Militia shout and wave automatic rifles to clear a way for them. A woman runs beside a stretcher. She wears a black robe. On the stretcher is a man's mangled body – probably her dead husband or son. His age cannot be seen because the bomb has smeared the skin and stubble across his face as if it were a mask it had tried to rip off. As the woman runs she screams and raises her clenched fists to heaven. Then she opens her hands – with the palms up and fingers spread – and shakes them over the body, pleading with the crowd to look at it. These are age-old sounds, gestures and expressions of grief – the image of the pain of war. And then she sees – half sees – men pointing a TV camera and sound-boom at her. Her right hand – with the open, upturned palm and spread fingers – sweeps down to the body in a gesture of display – then clenches to a fist and rises to heaven. In the same instant her left hand glides gently to her hair and – gently, delicately, with a salon gesture – pats it into place: she is on TV. The gap is filled. That is a TE.

The hand patting the hair into place is not a sign of vanity or insensitivity. The woman's pain was real. The gesture comes from her social situation. She is not a stage heroine acting out her pain in a privileged setting or giving it the 'treatment'. She must go home, shop, cook, clean, nurse children, bury the dead, mourn, go to work and get on with life – perhaps the patting hand will be held out to beg.

Often in theatre a scream has the wrong price-tag on it; almost always when working-class characters scream they indulge in the luxury of one they could never afford. Alone, neither the shaking fist nor the gentle, patting hand tells the truth, but together they tell the violence and waste of war. The gesture is too small to be noticed in most theatres, but it shows the power of TEs and the importance of using them properly. The gesture may be interpreted and performed in totally opposed ways: it depends on the philosophy.

It is often thought that art reveals a reality hidden behind the everyday. This reality is said to be the meaning of life because it secretly forms it and when it is revealed its value and significance are self-evident. It may be divine, Freudian, instinctual or something else. Certainly we do not always know why we act or forsee all the consequences of our acts, and we are wasteful of our biological potential for pleasure and our intellectual potential for creation. But art is not a hidden truth with a self-evident value, it is a negotiation between the subjective and objective which changes both. We do not have to show a hidden reality, but the nature and interconnection of the forces which openly surround us every day.

Psychological 'secrets' may be universal – as, it is claimed, is the incest taboo – or biographical, as they are in the plays of Ibsen and his followers. Biographical secrets are formed after childhood, which is rightly said to be a time of universalism. The child's psyche is dramatized and drama made the process of the psyche, of our intellectual-and-emotional life – that is why, to function, the psyche needs art. There are no dramatic 'solutions' to its drama. No one lives happily ever after, and the hero's death does not often incite others to die but may give them a better understanding of their life. The mere revelation of secrets is not creative – there must also be meaning.

Ibsen's revelations had meaning because his secrets were denied not only by his characters but also by his audience and the society that sent them to the theatre (this can be felt in a tension in the plays). But our society does not deny Ibsen's secrets and so for us their revelation has no value or meaning. Of course we can still observe the effects they have on the characters, but we have to supply a meaning that is not in the play. Iago is condemned to be tortured to death. In the world of the play's first audiences he *would* have been – but we give another meaning to the condemnation: it makes us reflect on society. For the first audiences, the torture closes the play's meaning. But for us, it opens it.

A secret can be told only once. Only once can Oedipus learn who he is. The secrets have become commonplaces, they tell us only what everyone knows. Far from revealing reality they are fetishized to make reality mysterious. That is why we have happenings and the theatres of the occult, silence and dreams. These are attempts to find a mystery beyond society and psyche, the secret of being itself (Havel wondered about it in prison). It is like an exercise machine with a circular band for a floor: you run but stay on the spot, the arduous journey is to nowhere. The endless repetition without meaning tires: puppets working puppets working puppets . . . It is done better by drugs (I believe). It cannot recreate the relation between subjectivity and objectivity, psyche and society.

The theatre of the absurd tries to show that life is meaningless, and that human values are only reactions – rage, pity (though even this is anaesthetized by the comic), boredom or catalepsy. We are like a legless fly trying to walk on the ceiling. If you believe it, there is less and less to be said. It leads to the autistic repetitions of minimalism or to the theatre of silence. The audience is told to intuit the unsayable in the silence. The silence is not Wittgenstein's unsayable – in *that* there is nothing to intuit. Wittgenstein said that whatever could be said could be said precisely. And the silence is not Lear's nothing because Lear speaks. In the theatre of silence there are not only no clothes, there is no emperor. Silence is the avoidance of meaning that is too painful, disagreeable or demanding. TEs say what the theatre of silence wishes to leave unsaid.

The secrets and silence are thought to be the subtext, which cannot or should not be made overt. But covertness cannot be art. Art requires an acknowledged understanding that changes the boundary between objective and subjective, history and individual. In fact Oedipus's subtext is blazed open to the public. If there is a denial it is the audience's that is Oedipus. Modern audiences do not deny this. Our pseudo-democracy obsessively exposes the psyche in order to *repress* social understanding. The subtext provides not meaning but mystification. That is why TEs do not use it – instead they use a metatext. When TEs are used it becomes clear that it is not the individual but society that is the more confused by secrets – and these are more dangerous than the secrets of Oedipus.

An actor finds his character in the text. In this respect acting TEs does not differ from method acting. But the *character* cannot be *performed*. The actor must fill the gap with metatext, and this is so even when the theatre tries to collapse the metatext into the subtext. The secrets of Sophocles's Oedipus are not even a subtext – they are more like unexamined state archives and even then they are already known to the audience. Oedipus's metatext belongs to the Gods and they hold the meaning. Ibsen's secrets were a metatext to his society and so they could be usefully revealed, and significantly Ibsen required a new approach to acting, just as TEs do. But even in Ibsen's plays the metatext is not the secrets but the meaning the audience gives them. In our theatre the metatext gap is still empty, yet society sends audiences to the theatre to see how it is filled – that is the difference between ritual and theatre. Theatre is meaningless when the metatext is misused, and almost all theatre now shown in London, and in some other places, is literally meaningless.

Theatricalization, psychology and biological determinism cannot provide a metatext because they impose predetermined, authoratative meaning. TEs show the relationship between psyche and society and reform the relationship. This makes theatre revelatory and gives it meaning. The meaning comes from philosophy, not metaphysics or nature. Philosophy provides the analysis for the TEs, and theatricalization provides their dramatization, articulation and insight. Philosophy should be as complete as possible; theatricalization is open-ended and a matter of artistry, skill and imagination. But theatricalization also defines philosophy, and so is also intellectual – just as the child's play is as philosophical as its questions (and far more disciplined than the good behaviour that rigidly follows rules). The intellectual truth of theatricalization is like a craftsman's truth and combines action and mind, in the sense that a 'true' line of bricks is laid. TEs are neither drab social realism nor fanciful. They can use all the theatricality of happenings, but not as an end in itself. Happenings have no meaning other than themselves; they do not have access to the 'natural' – nature is bound by laws and has no free will – or the 'supernatural' – *that* is derived from the material and must acknowledge what is material in it.

TEs use both character and happenings. To play TEs actors do not have to step outside their character or make it a generalization; they find TEs within the character's scope and use them to play the character. But actors should be *able* to step outside their character and become themselves if need be. They are asked to do this in *Red Black and Ignorant*. Really the actor's social self is the basis of the character, the negotiation between him and the character. It is the social self that makes the decision in the Palermo improvisation. The actor's ability to step outside his character into his social self is an extension of his ability to observe himself in performance. Actors from theatres as different as kabuki and Comédie Française understand the importance of being able to do this. An actor who cannot step outside his character is creatively rigid and may become uncreative. It is one reason why the method deteriorated into the treatment.

In *Red Black and Ignorant* the soldier returns home with his order to kill someone – anyone – in the neighbourhood. His mother represses her revulsion, dresses him in his uniform and sends him to kill her neighbour. The text gives her and her son's reasons for what they do. They may have other motives in a subtext (perhaps a writer is not always in control of the subtext). Does the son have an Oedipal relation to the father so that already he wants to kill him (as in the end he does) instead of the neighbour? Could it be unconscious guilt that makes him stand as passively as a child being dressed to run an errand?

The text (and any subtext) are written but a metatext is not. It is inferred and created by studying and rehearsing the written texts. It may contain many ideas, actions and emotions – because it is open-ended – and some of these may already be in the written text. The neighbour is a friend and the mother does not want him killed – that is text and subtext. But some things will only be in the metatext. Years ago when the mother sent her son on errands was she already training him in the obedience a soldier needs when he kills? In a way, when a soldier kills he is running an errand for his officers. That is a metatext question because it touches on the nature of society. The metatext of *Red Black and Ignorant* says that it takes a lot of culture to make us killers.

Suppose the soldier has a subtextual motive to kill – perhaps it's even why he joined the army, to be nearer to macho power. Is that the incident's meaning? If it is, why doesn't he kill the officer? The officer is far more like a father than the neighbour – the officer is strong and commanding, the neighbour weak. The soldier does not kill the officer because the officer is part of organized social power and the soldier would be punished if he did. And the order comes from society, anyway. So it is society that gives the motive its meaning. Otherwise it is like saying we drown because we breathe, when we should ask why a drowned person was in the water. Perhaps the soldier's fear of officers is repressed into the unconscious, where it could be attached to any number of motivations? The act's origin – its cause and meaning – is still social.

An Oedipal subtext would not explain what happens, any more than that we breathe tells us why we drown. What is relevant is not the motive but the cause. That is found by philosophic analysis of society. The truth is in the social world and in the metatext. Obviously that is what the acting should show – in action, gesture, texture – if it is to show the incident's truth. In this scene neither the mother nor son act on their motivations, they react to the officer as if he were Fate. The meanings provided by the subtext and the metatext are radically different. It is not a difference of artistic sensibility or taste. Apart from acts of radical innocence, the meanings of our acts are never our motivations for doing them. The reasons for our acts come from society: as good actors have always known, it is our *excuses* for our acts that come from our unconscious – that has always decided the texture of good acting. We act as we do because we are in a particular sort of society. Acts are like moves in a game: the rules of the game give the meanings of the moves and players move according to the rules.

The incident with the soldier is suitable for a TE because it contains contradictory imperatives, and their resolution increases or diminishes our humanity. Should the actress hand the actor his helmet as if it were a school cap? Or brush dirt from his knee? – reaction is obsessed with dirt because it believes that cleanliness is next to obedience. Should she hesitate to give him the jacket? If she gave it to him and then took it back, she would emphasize the mother's doubt. But she would not show us how the mother has learnt to deal with doubt. So she dresses him hurriedly and forcefully and is so intent – perhaps frantic – on getting him into his jacket that she drops it. At that moment the jacket is to her the most important thing in the world – but suddenly her hands are empty. The jacket isn't there any more! She is so surprised she doesn't know where she is. Its almost as if she's thrown the jacket away – or has someone come in and snatched it? An actress can use this moment. Then slowly she stoops to the floor to pick up the jacket. The stooping can be slightly metaphorized so that it seems as if she bows to the ground before the soldier. He stands ram-rod straight at attention. Is he awkward at being treated as a child as he prepares to 'act like a man'? At being in a killer's uniform in the family kitchen? At the sudden obeisance – which he demanded in his song but had not expected from his mother? For the audience his awkwardness is in the metatext because the mother's bow puts it there. The TE turns 'mother and child' into 'soldier and victim'. Does the mother's costume help the image? Should the costume be changed? TE turns everything on stage into a prop. There is no self-contained TE-design. TE-design identifies the text but establishes the structure of the metatext and makes it useful.

Usually TEs should be based on the play's philosophy. They join with it in a common language and this has a cumulative effect. But they *may* not share the play's philosophy. A reactionary interpretation of the jacket incident might base the TE on the way a medieval lady arms her knight for the crusade. This would conflict with the rest of the play, in which soldiers do not behave as knights are supposed to have behaved (they behave as they actually did). But a TE based on the play's philosophy might still use the incident in the same way. Then it would be satirical. The director should ask if satire was useful at that moment, not merely if it 'worked'. It would be useful only if it was consistent with the philosophical use of the rest of the play. Put like that, it seems obvious – yet in rehearsals such questions are often ignored.

Some TEs should be critical. When Gloucester is blinded in *King Lear*, a generous-minded 'retainer' is killed. The killing of the servant is more appalling than the blinding of the duke, though I have never seen the point made on stage. The TE should attack feudalism – perhaps guided by the way I treated the related incident in my *Lear*, when a soldier is ordered to assault Warrington.

The War Plays' philosophy is socialist, that is it is written in the understanding that there could be no reason in the subtext why the soldier must kill *anyone*. The incident's truth is in the metatext. That does not restrict the interpretation or make it doctrinaire. The subtext would be restrictive because its explanation is closed and invites pathos, which our age makes maudlin (as in Beckett's messenger boy and Cocteau's 'Poor Oedipus!'). TE-theatre expands texts and ramifies their social, psychological and theatrical possibilities.

The TE of the dropped jacket is drawn from the text and the characters, it is not imposed on them. It shows what the text cannot show and allows the actors to be in character. In fact it allows them to play the characters more intensely. This could not have been achieved the other way round – intense 'treatment' would not have produced meaning. The TE makes metatext and character one. It points to a tragic social truth: often in real life when people think they are most utterly, profoundly themselves they are merely playing a metatext which is empty because they did not choose it. They are like puppets who tie knots in their strings to remind them when to dance. Actors need artistry and imagination to choose incidents to TE and to work out how to TE them – society is cunning and awe-inspiring in its ability to conceal from itself what it does. The jacket need not be TE-d. There could be a TE after the soldier has left. The mother might tidy the room or use a dishcloth (impotence) in juxtaposition to the flak jacket (power). Like the son, the mother survives by taking orders.

TEs are not arbitrary. The text suggests them. They do not distort the text's emotional and dramatic structures – properly TE-ing it does not even distort its tempo. This is surprising. The explanation is that as long as TEs use the text's social truth they can develop it without distorting the text's structure. The structure is itself an analysis of the social truth. So the text lends itself to TEs because there is an intrinsic compatibility between it and them. If TEs do not use the social truth they distort the text and again make theatricalization an end in itself, they become product and not process. TEs are autonomous but what they add to a text is not unlike a musician's expressiveness. They do not have to 'stop' the text – though they may. They relate to it as other acting does, serving and expanding it. Each TE may be brief or extended but together they TE the whole play. This creates a style of TE-acting which becomes the language in which the audience interpret the play. TE-acting tends to be more graphic, direct, simple, theatrical and powerful than treatment or naturalism; and because it combines expression and demonstration it does not produce a false language of compulsion, sentiment and inflated emotion.

Art does not passively serve philosophy. It illuminates it. That is the function of TEs. The philosophy used to create the metatext must be consistent. Often in rehearsals the three texts are confused. An action based on one text is supported by an argument derived from one of the others. The result should be offensive but instead it is buried under slick theatricalization or hysterical treatment.

Multiple Theatre Events (TEs)

TEs change the way plays are written. The penultimate scene of *Restoration* is a multiple TE. If this is not under- stood it will be acted in a quasi-method, quasi-classical way. It will not work. Lighting effects and stage business will be used to make it work. They empty it completely. The characters have important things to say because *their situ- ation demands* that they say them. The audience expects it. The text can create the situation but the rest is performance – TEs. Each character must perform his relation to the scene's economic situation, because that relation is the only form society allows their humanity to take. This does not devalue the characters. An actor who wants to show that his character's *soul* is good and sensitive might think it doctrinaire to object to this. But the scene shows how good becomes bad, how sensitivity becomes callousness. A man drowns *because* he breathes; what keeps him alive in one situation kills him in another; the situation changes the meaning – drowning is another way of breathing. The *Restoration* scene must show the true situation. The last thing the acting needs to do is carry on a sentimental fight against the vulgar prejudice of innate evil. The whole play attacks that prejudice. Society corrupts goodness and souls may be in chains – it is why Himmler gassed people and when he overworked his killers sent flowers to their wives in apology. What do the flowers prove? It is a vicious platitude to show that each of us has a good, kind soul. It is like strewing Himmler's ashes on the ashes of his victims. Whoever wants to do that has not yet seen human ashes creep away from human flesh. To show someone's soul in chains we must show the chains and the wage paid for wearing them.

The scene is about getting a man ready to be hanged. Each character in it – including the victim and his devoted wife – must be shown as the hangman. We must show how they are forced to be that, and what their fee is. Not how 'underneath' the brutal are kind, but how kindness is made brutal and beauty ugly. When the devoted wife forces alcohol down her husband's throat it should be as if she put the rope round his neck; and that is not done nicely – it is sick to imagine that it is. The priest prays as if he were drowning a basket of kittens. He need not hurry his prayers – though he may – it is just that in his life there is no difference between killing and praying (he is like an army padre). The victim, his wife, the drunk, the priest, the up-and-coming apprentice, the respectable housewife – all must be taken to an extreme because hanging is an extreme. The action is chaotic, the cogs on the wheels devour each other – but it must be shown clearly, in accident-time (I will describe this later). If the relationships are not TE-d in this way there is nothing to play in the scene because there is nothing there but social truth; and this cannot be reduced to merely personal truths, even if they were relevant. At the moment our theatre cannot act this scene because it does not understand social truth or have the means of showing it. The old forms of theatre lose their vitality and are replaced by gimmicks, hysteria, fake-mystery and *Muzakals*, and are less and less able to tell the truth.

Bingo is subtitled 'Scenes of death and money'. Everything in the play has its price, the value the characters put on it; and its cost, the malaise and death it brings to them. The metatext's performance must be based on the subtitle and the actors should metaphorize the relations it exposes. It might be useful to rehearse some highly emotional scenes as if they took place in a bank and had to do with counting money. This would not produce the performance – that would be crude, a product not process – but it would give insights into the characters' prisons and suggest TEs.

The argument between Coombe and the Son in the inn will not work if it is treated as a good, old-fashioned slanging match. For Coombe, the Son is sent by the Devil. For the Son, Coombe is sent by God – God has appointed him as his enemy and sent him to be defeated. For Coombe, the son is a large debt; for the Son, Coombe is a large increase in income. Both men fear each other and are angry – but the Son's anger is glad, Coombe's is embittered and made even angrier by the gladness he senses in the Son's rage. (The Son's gladness is a reason why later he must confess to Shakespeare.) When this is understood the argument between Coombe and the Son becomes powerful and their non-communication more unbridgeable. 'Treatment' would merely make them angrier, and the more they shout at each other the better! – but this would obliterate their precise choice of words (people count money and measure land precisely) and all the audience would hear is noise. Once again the right TE gives the characters more intense life.

The relationships in *Bingo* are founded on money but this does not reduce them to money. That would make economic determinism into another form of fate – and then, for example, there would be no reason for Shakespeare's suicide, which is an act of free will. Economic relations drive people to new human insights and profundities, to the inscriptions stones on the bottom of the stream cut into the water, where characters read their own triviality or power. When the father's hands touch his daughter's flesh they are as cold as if they counted money. How do they throw snowballs? It says nothing that the man still has a child's happiness in his soul – even a child knows that. The snowballs are made in hell – where Shakespeare stores his happiness. They are counted like coins: one man cheats and is shot, one man judges his life and freezes to death. Both are 'happy'.

In *Summer* Xenia lives the emotional logic of the dead. Her interest in fashion is part of the logic. Why is she dead? Where is she buried? How often does she bring flowers to her own grave? How do the dead sit in chairs? Why do the dead lose their keys? How do they spy on the living? How do they give birth? How do their children live? And when the dead are spat on how do they die? (Those who say that Xenia should not be spat on do not understand that she wants-and-does-not-want to be spat on.) Xenia's death is psyche-social, and she hides it from herself and others. The actress who plays her must fill the gap with the TE of this death from her first entry. Otherwise Marthe's reasons for spitting at her are not clear: the spit is the way she finds of killing the dead. She knows that the dead want to take your life even when there are only seconds of it left – the dead are covetous of seconds.

Marthe's death scene brings out another characteristic of some TEs. Usually a director tries to assemble a play's different social worlds into one stage-world. Imagine a servant standing before his master: the servant twists his cap in his hands. The scene might win our compassion or make us laugh; and we might be made to object to the relationship. But if both actors are in the same technical stage-world we see only the surface of their relationship, and that they can be human side-by-side in the same world. If the actors are in different stage-worlds the dislocation is more radical: it is shown structurally. The sight is strangely disturbing. We see that the stage gap is not co-extensive with the social space. The gap contains two social spaces – as if two objects occupied the same space. Each social space must exclude the other *and* deny its humanity. The characters are in different worlds and there is no shared humanity because human beings can only inhabit one world: an environment is integral to its species. The psychological gap is shown physically and the two worlds are shown to be unbridgeable except in the act of making them one. Otherwise we would be able to change our species by changing our address. Another way of putting it is to say that the spectator is in two places at once and sees from two different points of view. He is still free to make his personal judgement on each world, but he *cannot* ideologically dissolve the barrier between the two. He cannot, for example, dissolve it sentimentally. It is seen as what it is, a barrier of violence. The psychological has been made physical. Ideological disagreements on opinions are commonplace; but it is more difficult to maintain for ideological reasons that, say, a square is round. Believing it is changes the believer more radically. He must accept more responsibility for his belief. Himmler would accept it by killing more people. It is not necessary for the audience to be analytically conscious that they are seeing two 'worlds'.

Apprehension becomes, partly, perception, especially when ideology is critically involved; but when perception is changed there has to be a new apprehension, a new choice of reality.

TEs can separate two worlds that meet in one room by basing each of them on a different form of theatre. A whole play may be structured on different forms in this way (*Jackets* is an example of this). In Marthe's death scene, Marthe's world is tragic and Xenia's is farcical. The scene is not tragi-comic, where meaning is unclear and the same thing may be seen in different lights. The tragedy and the farce are clear and distinct yet brought face-to-face. Marthe and David are played tragically, interpretatively and technically, and this decides their timing, voice, movements, gestures and so on. Xenia is played farcically – and her timing, voice, movements and gestures are based on farce technique. She is a dead woman who is angry that someone escapes from her by dying; and so not only is she dead, she has now lost her reason for living. That is her social reality, and it is beyond tragedy: it is farcical. The farce is her metatext but the point is also made in the text. For example, flowers are not left for the dead woman but for Xenia. She must handle them farcically. (The dead hate flowers.) Her situation is tragic but she is not: if she is played tragically her situation ceases to be tragic. The scene's tragedy and farce are like the hands of the mourning woman, one a fist shaken at heaven, one patting the hair – together they make the TE. The art is to combine the two worlds – tragedy and farce – technically and realistically into one recognizable social world. This can be done with skill and tact, so that it seems as 'natural' as the way the mourning woman used her hands. If the two stage-worlds are not combined into convincing social realism they are not process but product, and make theatricality an end in itself. Then reality is not shown. There is a simple acting exercise which gives the gist of this sort of TE: one actor sings a sad song while another sings a happy song, and each remains in his own 'world'. (Of course, not all TEs are based on the device of two worlds.)

The actress playing Xenia may feel that changing to farce for her last scene cheapens her character. Actors may still want to show the kindness of their characters' souls – and their own. I have argued that the 'kind soul' is a dangerous cliché. Its acceptance by any audience is sentimental because it denies appalling truths of their own world. Acting the scene's social truth requires technical skill and interpretative power which win more than well-meant sympathy for the actress and the character. A court judge does not serve the sentence he passes, but theatre audiences have to live their judgements – it is how the psyche punishes or rewards itself for making them. If Xenia is made conventionally sympathetic she becomes merely emotionally tragic. This does not provide the bitter lesson of classical tragedy, which showed the audience that the Gods were not moved by human tears, the characters' or the audiences'.

TEs help us to see which world we are in. If there were a God scientists would need to do tests on him to verify it. What else could our world do? The second coming would be announced not by trumpets but by a scientific report. How else could a civilization, above all a christian one, act responsibly? Christ would be a UFO – and might be an enemy from outer space. If he swept aside our scepticism with manna or brimstone, we would submit. But then why give us reason and scepticism in the first place? This sounds ridiculous but the point is serious. Society misuses its metatexts to provide false meanings. Religious belief can still be fanatical but it cannot be serious. Our society cannot base itself on God: the machines do not need him. When the illusion of God is removed from the metatext and put in the text, in the way I have just done, it becomes comic. The religious may not be consoled to know that in our theatre worse illusions pass unnoticed all the time because they are 'art'.

TEs are not simply Brechtian alienation effects. Brecht frequently revised his understanding of theatre, I am commenting on it as it is generally understood. Brecht wanted to found a Diderot Theatre Society. Diderot was a rationalist social-philosopher but a romantic artist. He said 'Poet be dark!', Brecht wanted poets to be light. Yet alienation theory depends on a philosophy of mind held by Diderot and other eighteenth-century rationalists. It appeals to objective judgement but does not secure the means of achieving it. The mind cannot get outside itself to be objective. The structure of mind is part of the continuum of society: both are part of one reality, and our examination of particular problems repeats the general problem – if not absolutely (since the examining mind must repeat its willed incorporation into society) then with a drag of distortion. Himmler killed out of love but organized the killing objectively. Objectivity does not penetrate passion or complacency. Theatre must infiltrate the processes which make the social mind; TEs attempt to do this.

Brecht sometimes confuses theatre with sport, and this confuses theatre with ritual. Sport is not alienated but partisan. Whenever it tends to alienation it does so on the basis of extra-ludic authority. Nineteenth-century cricketers believed the game, not winning, mattered; alienation operated as a bastion of authority not a means of questioning it. The philosophy of all ritual is given by outside authority. Brecht's confusion suggests it is the text which provides theatrical pleasure, and that the meaning is given by authority (as the meaning of football is decided by the ruling authority). But it is the meaning of the text which provides theatrical pleasure – the meaning is the way social space occupies the stage gap, and it becomes aesthetic pleasure in its embodiment in the texture of performance. But only the meaning of the text – not the aesthetic texture – makes the audience creative.

The masks of *The Caucasian Chalk Circle* weight one side of the triangle. The audience see the masks but the characters do not. On stage the two social worlds are properly separated but not realistically joined. The audience is given privileged understanding of the metatext, but it does not do the audience-work – that is done for it by authority. This makes *The Caucasian Chalk Circle* a fable, which clarifies but also obscures meaning by putting product *inside* process.

The point can be made by considering Brecht's use of music. Music cannot be alienated or even fully incorporated into alienation. Music has no grammar or meaning and does not lie or tell the truth. *The Threepenny Opera* music deconstructs romanticism but creates its own Grossstadt-romantik. The text of Wagner's *Ring* alienates the music as much as the music of *The Threepenny Opera* alienates its subject. In both operas there are gaps between music, subject and text. Wagner uses the authority of myths to explain the present. Brecht uses the authority of musical satire to dissolve the serious (but also, significantly, uses a Passion chorale to recapture it). Brecht uses music in the way Wagner uses myth. Both are external authorities. Wagner escapes from social problems into the spiritual operetta of *Parsifal*, and Brecht faces up to them. But the point, here, is means not ends.

Music does not precede speech historically, cognitatively or emotionally. Machines had to teach us to speak before we could sing or make any music. The first music was practical and used to organize action. Even religious music was practical: offering music to the Gods was as practical as offering them food – the equivalent of petrol we put in machines. Early humans related to the Gods not by being good but by having the right 'keys'. Musical instruments are quite late tools; but even the singing voice relates to the speaking voice as a tool: like the opposable thumb, it confronts the alien mirror-image of itself. We experience pleasure in music only because the intellect first confronted 'nothing' and gave the world meaning. In all music something is missing: the speaking voice. Music is a form of silence. It requires an external authority that speaks before it sounds. The sound of music cannot fill that silence and the neurosensory pleasure music gives cannot be that authority.

There is no musical reason why we should not belly-dance at funerals or sing comic-patter songs at *autos-da-fé*. There is no *musical* reason why we should not march to waltzes – the reason we do not is practical. March-music is march-music because we have the institution of marching, but we did not first hear march-music and then invent marching orders so that we could march to it. (Does anyone imagine we danced before we walked?) Sad music is sad by convention. Even funeral music is close to love music. Because music has no natural meaning it is ideal for authoritarian use. Authority establishes the meaning. We use music in the way we use food. We use food symbolically and ritually to bring us nearer God – but even worms eat. Eating is as purely practical as excreting, and of course children and primitive people have excreting rituals, use excreta symbolically and get equal pleasure from eating and excreting. When we use music to serenade, march to war or sing hymns, we are doing nothing in itself more profound than children do when they play with faeces.

Schopenhauer completely misunderstood music, which is why Wagner was able to admire him. Music is not the presence of 'will' but the absence of 'will' – and only the dead are more will-less than listeners to music. Schopenhauer craved the political security he got from his philosophical pessimism and determinism, and he tried to use music as proof of the truth of his philosophy, although he knew that its truth depended on being unprovable. Human beings created music, and the psycho-physical pleasure we find in it we ourselves have made possible. But we also made the musical barriers that divided classes and cultures – because music is 'spoken' by authority and is silent before authority speaks. Whoever changes the use or style of music speaks as authority. But because music already exists within complex cultural relationships, once an authority changes its established use (detaching it from memory, custom etc) it is vulnerable to other authorities. In any machine-society music is a class and cultural battleground. That is why it cannot be stabilized in alienation. But all alienation – in music, text, object, performance – is equally unstable, because culture is a symbolic network of conventional meanings.

Modern technology makes music more invasive but restricts its forms and uses less of their potential. The consumer is made a standardized product and impotence experienced as freedom. When a policeman stands on the doorstep and tells the mother her son has died in a car crash, the radio plays background social-*Muzak*. The policeman speaks the social-*Muzak* as funeral music. Potentially this frees the listener from authority's grasp – but only if music is part of a free social metatext: otherwise the *listener* is alienated. At the present time music is ghettoized as entertaining, religious, military and so on.

Brecht isolates music in various ways. For example, he flies insignia over the stage while a song is sung. The insignia do not alienate, they transmit authority. They are like the lights outside a dance hall: *here* you may dance *this* sort of dance. In Brecht's plays most of the songs are solos. Really he uses them as Shakespeare used soliloquies; but there are no Hamlet-like questions, and (unlike the *public* soliloquies in *The Worlds*) the authority of the soliloquies does not come from the characters. They are used in the way masks are used in *The Caucasian Chalk Circle*. Really, in Brecht, music is the mask worn by authority. However, his understanding of people and society is such that his plays are not restricted to the use of one authority.

These comments are inadequate and I cannot add much to them here. Brecht did not fully develop the use of metatext. His plays work even in unBrechtian ways, though far less well. His metatexts can be acted in a way that makes them parasitic on the text, as if the text were the metatext's subtext. Alienation does not provide an autonomous metatext. A metatext is not alienation but a commitment that involves the psyche-social processes of real life. The audience commits itself to judgement because it questions itself.

Many of my scenes – maybe all – cannot be performed unless the performance is based on the metatext; the metatext acting cannot be parasitic on the text because the text will not function as a subtext. It records modern society and the whole of modern society is alienated: you cannot alienate alienation. If the metatext is not acted there is nothing there. Because of when they were written Brecht's plays still have strands of traditional theatre in them. Inevitably some of the revolutionary break with the past was the effort to get away from it, not to construct an alternative with its own capacity for change. Since Brecht's time capitalism has become adept at weaving alienation and empathy into one self-negating experience. Modernism tried to find a metatext in the subtext, but the social-psyche of post-modernism does not have the structural means to do that, it simply does not know them: they were paths on a mountain that has been swept away. TEs are now the only alternative to fake-theatre.

The one overall structure in my plays is language. It brackets the text that is there with what is not there, the metatext. The language is in the metatext as well as in the text, and it exists for the characters only as a consequence of being in the metatext. The language is the play's not the characters'. This does not diminish the characters' importance or individuality. Shakespeare's blank verse belongs to the play not the characters (though the relationship between his characters and their plays is not modern), but this does not diminish the characters – it adds to their meaning. Because the language of my plays points to the metatext, if they are not TE-d the audience cannot hear the language – it is meaningless. The actor is like a comedian telling jokes to an audience with no sense of humour, except that it is the actor who does not understand the joke. Trying to make the text 'work' by theatricalization and the 'treatment' takes away even more meaning: the play will be like a musical instrument in the hands of a dead musician. This sounds daunting only because what our theatre does is meaningless and it has lost the tools of meaning. But often when schools and colleges perform my plays the approach is understood as if it were self-evident and does not need to be theorized. Youthful energy and imagination make the play theatrical, and the youthful need to understand the world makes the philosophical consequences clear. Professional theatres and players have more acting skills, more elaborate equipment and often use more strenuous treatment, but they cannot compensate for the lack of social truth.

TEs are biased but not authoritarian. The actor's philosophy cannot work as an external authority. TEs invoke the audience's real life socio-psyche processes, so that their dramatized psyche works for itself. Freedom of thought is not a matter of opinions. We do not have opinions about natural laws, we have them about society only because it is owned, and because we are part of it and create it partly by our opinions. Machines are not interested in freedom, they know only necessity. We will be free only when we understand what we do, and when we can abolish ownership and become autonomous arbiters of creation. That no longer has anything to do with Gods and Devils, and certainly not with good and evil as they are commonly misunderstood. Because the relations between freedom and necessity, mind and machines, people and society, are reciprocal, freedom cannot be imposed by force – it simply cannot be imposed uniformly, and at the same time, on all the structures of psyche and society. Humanness is created by the adaptations each of the structures forces on the others. So freedom exists only when it is chosen freely, and that is not yet our case – nor will it be overnight.

TEs cannot simply provide a better understanding in place of a misunderstanding. Audiences cannot be coerced into understanding by an aggressive or emotionally domineering performance. Emotions stand between concepts and feelings and, in this respect, they are passive. To change them you must change concepts, but each is locked in the other. (The problem is posed by Himmler's sermon.) Emotional appeals achieve only token responses, we cry at the superficially moving. TEs try to use the psycho-social processes of real life in a way that avoids their frequent circularity. They require the audience to translate their own language and discover what they know and believe.

The Real World and TEs

The processes of TEs are not exclusive or even special to
art. But in real life they may be 'automatic'. Then they
decide what *we* think and do – *we* are the group and the
individual understands himself as a member of it. He is one
of *us*. But the group is not a means of understanding but of
being understood. Even so, it only accepts the individual
under sufferance because it is itself artificial: broken frag-
ments of pot imagining wholeness. The group is able to
exist only because its members do not merely repeat its
understanding of things, they sustain it by belief and this is
never passive. The psyche is questioned by its experience
even when it affirms ideological answers. For example,
innocence must *will* guilt even when fear forces it to do so.

Nothing in the world is familiar but we must pretend things
are. In crises this leads to fundamental questioning; but
there is also the day-to-day questioning of the constant flow
of novel, unconceived experience. Familiarity increases
proximity and brings things into closer focus – but it is
always the familiar which is most strange. It is strange not
merely because its changes are unpredictable (otherwise
they would be part of familiarity and we would not see
them as strange) and therefore more disturbing, but because
the familiar always has one hand on 'nothingness'. Love
brings mortality, our present takes away from our future.

Ideology depends on the 'self-evident'. Yet always part of
our experience appears strange to us and threatens the self-
evident. It creates doubt, which leads to insecurity and
strife. Partly the doubt is ontological – it is as if the
periphery constantly drifts towards the centre – but there is
also an immediate, personal, day-to-day doubt. This arises
in the family and its generations and leads to strife amongst
'us'. Authority exploits this strife by reinforcing it with

ontological doubt, turning 'us' into 'them': the other class, other race, other culture, other creed and so on. This makes strife potentially universal.

The psyche itself has no need to combine personal and ontological doubt – obviously it would sooner doubt authority. But we live in societies of ownership and conflict and the psyche wants the security that comes from alliance with authority. We turn to authority to justify our doubt. We adopt its world view but at the same time we doubt it; and the more seriously we doubt it the more strenuously we deny the doubt – for fear of losing the self-evident and the protection of power. We are in an accelerating cycle that only complacency can retard. Both fanaticism and complacency are energized by doubt. The beliefs that cross class-barriers (such as patriotism) are the ones held most fanatically and brutally because it is there that authority is weakest and ideology most implausible.

Personal doubt and ontological doubt are made one. But ontological doubt persists in attracting our attention, the periphery drifts to the centre. It is forbidden to contemplate it because it is the unthinkable – it cannot be socially 'stabilized' by nigger-baiting, wog-bashing and all the seemingly petty dross of media agitation. Ontological doubt is related to radical innocence and cannot be resolved; it causes the instability in corruption. To gain authority's protection we try to believe its ideology; and so though we do not fully believe X we are forced to act on it. The puppet devours its own straw. And then the periphery, the boundary with nothing, drifts to the centre – and we doubt ourselves. The doubt is ontological. It is not simply that we doubt our right to exist – on this level of experience we doubt if we even 'are existing'. We become nothing. That is terror – and to escape it we make our commitment to authority total. The psyche becomes totalitarian. Reaction, fascism and even conservatism (which may cross the political boundary, though the bias is always to the right) are the psyche's shields against terror, the masks that face inwards. These forms of madness are at one with society's forms of ownership, and so they are at home in our social institutions – and as yet our institutional safeguards against them are weak. We have come some way in learning to distinguish between madness and sanity in the psyche, but not nearly so far in distinguishing between them in society. *The War Plays* are set in the future not the past.

Doubt is the cause of terror, but it is also the reason for hope. Doubt stopped us being the creatures of evolution and made us the creators of history. There are enormous risks in our situation – we do not have the security of evolution's eons, the hands on the clockface are triggers – but if we did not live in this risk we could not become human.

The connection between doubt, belief and authority is illustrated by nonconformist religion (and by what happens when the colonized adopt the colonizers' religion). Nonconformist religion regenerates the religion of conformity. It wills one per cent nonconformity but ninety-nine per cent conformity. In the nonconformist psyche the ninety-nine per cent legitimates the one per cent; and it is legitimated in order to deny the authority that legitimates it. Clearly this cannot be revolutionary. To be that it would have to destroy the alliance religious authority makes between ontological doubt and personal doubt. That means changing society, not merely its ownership. The one does not follow automatically from the other. Everything depends on the conscious reason for which ownership was changed. The psyche cannot be forced to be free; it is easily capable of experiencing freedom as tyranny, and so effectively turning society into a prison.

Theatricalization does not concern itself with meaning. It treats the spectator like a shop window dummy and pretends it is warmed by the clothes it drapes on it. Theatricalization remains its own effect and turns the audience into an abstraction. It is as if it treated a wounded man by tying the bandages between the wounds because it does not wish to soil the bandages.

In real life the 'gap' exists between authority and behaviour, speaking and understanding. Negotiating the gap is a social process. Ownership of society imposes imperatives in the gap, and so freedom is made protean – sometimes the most abject forms of enslavement are experienced as freedom, and of abasement as nobility. The real meaning of what we do is made clear in the end, when the machines insist on reality – but it may be understood before then. Artistic action opens the gap because it isolates it, experimentally, from social reality and makes it possible for us to negotiate it in imagination. This radicalizes (within the limits of the machines' world) the freedom in the socio-psyche process – so that we may become what we are in relation to the society that is owned and not to the forms of ownership. TEs use the gap to unite the furthest determinants of our life with day-to-day experience; we are even able to observe without panic the drift of the periphery to the centre – it can be shown in accident-time.

Actors pay emotionally and even physically for the social truth they tell, but they can prepare for this in rehearsals. The audience cannot. On stage the actor is the camp commandant, and the audience is the Russian guard; but for the actor the audience is also brother. The tinsel and sangfroid of theatre shrug this off, but it is true. We cannot experience much of the emotion in us because doing so would wreck us. It is why society sends us to the theatre – and why we go. If the socio-psyche is confronted, the audience confronts itself. Its members have to do this in real life, but need, fear, shortage of time, social pressure, tempt them into shrugging it off. This gives theatre its social importance. It cannot use the philosophy that holds society together even when it seems to use it. How could it tell the improbable stories of our lives without showing the failure of the philosophy? The gap always exposes society's philosophy as inadequate – as not truthful enough to make us human.

To reproduce social truth we need TEs because they are the way people live their daily life. Not even people in traditional, static societies saw the world as if nature or God had put labels on things. But our stage has become less dramatic than the street, and the actors less competent performers than their audience because they are in a lesser drama. The stage is not part of the process which creates social reality, as it was in classical Greece and Jacobean England. It has become empty entertainment, or seeks a pseudo-significance which shrivels in daylight as if it had been put in a fire. The audience is sent to the theatre to see social truth; but – because it is how we learn to survive when we are children – it will accept the solace of lies. It takes small effort to believe lies, but it is always an effort to believe the truth, and really we find much of it quite unbelievable – ultimately because we lack our machines' realism and their need of urgency. Now the audience, not authority, must create the performance's social meaning – that is the audience-work. If we trust the audience they become artists.

Theatre does not merely provoke reflection or offer exemplary and minatory examples. The audience's experience becomes part of the practice of their daily life. It is the difference between a photograph and a ring at the door. The audience turn the stage product into real process. TEs are not like seeds scattered by God or artists to grow, but more like machines designed for a purpose. Though machines create us through socio-psyche processes, we make the processes actual, not passively but by our understanding. We create our psyche and social reality at the same time: the potter spins on the wheel and the ground spins under the wheel. Society glosses over its processes with ideology, inertia and panic. TEs remove the usual determinants so that knowledge may be examined even when it merely repeats itself. Hamlet asks 'What am I – that I may know how to make?' TEs ask 'What do I make – that I may know what I am and may become?'

Ultimately it is the machines that send us to the theatre. They make it necessary for us to create a society in which they can work. This imperative fills the gap. The gap is like a dream-space or even a child's play area. The aim of children's play is to understand, when it comes, the call to come in – which says 'It is time to stop play'. The experience of theatre is made intense by the absent, waiting reality. We are the machines' imagination. They have no use for fantasy – for them that is a mechanical fault – but our imaginations are the way machines dream. Theatre is the place where machines dream of our freedom.

The metatext changes historically with technology. It has been occupied by Gods, Devils, the unconscious, chaos, silence – now we have to take responsibility for it. In our hypertechnology we must become more human, or we will become more brutal and there will be economic and ecological disasters. Machines make it possible for us to be more human. Sometimes they ask too much of us but they are on our side.

Bakhtin thought that lyric, epic and tragedy depend on a monologic understanding of human beings. He said 'the discovery of the *inner man*, "one's own self", [is] accessible not to passive self-observation but only through an *active dialogic approach to one's self*. There are no separate worlds of humanity or art. Heteroglossia would be empty chatter if it were not for the machines. Machines are monologic because only they have a self-sited soul in the traditional religious sense, but they provoke human dialogue. When we speak machines speak with us, so human speech is never monologic. Lyric is not the self's discourse with the soul but with machines. Tragedy is social because it needs a dispute between chorus (or its equivalent), a protagonist, an antagonist and Fate. Classical tragedy pretends that the protagonist monologically 'speaks for everyone'. But TEs can make this dialogic and useful. The process of distortion always preserves the truth – truth is born from the fossils of lies, it is the way in which the past is part of our humanity. The fossils of lies are all we have to base truth on – they are the relics of old machines. TE drama is dialogic in itself and in the audience's reception.

The War Plays try to free the audience's judgement. They do not show several versions of one event and ask the audience to spot the true version. Each play is a rewrite of the others, and repeats and varies a few simple events. This helps the audience to reach an abstract understanding grounded in material, particular reality – the events are not true but the metaphors become true. The combined events bring the analysis closer to the story. TEs tend to give priority to metaphor over strict realism, but in order to serve realism not fantasize it; the psyche's drama is in itself but about society, and it can only be expressed by poetry – the subject of poetry is not fantasy but fact.

The trilogy becomes more abstract by becoming more detailed, more macroscopic by becoming more microscopic, more general by becoming more particular. It is as if by

entering smaller rooms we put on bigger clothes. Or as if
real people appeared in a dream at the side of dream-people.

If we tell one event in several stories we do for our time
what the ancients did for theirs when they crystalized many
events into one myth with a secret, total mystique. For us
events are separate pieces of riddle, and Oedipus is not
waylaid by the Sphinx but carves it from the highway stones
as a memorial of his journey. Our stories should be as
specific as journalism and as general as philosophy; but as
TEs demystify art and life, the philosopher reports the
story and the journalist explains it – and then it is the story
of our common life.

TEs show how people are made to be what they are so that
things can go on happening as they do, not what must
happen because people are what they are. Society escapes
into fantasy and illusion. So does art when it avoids the
paradox and becomes style – Hitler's Greek, the theatre of
silence and so on. But the paradox is always there like an
horizon under our feet – and so it can be put on stage at
any time. Theatre is ruthless in creating its own reality. If
it lies and members of the audience believe the lie, they
must live it just as if they had voted for it when it was told
to them by a political leader. Then they take on a Xenia-
like deadness, with the monomanias and hectic obsessions
of reaction, and are the ghosts in the shopping arcade.
Within limits perception can translate its own language, so
evidence need not be kept in despair from audiences. If
audiences see irrationally they are confirmed in their reaction and must accept more of its consequences – the play
will make them become what they are. A good play
encourages fascists to kill more Jews and Blacks, and the
rest of us to stop them. In or outside the theatre there is no
common humanity.

Plays fall into two groups: they are like *Oedipus* or like the *Oresteia*. Oedipus's sufferings purify his society and the old order is restored. All Shakespeare's plays belong to this group. Lear's madness is old but Orestes's madness is young. When Orestes is made sane the old order is changed, but a Goddess has to rig the vote to change it. We have no divinities or devils to help us. Their part is played by the audience. TEs help them to play it. It is culturally disasterous when society chooses the wrong sort of drama. Our drama should be like the *Oresteia* and change society and its institutions. TEs have their origin in the *Oresteia* when a Goddess is forced to vote.

The theatre of TEs is free from biological and theistic determinism; does not regard art as metaphysical; is not a theatre of artists and spectators but of participants in creating psyche and society; is part of the social process and does not stand aside as mere entertainment or relief; is a theatre of politics, not withdrawal or redemption; and because society cannot be changed and made more human without comedy and tragedy, it uses both – but it is our comedy not the Devil's, and our tragedy not the Gods'.

The Plan of the Plays

The Palermo paradox raises questions theatre has dealt with from at least the time of the Greeks. We have to make the questions useful again. Questions of guilt may be solved, but who can solve the problems of innocence? Radical innocence is an answer that provokes questions. The answers are new ways of using the problems. The questions of the paradox are too deep to be solved, but they can be resolved in ways that make us and our society more human.

In time society's raw truths become myths and lies. If

drama deals with questions in obsolete ways, with obsolete means, then the questions are made monstrous. But the questions are the only source of our rationality. Theatre must make them useful and creative. The nazi commandant wished to stage a real drama, a military-religious rite. He unwittingly staged the paradox that questions how we live – and the camp square became a stage which asks how we make and use drama.

In *Red Black and Ignorant* characters confront the paradox. Later, in the other plays, these characters produce developments of themselves. I do not mean that they wrote the trilogy; but just as an audience cannot escape from reality when it watches fiction nor can a writer when he writes it. Society uses dramatists to create the drama it needs but a dramatist is not a conduit. He is responsible for what he writes, not out of duty but because discerning anything means evaluating it and this requires desire and commitment. What an author writes expresses the political position that informs his subjectivity. The way he writes shows his relation to himself, which is also his part in the social process. The relation 'creates' what he writes, the limitations come from the limitations of his skill.

Characters are part of their author's social reality and have the logic and independence this gives them. Art is fiction but it is also an event in real life and shares the dynamic of the rest of life. So sometimes characters invent the dramatic means they need to confront their problems. They redramatize the story. To put it another way, the various dramatic means used in *The War Plays* were created by my need to use the characters to solve the problems. The means come from the characters and their need to recreate themselves in further stories – and this would be so even if they were merely like corpses that pulled the shroud tighter to keep out the cold.

We can ask what is fiction? The borderline between writer and character, actor and role, audience and story, is not as impenetrable as the boundary which joins them. If I write of a holocaust, the dead of Hiroshima, Auschwitz and Dresden use me. Unlike other fictions the dead must be true to life – the machines demand it of them. Killers make good legends but victims do not. Only simple excuses are ever accepted but causes are complex. The reasons for which martyrs died become the reasons for which we live. By using fiction the dead let us live in the paradox. We can ask what is fiction?

The War Plays make up a haphazard history of theatre. When I could I used dramatic means from the past, the rest I had to invent. Perhaps that is the proper use of post-modernism? Truth has no style, but it does not follow that a random *mélange* of styles produces subliminal or transcendental truths beyond rational analysis. A writer must find the language in which his characters can talk to him, otherwise they have the limitations of real people and not the freedom of fiction. Post-modernism could take away the sacredness of the past and make history useful to us, so that it ceases to be our torment. It could release the dead from their prisons, free us from ghosts and at last let us talk to machines as equals. The danger is that capitalism is so powerful it can turn even our masters, the machines, into our slaves – and then we have no future: we become the dead who trade in coffins.

The Palermo improvisation and the story of the Russian guard appear in the trilogy many times in different versions. They are the basic T-event. For example, the third play begins with the paradox as it is used in the first play, but in a version closer to the Palermo improvisation. In each play the characters are T-characters in relation to the trilogy. The soldier son could be the same character in the first and third plays, but the Woman in the third play is less like his mother in the first play and more like the Monster's mother. In the third play Mrs Wilson resembles the girl under the wall in the first play but is older. And so on – these identities are suggestions.

With the exception of the First Woman in the second play (who also appears in a scene of the third play) none of the characters in any one play knows what happens in the other plays. To the characters the events are unique, to the audience they are TEs. Whatever the actor believes he shows, that is what the audience sees – because of the recurring characters and events. The trilogy uses historical time horizontally, but psychological time vertically: the passing of one time through the other TEs the plays. Even if they are played on their own the plays will still be seen as TEs because that is how they are written. The audience give the meaning – they have the role the Greek theatre still kept on stage and gave to the Gods.

The events of the first seven or eight scenes of the third play occur before the events of the second play. These scenes make up a fourth play, a political-military-family drama. In rehearsals it came to be called the Greek Play. It could be played in its position in the text or separately on its own. Or it could be played after the first play. It could then be followed by the second play and the rest of the third play.

Red Black and Ignorant

This play is derived from agitprop. A man who has never been born recounts the life he did not lead. The play shows incidents from his life. Sometimes the characters comment in the manner of a Greek chorus (many agitprop plays use a chorus). For the choruses the actors must be themselves – the choruses in the other two plays are treated differently. At the end a soldier, instead of killing the senile neighbour (who is as helpless as a child and will soon die), kills the wrong man – his father. The father praises the son's parricide. What is fiction? It tells easily truths that are hard to live – but what did the Russian guard do on the execution-parade ground?

Art reinvents death often. Fiction is a womb or grave, but cannot exist in the world of half-illusions between them. If it gives birth, it does so (in the end) to the audience. If it kills, it kills real people – because if we do not confront the paradox even when it is only in fiction, we enter illusion and become corrupt and dangerous. The child's psyche is dramatized at a time of radical innocence, and later it can never be indifferent to the paradox. Fiction has its own reality and the rest of reality finds new uses for it – but fiction cannot make amends for harm it has once done.

The christian God was crucified on a wooden crossroads to satisfy the father's will. That fiction cannot be changed because it is not art and does not have the historical protection of art. It remains a curse on christianity. But Oedipus is art. When the Monster praises his son it is as if Laius praised Oedipus. How else can the unborn father be given life? Perhaps the brothers on the execution-parade ground cursed one another as they died. But when the Monster praises his son we see that cursing was the only form of praise left to the brothers. We can teach the Sphinx riddles. What the Russian guard did was meaningless, but fiction can share its reality with it and give it meaning.

But it cannot change the Commandant. He is the only character in the trilogy written without sympathy or forbearance. He is the officer in *Great Peace* who orders the

killing. Every time the students acted the Palermo improvisation they began with the officer giving his order. His
presence in the improvisation was vital for its social truth
and meant that the end could not be fantasized. The
paradox creates a crisis that may corrupt radical innocence;
if it does, the burden of the destroyed innocence is added
to the corrupter's corruption. The longer corruption lasts
the harder it is to change. The acts of radical innocence are
unexpected, but those of the corrupt become so predictable
they could be charted like the stars. It is the mark of office.

The Tin Can People

This play is the middle of the trilogy in position and
method. The chorus comments on the action in an
informed, distanced way. This broadens the play's political
and psychological scope. In the chorus the characters are
like doctors examining themselves in other parts of the
play. Unlike the actors in the first play, the actors should
use the choruses as if their characters had been in the events
they describe.

The Tin Can society is the most advanced society possible
in the capitalist world. Nuclear war has brought the audience's consumer society to its highest state of perfection.
The Tin Can valley is heaven on earth. It gives labourless
luxury outside financial time – there is no instalment date.
It is said that the distortions in society are caused by
economic insecurity, that hunger and other needs feed the
beast in us. If this were so, the Tin Can people should be
happy in their ideal world. But because they do not relate
to the world through machines and their iron necessity,
they live in a dream. The human mind can hardly be
founded on a tin opener . . . They go to sleep in one world

and wake up not in the next but in the one before. When the soul loses its mechanical basis it becomes reactionary. Limitless free consumption, like heavenly manna, takes us out of the relationship which creates our humanity. We become like children without a reason to grow up. In dreams, objects are unreal but reasoning and emotion are real. But objects, not emotions, present reality to us. With the mad it is the other way round; and if we could interrogate the mad inside their madness we would immediately understand history because we would be in it but not part of its illusions. Too affluent people, in the play and in reality, share one thing in common with the mad: they have everything. But like the mad they have a sense of loss, the conviction that they have nothing. It comes from the insecurity affluence lays bare: the only instalment date is death.

The Tin Can people's story is the most modern of all stories, the story of luxury and death. So it is the last story – but I found that it contained the first story: the story of the God who is killed at each harvest and reborn each spring. The story records the first relationship the human socio-psyche created with the earth and seasons, space and time. Christianity turned the story of the year's cycle into the monolithic story of one day that had eternity for tomorrow. Christ made the diachronic and synchronic one, and mystified society and change: in the end is my beginning, I am the Great Tin Can. This is commemorated in Easter, a sop to human inertia and a reminder of state violence – an assurance that change is not needed and a warning that it is forbidden. The christian retelling of the story brought comparative political stability and some elementary regulation of war, and released social energy in humanizing ways. But in time fictional energy, like physical energy, dissipates its source – the form curls at the edge.

Christianity prepared the ground for industrialism, when people could no longer live with God but had to accept the Devil because the state needed him. And now capitalism dehumanizes people and makes war more barbarous.

The one being for whom there is no place in heaven is God. Heaven does not need him. If it did it would be a place of insecurity and scarcity, in need of a protector and guide – it would be another place of politics. The problem of the Tin Can people is that they are in heaven. So if anyone enters their valley he comes from outside heaven and must be Satan. The strange traveller disturbs the Tin Can people in the way industrialism disturbed christian feudalism. There are no angels in heaven because there are no machines: so only the damned go there. Satan is heaven's only hope of salvation – just as he was for the machineless-world of feudalism. And so when the young God enters the valley the Tin Can people turn him into Satan and heaven into hell. Affluence has not freed them from the paradox. No one is freed except by death. Even corruption does not free us. With the rewards of corruption innocence returns and brings the crisis corruption was meant to resolve. Society places the paradox in our minds and we live it, and may have to die for it, or we go mad – morally or clinically. Corrupt society is irrational. It breaks down in crisis, and then it is as if innocence swept away all choice and imposed itself as a penalty. The Tin Can people are the image of our time.

Section 2, scene 2, is a multiple TE. Towards the end of Chekhov's *Three Sisters* the characters on stage talk or fall silent, while off-stage their society – using Solyony as its agent – murders. In our theatre violence is on-stage because that is where it is in our life, not waiting in the wings as it was in Chekhov's. His characters hold an inquest on an accident that has not yet taken place but which they cannot prevent. *Our* stage is the site of the accident. So the scene is faster and more extreme than Chekhov's: it is set in accident-time. Now it is because things happen so rapidly that it is hard to prevent them or escape from them.

When people report what it is like to be in a serious accident they say that they were calm and that time seemed to slow so that they noticed things they would not have had time to notice if they had been strolling by. In a crisis reality resembles a TE, and involvement in it *is* alienation. If the scene is to reproduce chaos it must not be chaotic. Chaos is the absence of the unexpected, the Commandant's set face. Free will does not work in it; instead everything happens according to laws of determination. Chaos is the image of fate. In a TE of a man blown from a plane a mile above the earth, he reaches for his wallet – in the moment of crisis he puts his hand on his heart. Chaos is very precise.

In the scene a woman tries to prove she is dead and to find movements that will imitate the immobility of death; another woman tries to kill a man; he fights for his life; and another woman attacks him but then saves him by turning the spit of the first play into a gesture that embraces plague. The scene is violent, fast and chaotic. It is detailed, observed, imaginatively graphic – but very carefully organized, controlled and co-ordinated. The trajectory of each speck of dust in a falling wall shows how the wall was built, what its weaknesses were and why it fell. In an explosion each speck of dust points to the other specks and to the explosion – each event in the scene is about the other events. We can only understand history and chaos by reading the specks of dust, they are the only maps we have of history and chaos.

We must not imitate the camera's slow-motion. Time must be slowed by filling it with significant, graphic, metaphorized incident and detail. If we slow time artificially we distort the event: when a camera thinks for the audience they do not look but stare. We abuse facts when we try to make poetry of them, poetry *is* the facts. How we show the scene shows its meaning. We must allow chaos to show its cause. Some of the TEs may be stressed, at some points, over others, but the others must not be played down so as not to distract, because slowing or stopping *attracts* attention. Everyone in the audience must be free to choose what is significant for themselves.

We read a printed page by following the direction of the lines. We read a map by taking in the whole and then interpreting the details. Watching a multiple-TE in accident-time is like reading a map by beginning with the details. When the audience see these have meaning – that they are not mere noise and rush – they broaden their understanding to the whole scene. This reverses the usual direction of the ideologized socio-psyche but replicates its profounder working, when the periphery drifts to the centre and the strange and familiar constantly metamorphose into one another – but prevents authority imposing its interpretation. The audience see chaos in real-time, but slowed by graphic, metaphorized detail, and so they see as trained observers or people in accidents see. Perhaps it is the strangeness of accident-time that led to the belief that the drowning see their whole life. In a serious accident it is as if we become the hands on the clockface. Accident-time cannot be put on stage except by TEs.

The characteristic 'T' extremes of violence and stillness in the earlier scenes teach the audience how to look at this scene. Every play is in a foreign language and must teach it to its audience. It must make clear whether it is a comedy or tragedy, or comic effects will be tragic and vice versa. But more subtly, a play's language is not the same as ordinary speech, its codes are closer to a specialist language:

in reality, events are in space and time but on stage space and time are in events and language. Each play invents its own codes, and they do not simply drop into it from social reality. Drama reproduces events by interpreting them and it can only do this by analyzing them, well or badly. The analysis is the philosophy that fills the gap. But all philosophies are in a foreign language – that is what gives art its pleasure.

The play ends simply. The simplicity seems naive if we do not remember the extremity of the Tin Can people's experience. They believed they were the only people alive, they were God and then the Devil. Now if they are to be human they must be simple. Later they are destroyed and the paradox confronts the audience again.

Great Peace

The Tin Can People is about our affluence, *Great Peace* is about our destitution.

The characters are not protagonist-and-chorus. In the earlier plays the chorus contains the characters, in this play the characters contain the chorus. Their experience and their desire for sanity make them speak objectively and teach them how to. Writing the trilogy was the attempt to make them able to do this. This change, like the trilogy's other changes in dramatic method and form, comes from the characters' need to confront the paradox and become themselves.

The soldiers' chorus in scene 12 seems to be an anti-chorus, doubt and demonic possession driving out understanding and replacing it with ritual. It is a ritual for the soldiers, not for the audience. They see the world in the way the

audience see the accident-time scene in *The Tin Can People*.
In retrospect they witness their crimes as victims – they
victimize themselves. Their chorus obsessively preserves
the truth for the sake of a lie – a common social practice.
Later one beautiful morning the lie can no longer be
believed and the soldiers kill themselves in a last attempt to
believe it. Is it a refinement of the corruption of radical
innocence that soldiers kill themselves to make lies true? Is
killing themselves the only way left to them to claim the
radical innocent's right to live? Escape into corruption
merely worsens the problem of the paradox. The mass
suicide of the dead soldiers is the only way they can become
what they are. They are the guards on the nazi killing-
ground. Their death is implicit in the madwoman's imitation of death in the accident-time scene of *The Tin Can
People*.

The silence of the soldier with the empty cigarette packet is
also a chorus: the silence of radical innocence confronting
the paradox, surrounded by the yapping of orders.

After the Greek Play the dramatic form changes again. The
rest of the play is an Odyssey, or an imitation of the
medieval travelogues of Chaucer, Boccaccio, Cervantes and
Dante. They told stories within stories. Chaucer's stories
divert pilgrims from the rigours of their journey; Boccaccio's divert refugees from their fear of plague; Cervantes's
reassure his readers by praising life as Quixote travels to
death. Dante's stories do not reassure, they remind the
readers that the door to hell is in this world. But even he
only visits hell and has a guide to comfort him. The people
in *Great Peace* have no guide. They live in hell and you do
not have a guide to your own house. No existing philosophy
can guide them. No one has gone before and returned to
tell them to turn back. A sleep-walker holds out his hand
like a child that is led but no one leads him. It is the same

with the people of *Great Peace*. It is as if they had internalized their landscape and become the stories that wander over it. But that is how all of us live in a nuclear age, even before the bombs are dropped. Inside our head we browse through the maps of ruins.

Is it because like Chekhov's characters we are spectators of our lives? Certainly we are afraid. Our fictions live our lives for us; the people in *Great Peace* wander and scavenge in the ruins in our head. Chekhov's characters reassure themselves with stories of Moscow, but illusions – carrying naked candles in storms – cannot help the refugees of *Great Peace*. Their inner and outer landscape are one. What they do in one they do in the other, whether it is to build cities or ruin them. And though we do not see it, that is true of us. The people of *Great Peace* rid themselves of illusion – the baby becomes a rag, the survivors do not dream of Moscow but build a city. That may not be true of us.

Our technology needs fiction: it pretends the fiction is apples that grow on metal pylons and prove that it is not fundamentally changing the world. Its fiction becomes all pervasive. It infiltrates reality till we have almost become the light reading of our machines. Witches and heretics were burned; now good, law-abiding citizens wait for the nuclear fire or the chemical wasteland. We make hell, no God would dare to study its blueprints as calmly and assiduously as we do.

In *Great Peace* the people go to hell to take the world out of the hands of Gods and armies and put it into their own. They are our guides to the ruins.

The Sheet

The Woman is a mad chorus telling the truth
Her gestures with the sheet are a chorus
They are a TE and the sheet is her TE-prop
The sheet shows the shapes of metaphors
The sheet is the great map of nothing on which we write
The sheet is a shroud and a midwife's towel
It flaps like a bandage on the arms of the wounded wind
The actress shows with great beauty how the Woman
    abandons the baby to die in the wilderness
It is the opposite of the ugliness she shows when the
    Woman goes to murder her neighbour's baby in the city
The Woman opens the sheet and drapes it on herself
She covers a murderess's body
She dresses as a penitent and goes to commit the crime
When the Woman is most mad the TE-effect shows us her
    sanity and that in time she will take responsibility for the
    world
TE-acting shows us a thing and its opposite – what it is
    forbidden to show or what we avoid and what we desire
    or need
The sheet flaps like a dumb man's tongue
It tells us what the guard told the commandant on the
    parade-killing ground
And how the soldier left his neighbour's house and walked
    home through the Palermo streets and stopped to kick an
    empty cigarette packet
If we had passed him in the street we would not have
    noticed him
At the end the Woman is given a coat
Perhaps to worldly eyes she handles the coat in an ugly way
    but the audience see in the handling the beautiful ges-
    tures she made with the sheet

They have learned the play's language: the language they spoke but did not understand

Once the sheet was Hamlet's ghost: the spectre that came from the future and beckoned him to follow it to the grave

The Woman cannot turn back: her madness is not feigned

Radical innocence shelters in madness when it cannot suffer the paradox: mad people's teeth are the gravestones of lies

The Woman's journey to death is longer than Hamlet's

If it were not she could not become sane: she would die in a cage of dead soldiers' bones

History journeys through disaster: we block all other ways as a glove hides rings on fingers

TE-acting pulls the glove from the hand: as a sheet is pulled from a statue

Levels of Reality

Handling the sheet identifies it and alienates it. The audience know it is a sheet and cannot be asked to believe it is a baby. Instead they ask why the Woman needs it to be a baby and see how she uses her need. Otherwise using the sheet as a baby would leave the audience in doubt. It would be an empty theatrical trick.

Because the baby is shown to be fake it establishes the *theatrical reality* of the other baby, the baby-with-a-fist. When this baby raises its fist the gesture is *theatrically real*. It is made by a machine in the baby. This combines the social forces of people, machines and imagination at the lowest point of the Woman's madness and the start of her journey to sanity. The combination vibrates in the mechanical-magic that floats like mist in the socio-psyche; it is as if a human hand had gestured, setting up waves in the mist. The TE teaches the audience the language of the Woman's journey and prepares them to go on it with her.

The audience and the Woman must each keep to their own level of reality if they are to make the journey together. To protect her mind from the ravages of its madness the Woman needs the fake baby to be real. During the play she recovers from madness, and then she needs it to be a sheet again. The audience need the baby-with-a-fist to be real so that they may carry it with them on the journey. They go on it because they need to carry the baby-with-a-fist safely through the play – that is their audience-work. They cannot let themselves abandon it as the Woman did. But when the play ends they can abandon it and go out into the street – it is only a prop. That is also why in the end the Woman abandons the sheet – it is a prop.

The gesture of the baby's fist is the most paradoxical TE in the scene. When the mechanical prop gestures it makes the audience real – as if the machine were a conjuror who lifted the audience out of a top hat. The audience and the Woman need different levels of reality to understand, without fantasy, the real world. Each needs their own level of reality to become what they are in relation to the play. The audience use the theatre in the way the Woman uses the sheet.

If the psyche's different levels of reality, in and out of fiction, are not respected, the audience cannot use the play properly. The use made of levels teaches an audience a play's language. If the levels are respected and the borders between them crossed only for logical reasons (to produce process not product) the imagination turns art into reality instead of into fantasy. Levels of reality are rarely understood in our theatre. Empty tricks are played with them to create fake theatre and make the play work. Our theatre is so destitute that it even regards the tricks as the essence of theatre.

When theatre pretends to be 'real' it is not art and drops out of social reality. It becomes fantasy. When it accepts and uses its artificiality it has access to many levels of reality. These levels are the reality once sought by ritual: for us they are in the social reality of this world. The rest is fake.

The Meetings

To understand themselves the trilogy's characters create dramatic devices. They do this in the way society creates drama. The characters are in the theatre with the audience and the theatre is in society. As in *Oedipus*, the audience is the character and investigates the reason why society sent it to the theatre.

Greek theatre used the dramatic device of the strangers who meet and share a common fate. The stage hell of *Great Peace* creates its own dramatic devices, just as in a real city the ruins and stragglers would have dramatized the Woman's life. In the Greek Play the Woman is not corrupted by the paradox because she acts not for herself but for her child. Instead she becomes mad. Unless she understands why she was mad she will not be completely sane. But to understand the events that drove her mad she must meet the others who took part in them. They are dead, except for one soldier. But when she meets him she does not recognize him. It is too early, she is not yet sane enough to need him. But even if she could go back in time to meet the others, they could not help her. When they committed their crimes they were too corrupt to see what they did.

They would not merely need to know that they too were victims (a cliché) but be like Orestes – victims who justly accuse the innocent. The only people who can talk of the terror of that are those who have lived in the same wilderness as the Woman.

So the Woman invents a new dramatic device. She turns the people she meets into the people she needs. It is as if a stranger came up to you in the street and instead of asking the way to such-and-such a place asked 'What is the purpose of life? How should I live? What is crime?' It is a sign of the Woman's need for sanity. The soldiers are not allowed this need. The Woman achieves it only by going insane. Now she stages each meeting when she is sane enough to need what further sanity the meeting will give her – but in each meeting she risks losing the sanity she has already won. If she had met other people before she needed them, she would have seen them as stones or trees, or turned away when they stepped over the horizon. Now she turns the sick woman and her daughter into her dead neighbours; and a young man into her son, who died for an empty cigarette packet. And because they are also in the wilderness the names she gives them stick and they name her in return.

From her first step in the wilderness the Woman's madness is a journey to sanity. When she abandons the baby we cannot blame her, because we drove her mad. Madness is a matter of politics, uniforms and weapons – even when these causes are filtered through a mountain and appear as the arguments in a kitchen. If we do not understand her, she would point to our bombs and call us mad. She pretended her rag was a child, we pretend bombs are our salvation – and do it on the say-so of rulers who own our culture and decide what passes for moral sanity. Perhaps those to whom the paradox cannot speak cannot live without a nurse or leader – or followers. Perhaps they are incurably mad, although we do not put them in strait-jackets but in uniforms. That will be the Woman's question when she is sane.

The stranger is too young to be her son. But psychologically and socially the relationship is inevitable. The Woman's innocence conceives the son in her madness, when she·is alone in the wilderness. The paradox creates the relationship but it is not outside social relationships. It is not important who she calls son, any man would do – but then, everyone must do. She does not return to the past to find she is innocent but to find what crimes her innocence drove her to. She confronts herself as mother and neighbour, her son confronts her as citizen. The paradox is political and makes the roles of mother, neighbour, stranger and citizen one, the house and city one. We do not allow that and that is why we are not human. The Woman cannot be a good neighbour *and* a good mother. Like the audience with their bombs, she is monstrous. To understand herself she must understand society. Then she can be sane and all strangers can be her children. There is a seriousness in what the son tells her that cannot be added to.

The Lens-in-the-Head

The plays move from agitprop in *Red Black and Ignorant* to a camera in the last scenes of *Great Peace*. We see so much film that we have a lens-in-the-head. This lens does not shrink the stage of *Great Peace* to a screen but expands it to a city, the ruins and the wilderness. The lens-in-the-head always focuses on the horizon even when it is in close-up. Close-up widens the field of vision by focusing on detail and puts what it sees into accident-time. This makes the camera a chorus, but the characters in *Great Peace* are still their own chorus because the lens is in their head. The lens-in-the-head follows their wanderings, struggles, reconciliations and departures and closes in as they come nearer to the paradox. Its focus is so close that it shows the soil in the map. A chorus need poetry to analyze their situation and speak about it to each other – poetry is the most public language. Survivors of great atrocities cannot speak of them – or even of what caused them – without poetry. The lens-in-the-head of the people of *Great Peace* helps them to speak as poets.

What is important about a camera is not what it sees but what it says – its analysis of the story. (Often in films cutting puts back the chaos, and its mystique, that the camera had got rid of.) At the end of *Great Peace* it is as if a camera in the dead woman's hands went on recording. The change to the last scene is written as a structural TE. Each individual production must solve the problem this creates. If the text solved it it would intrude on the structural dynamic of each individual production. It would even break the rules of the Palermo improvisation.

One of the camera's great gifts to aesthetics is that it can show emptiness – Lear's nothing – in all its domestic, bureaucratic detail. A camera at Auschwitz captured Himmler chewing his thumb.

The Pram

The Woman's pram is a psyche-x-ray of Mother Courage's waggon. This does not reduce the waggon's economic function. In the wilderness and in the Greek Play children are a source of profit to mothers and soldiers. (And in the wilderness the Woman wants a scarf in payment for her kindness, and might have strangled the sick woman with

it.) When the waggon was finally used as Mother Courage's
hearse or burned, it still had an economic value and
measured cost. But when it is gone, what becomes of her
obduracy? What do we see in the burned grass where it
stood?

Mother Courage must choose to be the Russian guard or
the commandant – and *we* must, even if we are spared the
confrontation. The choice is posed in the building of camps,
the stitching of uniforms, the payment of taxes for bombs,
the training of children. In the human farce of consumables
and durables a pram is trundled round as if it were a coffin
on wheels in the mother's hands.

Mother Courage's daughter Kattrin pines for a baby – it
might be her baby in the pram in *Great Peace*. One night
she climbs onto a roof and beats a drum to warn people
asleep in a neighbouring town that soldiers are about to
attack them. She will not stop drumming and so the soldiers
shoot her. Would she have beaten her drum if her baby had
lain beside her on the roof – or in her belly? When Kattrin
beats her drum she is beating her baby to death. That, at
least, is what we ask of the Woman – and of those who
make bombs. Fictional characters show us what we do but
cannot live our lives for us. So Kattrin beats out her baby's
brains. How else can the town be saved?

Names

Very few of the plays' characters are named. Why are the
other names not given? The characters are not meant to be
generalizations but individuals with holes in their clothes
and dirt under their nails, and their extreme experiences
sharpen their political and social individuality. It's their
extreme individuality which makes them representative.

Antigone and Creon are named and their individuality is beyond doubt. But they are also generalizations – and their names may obscure the way in which the ruling class is used to represent the social psyche – as it still is in *Hamlet* and *Lear*. That is how Greek drama could best serve democracy. But our social and psychological crises cannot be acted out by royal families – *they* can only act our soap operas. The direction in which creative psychological and social forces run is from personal repression to political expression; for the Greeks it was the other way round. Art was still a means of repression used by the ruling class (folk art always criticizes this sort of use but succumbs to it). Unlike the Greeks we must clarify the meaning of social divisions if we are to understand ourselves politically and free democracy from chains.

The characters are not named because although they are not symbols their lives are social forces – and the forces are clarified by the crises. But there is another reason. They have lost their names because they have lost themselves. Names are a sign of our humanity. In a nuclear age we still have to create our humanity. I would have felt I was christening bits of limbs I had dragged from rubble.

When a woman's body is dragged from a bombed house authority rushes to name her and enter the name on its form. Who names the airmen who dropped the bomb? War memorials would be more useful if after the name of each dead we put the names of those they had killed. I suppose the administration would find it too difficult to get the names – or even the numbers. But it would make the memorials T-memorials.

Conclusion

The Tin Can people should have been happy – and even good – because they wanted for nothing. The woman has wants but does not satisfy them as we would. Is her hunger only satisfied by hunger? She has no one to coerce by a hunger strike; and she eats so that she is strong enough to feed the rags and become sane – and with the soldiers on the morning when they saw that they could only find out if they were alive by killing themselves. What she needs more than food is the right to hope.

The people in *Great Peace* are in hell. There is no God to take them off to heaven and they have no use for Faust's contract. It is easy to use technology to build hell. But you cannot build heaven by technology and commerce alone. If you try you build hell, and when there is a hell everyone is in it. Tertullian said that one of the joys of heaven would be to watch for all eternity the sufferings of those in hell, as if hell were God's colosseum. That is one historical, fairly limited response to the problem of being human. The paradox does not allow the sufferings of others to give us happiness – not for eternity or even a lifetime, but only for a few bleak, raucous years serving tyranny or quietly going mad in a false democracy. The corruption of innocence does not last, the tormentors tire or the victims rise against them.

Democracy cannot give security and freedom while rich and poor are divided in all things except sentimentality, patriotism and brutality. Victims do not seek revenge for wrongs but because those who wrong them turn their backs and walk away to the feast. Strike someone with a knife and give him the knife and he may kill you. But if you strike him with a knife and then walk away to the feast, the killing will go on for generations. A world divided into rich and poor cannot be at peace. Nor can societies divided in that way. The corruption of innocence which creates unjust society, destroys it. The injustices are terrible, but the justifications of them – the excuses, the twisted reasoning – are far, far worse. They are what finally destroy society. And first they destroy the human image. Injustice cannot protect civilization. One day people will be astonished that we thought it could.

The son is not building a utopia for saints but a city in which we may be human. He loiters like Hamlet on the site of the city, till he sets out to fetch the Woman. Why won't she go back with him to build the city? It is a matter of the paradox. The paradox is demanding, but it is the foundation of our lives. When the Woman abandoned the baby to die she drew the plans of the city for it in the dust. She goes away from the city to be one of its foundations. I wanted her to come back, but it was not time.

l

Poems for *The War Plays*

After the Raid

For a while I stopped running and trying to find direction
I stood by the street and watched others pass
Many carried small bundles like birds with debris in their
    beaks seeking a tree for their nest in a burned forest
Children had lost their parents and parents had lost each
    other
The old stumbled with the weariness of blind infants
Carts creaked by – their wheels were large so that one beast
    could draw them in rough country
Now people drew them in ruins
They were piled with the dead
I asked what liquid ran from under the carts
The bodies on top pressed it from the bodies below
It was the chyle of the dead
The city was silent except where the buried moaned so that
    it seemed the ruins sang to themselves
Black smoke unfolded in the sky
On the broken walls huge shadows glided and leaped among
    those who went by as if the living were being taken
    prisoner by the dead
Already in the past there were signs
The merchants built high towers but where money came
    from even the bankers didn't know
It was as if the heavy ledgers squeezed it from the rows of
    figures
Twelve years ago I came to this city
On one side of the road a line of carts with big wheels
Each with a farmer hunched over his whip facing the mule
His family behind him facing backwards
All silent after the day's work
On the other side of the road a long line of automobiles
With drivers in coney-island shirts and passengers bent
    over maps

Even then the river and port had been deserted
One or two pleasure boats
In a few years people started to flee from the soldiers: each
    soldier was an ant colony shut up in steel
And birth was labour chore beside the coffin
I started to walk again
When the tall towers had reared up and thrown the earth
    like a blanket over their shaking shoulders
Fire had burned off the leaves and blackened the bark of
    an apple tree
But the burnt fruit still hung on the boughs
No road led from ruins
The skeletons inside people chose the way the people went
    and those who wished to go another way fought with
    their own skeleton
Or perhaps the skeletons were trying to flee from such
    pitiless flesh
It was the end of time

Dead Soldiers

I

Often its hard to believe people have done what they've
    done – yet the reports are accurate
The mind has contrived reasons for whatever the body may
    do
Or will contrive them in certain circumstances
To understand anyone's action – human or inhuman – we
    have only to describe it precisely

II

The dead get on with the business of living
Eat – sleep – tie up their rags – breathe
Contradiction is a sign of life
The dead acknowledge stages of dying – sometimes they lie
    still and rot or fall behind and are lost
Many dead die again as if the body's weight squeezed out
    the last shreds of life

III

From the hillside we saw the mist in the valley – a stranded
    sea creature
It came slowly but to us it seemed rapid as if speeded up by
    a projector
When it was close we saw the edges were blurred
It fell on us – licking our faces – inside our cuffs and collars
    – the tongues seemed to be in us – the body eating the
    inside of its own skin – the muscles sucking the bones –
    exactly like that

It passed and rolled up the hill – things sticking out –
   furniture – clothes – radios – a goalpost
Like gravel stuck on a snowball
We were silent for half an hour
We heard the drops of mist running down the stems of
   grass
Then we understood we were dead

IV
Sometimes the dead hold a formal discussion
When you're alive you know you're alive and now we know
   we're dead
Prove it with a rope round the neck? One of us starve?
He'd rot and vanish but he'd still see us and know we're
   dead
Vanishing? Rotting? How does that prove you're alive or
   dead?

The Walking Woman

Think of it!
Walking seventeen years clutching her bundle and asking
    why?
And when she was as dead as the land she trod she took
    new life as a dry bush twists in fire or a stone worn down
    by water takes on the sharpness of dragons' teeth
Her hair was a wirebrush for scraping out engines – her
    eyes peered from under it as if a night-creature had gone
    to ground in her head
Her small plump feet took short steps in the rhythms of
    little scurries of rubble dislodging in ruins
Her hands were old and unskilled except in the craft of
    time – they grabbed or the fingers stuck out defensive
She wore a scarf against the wind

The world was grey with ash and the dust of cinders
At night and in storms – great darkness
Sometimes the clouds thinned till the sky was threadbare –
    then the light was bright
She said the military are mice – their droppings are
    everywhere – you can tell the places they have infected
She said teach children to avoid soldiers' shit

Nothing could happen to her that needed a response she
    had not already given
She experienced all she had to experience
She drained the cup – she tugged the tether to the end
She was more stone than stone and water than water

Years passed between her few meetings with others
One woman told her that child's a bundle – you feed it but
    the gruel stays in the bowl of the spoon
She answered what the child leaves I eat to teach it thrift
The woman said you eat to empty the spoon
She agreed and the woman left
Then she fed the bundle and said I told her you were rags
    to get rid of her

When the bundle spoke she grinned for days like a class-
    room of children
The rags would explain the mystery of the world
When it fell silent she wept and raged
Was it sickening? Sulking? Dead? How could she tell when
    the signs of life were so little
She straightened the rags and went on

She was not yet empty and had not yet experienced all
    things that were in her to experience when a young
    woman who had taught her not to kill questioned her
She answered what do you want with an old woman with
    hands like the skulls of birds on withered sticks?
In saying this she mourned for her life which must be held
    against her – but she had not yet experienced all things
    that were in her to experience
The young woman said: then turn away
She gave as answer: although she would not go with the
    young woman the young woman would be her friend

When she was old she met her son
He sat on the ground with his face bowed on his bent knees
    and his hands clutched over his crossed ankles
She embraced him and held out the bundle
He stood and held out his hands to take it
He said come with me to the settlement – you're needed –
    much to do – work – teach
She would not

For seventeen years she asked why? why? why? and found
    no answer
Now when her son befriended her she asked him the
    question and he gave her a coat from the settlement store
A coat – for her!
She wheezed and pointed – a coat!
Once she'd've grabbed it and run
Now she pointed a finger as long as a thigh-bone and
    doubled over with soundless laughter – a coat!
For the woman who'd eaten the fruit that grows on the
    burned bush!

When all she had left was the bundle she gave it away
And when she was empty and had experienced all things
    that were in her to be experienced
When the world was dust yet she could have found in it
    one grain she sought and told each grain from the others
(For in us there is much that we may experience)
She hoisted the roads she had walked onto her back as if
    they were a bundle of sticks
And went on

Great Peace

Yesterday she died
Slowly towards evening she saw she must die
Like all those who reach her age she had died several times
 without learning much from death
The dead were dolls – discarded pieces of plaster bound in
 the wire that had once set them free
She left part of her mind as you might leave a room to
 others to live in but still listen to the voices that sound
 through the walls like the creaking of trees beyond hedges
She spoke of hope – now she's dead she knows its not
 needed
A few days of confusion and funeral fuss till the dead
 flowers are thrown away and the undertaker is paid
The dead are freed from time but patient with the living
Their death has put them in great danger
If they see legs in a ditch they climb in and pull the man
 from under the gun carriage
They take down the wounded's groans in a script that is
 read back as words
Their gestures seem to fight with the wind and tug at its
 hair
Do not watch for them – they are not themselves and have
 not become someone else
No nirvanas heavens or toys
In winter when bonfires were lit in the kent orchards black
 shapes tended the glowing braziers and white smoke
 drifted under the frosty trees
The sloes rotted and dripped
But out in the lanes the hedgerow apples ripened as if a
 mouth breathed in the ice and the ice protects the breath
 that melts it.
And there is a pale red glow in the frost on the fruit

Silence

Each year two minutes' silence before the fallen millions
Perhaps if we stood in silence before those yet to fall
The father's silence before his child might last three
  minutes
The woman's silence before her lover might last a week
And the silence of strangers before each other might stretch
  to a month
So that as we stared at those who had not yet fallen our
  daily tumult would stop
And a great silence spread
And later when we went about our business perhaps we
  would deal justly with one another
So that the long chain of distortions – the orders – the
  threats and cajolings – the wages and medals – would end
  and the price of freedom no longer be death?
Without justice there is always war
It is decreed in the infant's stammer and inscribed in the
  atom even when it's split
When we live in justice we will not need to be silent before
  the fallen
They will not fall

Choruses from After the Assassinations

Author's Note

After the Assassinations is the title of a play. I decided to publish only these choruses. Originally the choruses were speeches of the play's characters. I have called them choruses because I hoped they would encourage a reflective attitude.

The play concerned an event in the year 2030. When the play was written this event was fifty years in the future. A soldier deserts and kidnaps an armaments factoryworker's daughter to protest at the making and trading of armaments. Among the other characters were the soldier's and daughter's parents, other soldiers, government officials, right-wing fanatics, left-wing protesters. I have not kept a copy of the play. If I remember correctly the soldier was shot and his was the funeral at which the final chorus was spoken.

E.B.
December 1997

THE FATHER TALKS OF HIS SON

I am seventy years old
This is my dead son
He is not yet born
What I shall tell you has not yet happened
But it is already true

Don't pity me
His mother and I share the grief
You have seen white faces in undertakers' cars passing in
    the street
Would you wipe the tears from those faces?
Strangers may comfort mourners as surely as whores
    comfort their clients but lorries and hurrying shoppers
    pass the cortège
You may mourn but that will not change the story

It is the worst of crimes
As if when people opened their mouth you saw a desert
And when they snapped their fingers you heard walls fall
The scene of the crime is the world and each step and
    gesture of its people is part of the struggle of killer and
    victim
A misprint on a calendar would shock you: if three were
    printed before two
But what I shall tell you will not shock you
That is why it will happen

Imagine a forest where a storm blew but only a few twigs
    moved
The rest are still
Most of my son's generation had no work
Those without work are like still twigs in the storm
It is against nature
Yet we are creatures of nature

When the horse is led from the shafts it should run on the
    hill
When workers are loosed from machines they should
    peacefully walk home through their streets
But the hill is owned
The grass on the hill is owned
The horse does not even own the grass in its belly
It is led from its shafts at the door of the abattoir
And the city is owned
The people don't own the streets they walk
And as they don't own the streets they don't own their
    house that stands on a street
In this city no one knows where the street in which he lives
    leads
Or where he goes when he enters his door
On the ramparts flags crack like whips

Master and servant – owner and owned – are the four
    corners of the shroud
Do the owners honour the owned?
When did you teach them to do that?
Do the workers have power?
Who gave it to them?
Then how will the workless get power?
The workless are paid but coins were put in the mouths of
    the dead
Who will teach the owners to honour the workless when
    they have still not honoured the workers?

In this city towers full of files throw shadows down on the
    clouds
In laboratories seventeen thousand doors beyond the atom
    have been opened
By scientists who were thieves picking locks to plunder the
    future

Write on your tombstone: 'I Was Free' and generations
   would laugh
You don't even own the food in your belly

And if I stand by my dead son who is not yet born
It is written in the stars
And if I hope it is this:
Stars fall

THE SON TALKS OF HIS FATHER

When my father looked at the stars he thought of the holes
   in his pocket
When he heard the wind he remembered his hunger when
   he was young
He didn't own the machines but they taught him how he
   lived
They put tools in his head
When he sat at table his elbows knew the carpenter's plane
When he held his plate his hands knew the potter's clay
When he ate his teeth knew the cut of the harvest scythe
He walked on the street and his feet knew the quarry floor
Look at my hands
Dead leaves on a river or stones on the bottom
I cut my leg: blood has no feeling
The houses are pictures cut in prison walls
The trees are signposts floating at sea
I am a dream
My life is a joke played on the dead

THE MOTHER TALKS OF HER SON

My son had to find his own way in life
It was easier for my generation
We struggled to keep a job and that decided the whole of
    our life
We ate and slept and rose when our work needed us to
And so we weren't paid only for working but for living the
    way we lived
We did not ask why we were living
We asked for a rise or a meal or better working conditions
And when we asked for these things we asked for justice –
    because our work was unjust and this made all of our life
    unjust
So all of our life – even sweeping the floor and eating and
    sleeping – was part of the struggle for justice
My son's generation has no work
So what decides how they should live?
What's justice for them?
What does it mean when they sweep the floor?
When they ask for justice they ask why they live
But who taught them to be Socrates?

THE NEW SOLDIER TALKS TO HIS PARENTS

I've joined
I'm a soldier
I'd 'ad it up t' 'ere
I did nothin all day but felt as if I'd flogged me guts out
Went round like a coffin pushed in a wheelchair
A few more years an' my life's over!
What've I got out of it?

I'm sorry: they should've left me on the tip when they 'ad
    me

I know soldiers shoot civvies
It's government policy to fire at every riot
Would you be 'appier if I was on the street gettin shot at?
That's typical civvie!
I'd rather do the shootin!
Yes I may be shootin me mates
But if they start bother they can't complain when us poor
   corpses 'ave t' stick our necks out t' mop it up

So I joined the bone-queue with the other mother-
   stranglers
Right?
What I was before is over
Who I was is gone
Lost
Not missed
Don't ask me no favours
If they say shoot down your street – get in a doorway
I'll shoot
They tell me t' turn your room over? – I'll empty it
   through the winder an' pour you out after it!
I'll be so different inside their uniform me own mother
   won't know me!
She's no more t' me than one of the corpses!
I'm so full of parade-attention-at-the-double-present-arms
   the rifle's more 'uman than me!
So lock your door!
I'm your protector now!

THE MOTHER LOOKS AT THE SOLDIERS

Was there ever a time when civilians did not stand in
   silence before uniformed men?
Or a time when uniformed men did not lean on their arms

on the village square while the shadows under the stone
  pines darkened at noon?
Was there ever a city gate through which the uniformed
  men did not march shouting orders like the street cries
  of traders selling tyranny?
What daughter first saw her father limp home in a uniform
  as ragged and thin as the bark of a silver birch?
What scavenger first stripped uniforms from the dead
  while crows cawed as the bared skin turned the field
  white with the winter of death?
A uniform is a skin
Who owns the uniform owns the wearer
When people first arm themselves against their owners
  they do not wear uniform
They tear off a strip of curtain or dress to tie on their arm
They wear a piece of their home or the clothes of those
  they fight for
Such soldiers put on their own skin

THE ARMY JOKER

The rockets ain loaded
When yer think of it why should they be loaded?
They settled it with the enemy: both sides 'ave empty
  rockets
Made a pact!
They don't even make the war 'eads
Save all that money
When yer think about it it's all a bluff
All the Carcass Faces – both sides – met an' sorted it out

It's all politicians t'gether ain it?
If they tell us it's white it's bound t' be black
I bet they're all big drinkin buddies

I say corpse off t' the lot of 'em
I ain worried
As long as I get me lolly they can do what they like
That's what I'm in the army for
An' if the rockets *was* loaded our lot couldn't fire 'em
We're useless!
Our officers couldn't run a crematorium in the land where
no one died an' that still don't stop 'em talkin more shit
than a corpse with diarrhoea

Why they bluff us?
Solves all their problems
They 'ave t' stay out of each other's patch t' make it work
– but now it don't cost nothin an' they don't 'ave t' blow
each other up
As long as the rest of us think the rockets are loaded it
works
We're corpse scared of the other lot so we put up with our
lot
That's why they 'ave 'em: not t' scare the enemy – t' scare
their own lot till the ash runs out of their arse
Then they stay on top an' we stay down 'ere!

If the rockets was loaded we'd only deter ourselves!
Who'd let off all that lot?
The food'ld melt in the cans!
Everyone'ld be tryin t' get out of the city an' the streets
would be one big traffic jam
'Orns blowin like judgement day an' corpses standin by
their cars wavin their fists at each other
Then the cars'ld melt
'Uman toad-in-the-'ole
The world cremated in twenty minutes
No one'ld do that!
The rockets can't be loaded

THE SERGEANT TALKS TO HIS SOLDIERS

Modern war's technology not soldiers
Press this button press that
Unmanned planes unmanned tanks
Dead untouched by 'uman 'and
When the Big One comes our chances are better than the
  civvies'

Think of an 'ill
The scanner shows up 'uman meat
The commander calls artillery
They take the 'ill out as painless as a dentist takin a tooth
  out of a skull
Then there's a river
Yer can see where the light picks it out
The commander calls up airarm
'Eavy transports bigger than flyin factories drop concrete
  between the banks
Rapid-set
It closes the river over like 'ard skin 'ealin a wound
That stuff can turn a 'ole ocean as solid as a squaddie's nut
  in a matter of hours
The army drives over an' comes to a city
They don't bother t' scan
Just knock down all 'uman 'abitation an' move on
Like an army of locusts
It ain a front line
It's a picnic

Next a company of squaddies comes to a lane that once led
  to a village
Somethin moves – not yet dead
It's 'uman but looks like a burned toilet-brush
Sort of ashes stuck on a stick
It can't 'ear but it puts out a bone an' grovels in the earth

as if it was a coat it's tryin t'pull on
Three soldiers puke
Three!
Bent over a ditch an' retchin their stomachs up like
    squaddies celebratin Passin Out
The sergeant 'as t' kick it away
What do we learn from that?
We learn that doin it face t' face ain like pushin a button

Now there's so much unrest in the cities it wouldn't notice
    if there was an earthquake
Yer can't always use 'eavy stuff on a riot
If it's workers' estates yer spray shells from a chopper
But some areas yer 'ave t' miss the offices an' big 'ouses an'
    galleries
That's when fightin can end up very old-fashioned
Putting steel in tummies
We don't want you mother-stranglers corpsin out just
    because yer seen yer brother in the mob
So the army's steppin up trainin
Yer all killed a prisoner as part of yer basic
Now yer're going t' take a refresher course

THE DESERTER LOOKS AT THE STARS

Look at the stars and the empty wind!
The bastards!
A map of a sea without a shore
A city without a gate
Watch it from your roof till your house falls but no one can
    enter that city
The stars have written themselves on the sky
They follow the laws so closely they are the book of the
    laws

If they looked at men and dogs they would see no
    difference
They write their laws on ice and when it melts they are
    written on the water
In the storm the drowning sailor stares at the beacon and
    must be content with drowning
The stars are the laws of the earth
When we walk on the earth we tread on a book and scuff
    the pages with mud
When the execution rifles crack the crows rise a few feet
    from the prison wall and settle again
Pigeons strut on the hospital roof
They hanged men on the tree till it fell then used it for the
    pyres
Soon the newspapers will announce the Carcass Heads own
    the sun
They'll fire a laser beam that covers it with a black disk
The sun will cross at noon: a black eyepatch on the sky to
    tell us the rulers own it
And then they will fire their rockets and turn the sky as
    red as the inside of the mouth that devours the earth

THE GUERRILLAS TALK TO THE ELDERLY PARENTS

They took your son from you as an infant because he
    couldn't learn
Now they discover he couldn't hear and has something
    wrong with his throat
They needn't have taken him from you
But the damage is done
He's grown up and hardly recognises you
You told them he wasn't spitting his food: he wasn't able
    to swallow

But you couldn't pay for a specialist examination
Now they say you can take him home if you can pay for
    the training
He must learn everything from the beginning
Otherwise he'd be a danger in the community
Your son has been shut up for thirty years
If he'd been outside would you have given him a good life?
He'd have lived in your damp house
Been sent to a slum school
Got a bad job – or been out of work
It would have been half a life!
You yourselves haven't worked for years
If you had you'd still have been as trapped as your son in
    the madhouse

Listen carefully: there isn't much time – but enough
In the past people worked or starved
The rulers owned the machines so they owned the workers'
    lives
You were in the palm of their hands as surely as the line of
    fate
Now machines do the work and there's mass
    unemployment
Workers are paid a little more than the dole
The government set the wages
The workers save to pay for better schools hospitals food
    and clothes
They are afraid to strike: others would take their jobs
The government has even abolished the law against
    striking to prove they're democrats
They don't need storms or famines to keep you poor
Technology keeps you poor as long as they own it
But now you don't need to be labouring beasts: for the first
    time no one needs to be owned
All can be free

Yet you still have the same rulers and you still let them rob
    you
You know the robbers who'd take your wallet
You don't know the robbers who take your skin

The government is the administration of violence
The country is like a sundial with a rocket in the centre to
    throw the shadow
You say you are too weak to get rid of rockets?
In the past great armies waged wars
In 1914 how many millions of soldiers were taught to shoot
    rifles?
Now a few thousand men can blow up the world
That's all they need to fire the rockets
What if they had to train millions to press the buttons?
People would say no and the rulers could not go to war
They rely on a few elite psychopaths
The rest of us could stop them
We will show people how to resist
Only one thing could stop their resistance
The government could use nuclear weapons against them
If they don't they'll be the first weapons governments have
    not used against their own people
That is why we must fight before our rulers panic and go
    mad

THE MUNITIONS WORKER ENCOURAGES HIS CHILD TO
SING

Sing dad a song before the others come home
Which one do you like best?
Do you remember?
What?
Yes I like that best too

Sing then!
You've got your finger stuck in your mouth like a skeleton
    counting its teeth
If you stand like that the rats'll think you're dead and
    come and eat your tongue
Then you won't be able to sing – there!
We'd better get the death-doctor to cut her up and see
    what she died of
Come on luv you're not in the chapel of rest
Well if she's dead we'll have to put her in a hole
Shall daddy fetch his corpse-spade?
We'll put a big stone on her so she can't get out
There! – that made her sing
. . . Very good
She hit that tune like an undertaker nailing down an
    elephant
We were lucky to get her into that nursery
They teach the kids all the old songs

THE TEACHER

I teach
The world is full of simple things
In the morning curtains wave in open windows as the
    houses greet each other
And the light falls on mountains and water and factory
    chimneys and trees
And in the night the moon crosses the sky like an eye
    scanning a book
It should be easy to teach these simple truths
But the rulers wish the world to be ugly so that they may
    rule in it unseen
They have issued an order: the clouds are yellow and green
And the grass purple and orange and black

I watch the children squint till their eyes run with tears as
    they struggle to see the pink and blue stars
And their backs stiffen and brows furrow like lines in a
    book as they strain to see that each drop of rain is a
    different colour
And their fists clench as they recite the grass is black
I teach
It is my profession to counterfeit the appearance of things
While the beetle shouts at the sky you are green and
    scurries into the dark

THE MUNITIONS WORKER TALKS TO THE PICKET

He asked me how many cities I could personally flatten
He said they ought to twin towns: Vladivostok to bomb
    Coventry and Coventry to bomb Vladivostok
I told him if I didn't make the bombs someone else would
I said they're queuing up to drop them
Every time the pound or the stock-market fall they're out
    on the march shouting
Drop the Bomb! Drop the Bomb!
He said they don't know what they're talking about
I said that never stopped anyone talking

He wants me to throw up my job
I've spent my life clinging to it!
If I work I haven't always got one foot on the wrong side of
    the poverty line
I can give my wife a few comforts
We eat better
The job's something for the kid too
I can pay for the private nursery
She won't end up flogging her meat on the street

I've seen mates lose their job
When the redundancy's spent they *sit*
One of them had a hole – the wife'll tell you – in the ceiling
It was summer so winter was a long way off
He put a bucket under the hole
Winter comes and he gets a bigger bucket
He'll be sitting and counting the drips when the ceiling
   falls in
When he was working he'd've fixed it the first weekend
I don't blame anyone
I'm nothing special
Just common human muck
I'll give up the job when you give me one that pays as well

IN EVERY CITY

In every city there are children
In every city there are toys
In every house there are the simple pleasures of the table
The work of the house
Washing and mending
The stillness at night
And feeding the children
One being giving to another all that it needs
Yet in time this changes and nothing is given
All that is worn and eaten is bought like a ticket to
   nowhere
To live money is needed
But where there is money all things can be bought and sold
Curses fidelity truth and labour
The widow's roof and the poorman's door
And death
In every city there is money
In every city there are weapons

In every coin there is life and death
And who can name its value?

THE MUNITIONS WORKER'S CHILD

I look at this child and the letters from all the graves in the
world
Fall from their stones and rush to its father's house and write
on the walls
Don't
And I can't tell how the father can't see what's written on the
walls of his house

And for this child's sake I would like the newspapers to be
printed in letters from war memorials
(There would be enough letters)
So that as the newspapers were rushed in trains and vans
through the night
The letters changed their places and turned the lies into
truths
And when you opened the newspaper in the morning you
read
You are mad

THE PIED PIPER

If you knew your father worked in the bomb sheds
You would say no
Any child would
But you grow up
Your mind is changed into the market place
Where people sell each other and haggle over the change
The bombs aren't to protect you: they're a cosh the burglar
slips into his jacket in case he's discovered

Children followed the pied piper out of the town
If children knew how their parents lived they would get out of
    bed and leave the town
They would not need music
They would be singers who followed their own song
In the morning there would not be one child left to kill

WHEN A CHILD

When a child is brought up in a house with a leaking roof and
    rotten floors and is not dressed or fed so that its limbs grow
    straight
But battered until it is too scared to think
You take children from such houses
And neither is a man who complains of violence in the street
    but lets his country make H bombs
Fit to keep a child in his house

THE GOVERNMENT REPRESENTATIVE

I am the government representative
I'm sorry about the soldiers on your front door
I've asked them to be as inconspicuous as possible
Your son has deserted from his unit
He is very disturbed
Nowadays soldiers work under wartime strain even in
    peacetime
We have to accept that peace went out with the petrol driven
    car

Your son went to the city and ingratiated himself with a
    worker in an armaments factory

Two days ago he abducted the worker's daughter
She was four
Your son sent the parents a letter

It said the father and his colleagues should stop making
    rockets
Or the child would be killed

Your son's behaviour is typical of anti-government agitators
He wants to help the child but ends up killing it
(Unless we stop him)
I deal with such absurdities every day
So many people walk into the pit they've dug in front of their
    feet
Your son acts from a feeling of compassion so strong that it
    makes him fanatical and fanatics simplify issues
He believes everyone else is inhuman
So – brimming over with love – he puts his fist in our face
His actions are the opposite of his motives
No wonder he is bewildered and dangerous

I'll arrange for you to broadcast a message
Ask him to give himself up with the child
The Home Office psychiatrist will tell you what to say
We can't leave it to you – you might provoke him to
    something worse
Your wife will sit at your side while you speak
When you've finished she can add something
'Please son you're breaking two mothers' hearts'
Anything direct and simple
She'll be too emotional to say much
We may safely trust to her feelings

THE MUNITION WORKER'S WIFE WAITS FOR HER
KIDNAPPED CHILD

I made her bed this morning
I cooked her a meal
Soup so it's easy to digest
Only needs reheating
Then I gave her room a good clean out
It was overdue
I can't clean it when she's here
She goes behind me untidying it
It's our game
I saw a dead child years ago
In a cot in our neighbour's house
The sheets were as smooth as her face
She couldn't untidy them any more
White

The letter said if the factory didn't strike he'd kill her
The doctor wrote my husband a medical certificate and told
    him to take the week off
The factory's working
They couldn't stop the whole factory for us!
There's miles of it!

I should've spoken when he was arguing with my husband
My husband doesn't say but he doesn't like me to interfere
    with work
She's my child
I could've said I loved her
Mentioned it in a way that didn't sound silly in company
You have to say things like that now
You can't take it for granted anyone knows
If I could go back I'd say it on my knees!

We have rockets for the sake of our child
We love her

If my husband reads of a child being battered he flares up so
   much I send her out of the room so she won't see him in one
   of his states
He wouldn't hurt a fly

We have to eat
You can't think of rockets when you put food on a child's
   plate
We couldn't live like that
Perhaps we should?
He might telephone to threaten us!
I must work out what to tell him
Then I'll be ready!

My husband was a baker till the firm went bust
He tried the police but he's too short
I wouldn't let him go on the lorries because it meant sleeping
   away from home
The papers are full of houses being broken into and women
   terrorised all night
And he wouldn't be safe on the roads – drunken lunatics!
Why are people like this?
Why do we do such things?

When he got the job on the rockets they said it was permanent
We couldn't believe our luck
The factory was so big
I pointed it out to my daughter from the top of the bus
We were proud of it
That's why we were so –
No he won't listen to that!
He'd laugh at me!
Please please please let me have her back!

I must think
That's how to help her
Let him see I'm not a silly woman
I've thought what might happen if they fired the rockets

Not might: *would*!
I mustn't lie
The children's skin will burn like bad sunburn
Scorch so it smells of ironing
Babies will be thrown out of windows and over the houses
They'll fall in other people's streets and die with strangers
Houses will drop on them
They'll lose arms and bleed
And scream
You see I understand what would happen
And then I'll explain that we have the rockets so that these
    things won't happen!
That's why my husband makes them!
I mustn't get angry – it won't help
If they fired their rockets we'd have to fire ours
They wouldn't be so cruel as to make us do that
No one's that cruel – we can trust each other more than that!
He's cruel!
He took my child!

It's too complicated
I'll say I love her
No! he'll kill her if I don't make him see I think of other
    children
The government says the enemy wants to come over here
We must stop them
It's better to be dead than red
But if it's better . . . why don't their people ask us to drop our
    rockets on them – if it's better to be dead than red?
That's always worried me . . .
It's simple really:
If we dropped our rockets they'd drop theirs so we can't drop
    ours even though they want us to as it's better to be
    dead . . .
Does that mean *none* of us should live?

THE MOTHER

I didn't want my son to join the army
When he was a child he waited months for a hospital bed
I couldn't heal him any more than a vagrant woman who lives
  in doorways and covers her child with a silk scarf found in a
  dustbin can keep the cold from its head
At school they taught him he was a fool
I knew he was clever
I should have taught him to leave school
He had no work
I could not give him work or build a place where he and his
  friends could study and think
The city in which I reared him was a jungle
Yes a thieves' kitchen!
A bitch that whelped in the gutter of that city would have
  taken her whelp in her mouth and slunk through the
  streets eyeing the sidewalks till she was out of the city
I did nothing
I did not have the power to be a mother or teach my son the
  mother tongue

THE DEMAGOGUE

Party Members!
A Great Nation can Never be Destroyed!
The Moral Weapon is our Greatest Weapon!
Moral Disarmament is our Greatest Danger!
A Nation without Moral Leadership is lost!
Our Leaders are Moral Spastics and Intellectual Cripples!
Our People came from The Soil!
Return to The Soil in the Time of Great Challenge!
The Mother Fortress will Protect Her Race!
Our Leaders have No Fingers!

We're Ruled by Leaders with Mitten Hands!
Mitten Hands!
Mitten Hands that can't Press Buttons!
Without the Courage to Use Our Bombs we are Already Lost!
Burn out the Socialist Virus!
Disinfect the Species!
The Future shall be Red-Free!
     Up the Law!
     Go to War!
     That's What Britain Makes Rockets For!
     Drop the Bomb!

LOVE

People marry for love
Then go through a life of slavery to pay for the bed
They end up angry and stupid with hatred of the world
They have kids for love
Then they curse them and some of them break their arms
A punter gives his last few quid to a girl in an alley and
     afterwards kicks her senseless to get it back
Love took them up the alley
Don't say love is purer than that
Generals have rockets because they love us
When we fry they'll weep for us in their bunkers
You can put up with any hovel as long as you love in it
As long as you can say love makes you human you don't have
     to bother to act like a human and clean up the mess
You flounder about on your middens and call yourselves
     saints
If a god made the world he put love in it so that we couldn't
     make it any better and show that we don't need gods
Well if god made the world I hope he washed his hands
     afterwards

Where did the madness start?
There was an age of miracles
All the time reports of miracles coming in
The sea's divided and an army's crossing!
The blind can see and they're jumping over their sticks!
Dead popping up like escapologists!
Five thousand unemployed on the square?
Fine – feed them from this little basket of bread and fish
Storm at sea? Don't build a lifeboat – let them walk!
Bad neighbours keep borrowing your lawn-mower? *Give*
    them the lawn-mower
Now they blacken your eye because you didn't *mow* the lawn
    for them?
Turn the other cheek!
Another miracle! – why not?

The age of miracles is dead and it'll take more than a miracle
    to bring it back
That's why men have gone out naked on the heath to howl at
    the storm
Now the rockets are on the heath

THE PRIME MINISTER'S POCKET

When you have forced the government to get rid of H bombs
    you have not solved the problem
H bombs are dinosaurs
Any government would be glad to get rid of them!
While you celebrate your victory they will invent a nuclear
    weapon so small it fits into the prime minister's pocket
He will take it out to show to his grandchildren as they ride on
    his knee at Christmas
Your problem is not how to get rid of H bombs
But how to change society

THE OLD PROTESTOR

Sometimes your life is like someone else's biography
While you read on page twelve you're at school – page ninety
   already says there's a war or you're lamed in an accident
If you tear out the page the end is the same
If you tear them all out and commit suicide it only means a
   surprise ending
Their democracy is the freedom to turn the pages

Perhaps they will send me to prison
Well when you're old there's no time to correct mistakes
You must live in such a way that your life is a judgement on
   the way you live

My parents became children when they were old
Not senile
My mother laid the table as earnestly as a girl laying a doll's
   tea-set
My father worked at his plants as if he were making daisy
   chains
They wore old-fashioned clothes and their bodies had shrunk
   so that they were too big for them
They looked like children dressing up
Their lives became a game
I wanted to end like that

A STORY

There was once a rich man
To get rich he did bad things
He stole a dustbin from an old woman and sold it back to her
   with an anti-theft device
He lent money and made the borrowers repay twice as much

He made the poor work for him and took half of what they
    earned so that they paid him to keep them poor
But he didn't mind: he was rich
Only one thing worried him
Down the road lived another rich man
Now our man knew how he'd got his own money and he said
    to himself
This other man must be as wicked as me
So he didn't trust him: he slept with a pistol under his head
That should've made him feel safe
But it didn't
Did the pistol still work?
Were the bullets dud?
Perhaps his neighbour could creep like a cat and come with
    his gun to rob him
So he sat up all night trying to keep awake and nodding off
    over his pistol
Sometimes he woke with a start
Sometimes the pistol fell from his hands and he snatched at it
Once he saw a shadow creeping towards his bed
He fired
The safety catch was on
After that he tried to stay awake with the safety catch off
You could see him bent over the muzzle
Gaunt and tired
Grizzled stubble on his chin
Nodding and muttering and cursing his neighbour
The man who knew what thieves were because he was a thief
    and who put a pistol under his head so that he could sleep
    in peace
Lived in terror
And one night shot himself

THE MEANING OF HISTORY

Twenty countries have H bombs
Each to protect its way of life
When you say 'our way of life' you mean 'our theory of
  history'
Somewhere history may be turning a continent upside down
  to shake it out
But you say 'history is our way of life' like a dwarf telling a
  giant to put the continent down
And soldiers will kill millions for the sake of the meaning of
  history when they can't tell you three dates in it

THEIR TIME TO FALL

Seventeen thousand gates have been opened inside the atom
Those with the keys have great power
Whatever laws are passed
Whatever weapons are used
Whatever is made by machines –
All is ordered by the rulers
They count the heartbeats in the factories and the breaths in
  the streets
The steps of each person's life are recorded and filed
If an agitator disguises himself the outline of his shadow is
  read and the agitator it hides is computed
Shadows are read in the dark
And if the rulers see and order all things the gods and myths
  cannot be blamed for the chaos
The blame of the rulers is clear
So in the time of absolute tyranny ignorance withers
The people begin to understand their rulers
They will be the generation that cannot be lied to
The old rulers invoked gods

The gods are dead
These rulers have the power of gods
And so their time to fall has come

PEOPLE WHO CANNOT BE LIED TO

In the age of computer control and the technological eye
We are watched as if the whole earth were a face
There is nowhere to hide any more
Good!
Things are better like this
We know where we are
We are all under the same eye
We are the people who cannot be lied to
The stars have written a new law
We cannot break it
If we could break it the world would vanish
We have been written into the book of laws
If they wanted to tear us out they have to tear up the sky

THE CONDEMNED PRISONER

You who live under tyrants
Who do not own the food in your belly
I grew gnarled and strong as a tree on a mountain
In the wind I grew like a fist
I did not bear fruit
My strong branches are my fruit
The tyrant hounded me to the edge of the grave
I speak from within it
I could not be lied to
Walk out of my grave

AT THE FUNERAL

Why should we speak of the dead?
The time is short
Shouldn't we use it to give instructions to build the house?
Or list the food to bring from the stores?
Or name the times for meeting friends?
Yet the dead speak in us
Our pain at death does not use the common tongue
It is sighing and tears but also joy
We speak words that come to our mouths as if new keys
    turned in old locks

The Greeks said all things die
That is a simple truth and it is all
Yet it is worth saying since only we can say it
From the womb to the grave is a short journey but much is
    done on the way
And our hands reach further than our legs take us
We see the fields beyond the roof of the house where we go to
    take lodgings
It is wise to hope

The river that turns the turbines at the cataract runs to the sea
    and is lost
The tree falls to the ground where its seeds have fallen
Long after the marble pavement of the courtyard sinks the
    steps are still worn by those who come to honour the ruins
Hunter and deer and dog run in the same forest
All things die: and that is all
But no one can conceal his crimes in death and death destroys
    no one's beauty
If you would judge judge what was done and thank and
    condemn the doer and live accordingly

How will you honour the dead?

Bury them but you cannot open the earth with a freeman's
    spade
Burn them but you cannot gather the ash with a freeman's
    rake
When the earth is not owned you will honour the living
And then the ashes and bones of the dead will be honoured
The one thing worthy to outlast the stars is humankind
We are the book of laws
Our words will last longer than any granite on which they are
    written
You who do not own the food in your belly
Whose sky may become the inside of a mouth
Call no man happy till his neighbours are free